Michael Fuller was the first ever ethnic minority chief constable in the UK. He joined the Metropolitan Police Service in 1975 as a cadet and served in uniformed and CID positions throughout London. Michael has helped set up the Racial and Violent Crime Task Force and Operation Trident.

A SEARCH FOR BELONGING

Michael Fuller

535

Published by 535
80–81 Wimpole Street,
Marylebone,
London, W1G 9RE

twitter.com/535Books

Hardback – 978-1-788700-84-9
Paperback – 978-1-788703-55-0
eBook – 978-1-788700-85-6

A CIP catalogue of this book is available from the British Library.

Designed and set by seagulls.net
Printed and bound in Great Britain by Clays Ltd, Elcograf S.p.A

1 3 5 7 9 10 8 6 4 2

First published by 535 in 2019 as
"Kill the Black One First": A Memoir.
This edition first published by 535 in 2020.

535 is an imprint of Bonnier Books UK
www.bonnierbooks.co.uk

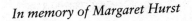

In memory of Margaret Hurst

As I watched the crowds enthusiastically cheering us, I now felt that our contribution was finally being recognised. For the first time in my career I felt kinship and a sense of belonging ...

PROLOGUE

I stared at the hostile crowd again.

We were now alarmingly outnumbered. Law and order dwarfed by the mob. We didn't want to appear scared, but we were. Around me I saw grim jaws and unsmiling mouths and I knew a lot of officers were psyching themselves up for a fight.

"There's 30,000 of us," they told each other. Trying not to feel intimidated because in fact, at this moment, here, now, there were only 30 of us.

A few kids were baiting us, shouting things, and a constable stepped forward. From his accent I could tell that he had been brought up as a member of the ruling classes. It would be interesting to know what route he took to get here but there was no time to think about that; he was stepping forward to reason with a group of mouthy troublemakers. I wasn't sure if he was brave or stupid. This was resolved within 30 seconds when they pushed him through a shop window. The rest of us stared in disbelief. Even the lads responsible watched open-mouthed as his body passed straight through the plate glass as if it were water and he some sort of toy. But, unlike water, the glass shattered into a thousand pieces.

There was a moment's silence.

Beyond the sight line, people were still talking and catcalling, but anyone who had witnessed the uniformed copper sailing into a shop without using the door was left speechless. Then, astonishingly, he picked himself up and walked out through the hole he had made on his way in, apparently unhurt, except for his pride. He must have been hurt. He had just been assaulted. It was our job to call an ambulance and arrest the suspects.

But we didn't.

Instead, incredibly, some cops laughed. Nervous, inappropriate laughter, because they had understood that arresting someone now, when we were heavily outnumbered, could get us into serious trouble; could be the tipping point we all instinctively feared.

So while the posh copper, staggering a bit, was led off towards the medics, we were sent to the bus to retrieve our shields. Then, gradually, instinctively, without anyone telling us to, we arranged ourselves into a ragged line. The black people we were supposed to cordon, perhaps mirroring our movements, also formed a line of sorts.

So now we were facing each other and, before we knew it, we had battle lines. Which meant there was probably going to be a battle. The crowd now numbered well over a hundred, so we must lose. What would that mean? Was this war? Would the toll to the loser be injury, even death?

I felt sick. I was intimidated by the size of the mob. The nearest were about six metres away, close enough for me to see the expressions on their faces, and I was shocked by them. We were the police but they were staring us out as if we were an occupying army.

"Babylon! Get out of Brixton!"

Our shields went up, not in response to missiles but like a signal to the crowd to start throwing them. And there were plenty of missiles available. This was a run-down area of south London with building sites everywhere, so it was easy to pile up wood, metal, debris.

And then, as if a spotlight had suddenly picked me out, as if all the people were one person, the crowd noticed my black face.

"Oi! You! Yes, you! Coconut!"

Coconut. A familiar enough insult from my days on the beat. Coconut said I'm brown on the outside but white inside. A traitor to my community. It always cut me a bit, but there were more insults to follow. I didn't really know exactly what they meant but I knew they were Jamaican and they were especially for me. Rasclot! Bumbaclot!

So they had singled me out.

A strange lull, then suddenly a single cry rose from inside the crowd.

"Kill the black one first!"

There was a roar. Guttural, like laughter, like fury, the fury of the mob.

ONE

I was born just before the 1960s began and for most of that decade I was a country boy. I had grazed knees and a keen interest in animals and I was all too familiar with stinging nettles. Climbing trees, seeking treasure, looking after an injured bird, watching tadpoles turn into frogs, roaming anywhere I liked so long as I was back in time for tea; my rural childhood was idyllic.

I even loved the village school. I won a prize for my joined-up writing and was discovering how good it felt to run races, and better still to win them. There were holidays and lots of friends, and sometimes holidays *with* friends. My best friend Kevin's parents took me along to Devon and we watched steam rising from the car's bonnet as it argued with the steep hills. Of course, there were birthday parties. Outside the rambling house of a girl called Edwina, her pony nodding at us over the fence, we stood in a circle in front of her father. Snap! I still have that black-and-white picture. A huge group of happy, laughing children.

There were just a few things I really, really did not like. One was tripe for tea. There was no escape from tripe, I had to eat it. Another was social workers. No escape from them either for a child in care. And, something else, as bad if not worse than tripe. Visits from my mother. Once again, no escape. When she said she was coming, I had to see her.

I waited for her on the living room sofa, swinging my legs, wishing I was outside with the other children. I heard a car pull up outside the Lodge, where I lived. There was a pause, the engine running, then it moved off. A taxi.

My mother walked in and sat down without hugging or kissing me. Now I see from photos that she was tall and attractive, with a strong face. Then, her physical presence meant nothing to me, except a consciousness that she had dressed up for the occasion.

She sank into a nearby chair, barely seeming to notice me. There was a cigarette in her hand and at intervals her mouth sucked on it furiously. Smoke billowed across the room as she exhaled. She launched into a complaint about the cost of the train ticket, the fare from the station. Soon, the air was full of smoke. She opened her handbag and withdrew a rustling packet and from the packet she produced another cigarette. I stared, fascinated, as she puckered her lips around it and a tiny orange bead of heat passed from one tip to the next. She inhaled deeply on the old one, as if she was bidding it a passionate farewell, before stubbing it out in the ashtray and starting with vigour on its successor.

Eventually, she changed to another favourite topic. My father. He had other women, he gave her hardly any money, not enough to keep me, not enough to keep her.

I stopped listening after a while.

Then I heard her roar: "*Tell him!*"

I looked up at her, blinking.

"You just tell him that," she insisted.

So I was supposed to not only agree with her but pass all this on to my father.

He was a distant figure but nevertheless I admired and loved him too much to challenge him. In fact, it was impossible for me to think of him critically at all. Wonderful meals would appear from his kitchen at any hour of the night. His house was filled with music – reggae and soca. Friends listened and laughed and drank rum together in his living room. And he arrived at the Lodge – this was very important and it made me swell with pride – in a blue Jag. He would take me back to south London for weekends, windows open, Dad's fingers tapping on the wheel, the whole Jag seeming to throb with Marvin Gaye as the green, green world outside gradually became the colour of brick.

There was no way I could pass any of my mother's complaints on to the icon which was my father. So I sat quietly on the sofa, swinging my legs.

Suddenly she leaned towards me, eyes wide, mouth taut with anger.

"Do they give you pocket money?"

Stupidly, I nodded.

"Do you save it up?"

I nodded again.

"Show me, then!"

Her eyes shone.

I studied her uncertainly but without suspicion.

"Show me!" she cried.

I was very proud of my pocket money and carried it around with me in my trouser pocket, enjoying the clinking sound it made. After a moment's hesitation, I withdrew it. A couple of shillings and a few sixpences shone in my palm.

She said: "Give it to me."

I stared at her.

"Michael, give it to me."

I said: "It's my pocket money."

She said: "I need it."

She opened her eyes wide and I saw in them the possibility that, if I didn't do what she wanted, she would become very, very angry indeed. I was already frightened enough of her cold detachment. I didn't want her to get any scarier.

Slowly, I placed the money in her outstretched hand. She assessed it with professional rapidity and then her handbag snapped shut and it was gone.

I volunteered nothing and my mother asked me few questions. She had little interest in my short replies. We took a walk around the rolling grounds of Fairmile Hatch, circling the great house. Inside was the nursery and its dormitories where I had lived before joining my new "family" in the Lodge. I remembered the nursery well: its sweeping staircase, rocking horse at the top, the rubber sheets and heavy curtains, the nursery nurses in their spotless aprons handing us a glass of blackcurrant juice very early every morning to keep us healthy.

We strolled on, past the sandpit and the gypsy caravan, past the flower borders and the woods, past the air raid shelter with its ancient ammo boxes containing ragged uniforms, which we dressed up in.

My mother talked. I was silent.

We stroked the donkeys, Neddy and Peppy. And sure enough, she started talking about Jamaica. She always did. She was keen for me to hear about the wonderful places and people there who were my relatives. And I knew why. My mother wanted to go back to Jamaica and she wanted to take me with her. She said that an aunt, a member of her huge extended family, would take care of me while she, my mother, worked. There was even a repatriation programme for children like me. My mother wanted the repatriation programme to pay my fare.

I barely listened if at all and said nothing about this Jamaican Shangri-La. I was glad when she left. She wasn't warm or kind or caring. She wasn't like Auntie Margaret, who looked after me at the children's home and whom I loved very deeply. I had no idea what you were supposed to feel for a mother; I just knew I felt nothing. Or nothing nice, anyway.

When she had gone I returned to the Lodge. Auntie Margaret was in the kitchen. She was wearing an apron and was busy making tea, clattering large saucepans with one hand, stirring a pot with the other, but when she saw my face she paused.

She said: "I don't think you'll be moving to Jamaica. Your mother would have to go to court and ask the judge and the judge would say no."

She grabbed another pan and I noted that we had shepherd's pie for tea. What a relief it wasn't tripe. That would have been too much today.

"Repatriation," she explained, over her shoulder, her head disappearing in the steam from the vegetables, "means going back. But you can't go back to Jamaica if you've never been there, can you? You were born here."

I nodded.

She knew, without turning around, how I felt. A few words from my mother or a social worker – Jamaica, foster care, move, words like that – could turn my world upside down and make me feel, literally, seasick.

I said: "I don't want to leave Fairmile Hatch."

That was the name of the sprawling Surrey mansion and associated cottages which housed our London County Council children's home.

"Now just stop worrying about it," she said.

She left the pots and pans and deposited the big slotted spoon on the counter and wrapped her arms around me in a kind and reassuring hug. How comforting her hugs were. I hung on to her tightly.

"I know for a fact your father wouldn't let you go all that way; he'd certainly oppose your mother."

My mother. That word meant nothing. Anyone could see that Margaret was my real mother. She loved me and cared for me and supported me and did everything mothers were supposed to do. My biological mother was just an angry woman who visited sometimes.

The other children appeared in the kitchen now. They could smell the shepherd's pie and that meant it was time for chores. Margaret had a strict rota of chores and she was strict about everyone doing them. I was on washing-up duty.

"I'm laying the table," said one of the smaller girls, reaching into the cutlery drawer although she was barely tall enough to see inside it. She pulled out some knives and forks awkwardly. Her hands were tiny.

I was always the eldest and there were usually six of us, but children did come and go. Some arrived very angry and disturbed and I watched as Auntie Margaret calmed them in that special, magical way she had. Gradually, those children screamed less at night and made some friends. But sometimes they would disappear: taken off to foster parents or different homes or perhaps back to their parents, although this seemed unlikely – very few children were even visited. I saw envy in the eyes of some when they heard about the maternal visits which I dreaded so much.

I helped the smaller girl with the knives and forks (just in case we forgot that we were in care, London County Council had stamped its initials on every knife, fork and spoon) and she smiled broadly and it was good to see that smile. As the big boy in the Lodge, I felt protective about the little ones and some of them reminded me of the injured birds I sometimes found.

And, as the big boy, I had been given a bicycle for my birthday. I cycled to my friends' houses, I cycled along the quiet Surrey lanes, I cycled through woods and across heathland. On my bicycle I was independent. I was free.

Social workers were disconcerted by this. Social workers were the enemy. Social workers were people who arrived to ask Margaret and the other staff questions about me. I would be standing in the room, or within obvious earshot, but they didn't ask *me* about me. They didn't talk to me at all. Instead, they talked to the staff, nodding their heads, writing notes and making comments which would sometimes develop into an argument with Margaret.

"You mean you let him cycle through the woods?"

"Yes." Margaret sounded serene.

"*Alone!*"

"Certainly." Her voice was rising a little in volume now, to match the social worker's.

"But—!"

"I can trust Michael to take care of himself."

"So he cycles from the Lodge through the woods *alone*. He goes to the singing teacher's house and the singing teacher is a single man, and Michael is *alone* with him at his house. And then, *in the dark*, Michael cycles back to the Lodge *through the woods alone*?"

"Yes," Margaret said.

Well, it was true the singing teacher was a little odd, but I certainly wasn't scared of him. I was growing into a tall boy and was easily capable of standing up to anyone who tried to hurt me. And the woods weren't scary at all, night or day.

Margaret repeated: "Michael can take care of himself."

I could hear the social worker's pen scribbling. Next time, it would be a different social worker. They were always moving on, changing jobs. They didn't know me at all. But they had a hideous power over me. Despite Margaret's reassurances that she would be there for me always, and her courage in arguing with them, we both knew social workers had the power to take me away.

They never did succeed, but they came close a few times, and this was extremely unsettling, as if they were capable of melting into liquid everything I thought was solid in my life. They were always suggesting something. Boarding school?

("No," said Margaret, "that would be wholly wrong.") A children's home nearer Mum and Dad? ("I don't think Shirley Oaks is the right place for Michael," said Margaret.) How about a foster family? This one was particularly hard to take because I already had parents, as well as Auntie Margaret.

Thank heavens there were periods when no social worker or parent visited, when life could settle down. I was always curious, always busy. Cubs. Exploring in the woods with my best friend Kevin – he actually lived at the children's home, but in a separate flat with his parents because his mother was superintendent of the nursery. Playing. Parties. Chores. Swimming in the pool of some friends of Auntie Margaret. Church. Sunday School. Pocket money. A walk every Saturday to Brown's sweet shop. An annual holiday with Auntie Margaret, sometimes to the seaside on the south coast. Listening to Elvis Presley, a favourite of Margaret's, as well as Mozart. And, of course, The Beatles. Kevin's mother took the pair of us to London and we went to a shop in Oxford Street, where Kevin and I together recorded an appalling version of 'A Hard Day's Night' which made us cry with laughter every time we played it.

In the evenings, Auntie Margaret sometimes watched TV with us. She loved police programmes. So my diet was *Dixon of Dock Green*, *Softly, Softly*, *Z-Cars*… I sat next to her as we followed the crimes and characters in reverent silence. When the familiar music signalled the end, we felt sad it was over and talked about the programme to make it last a little longer. These cop shows always shared with Auntie Margaret a clear moral message. Remember the difference between right and wrong. Then do the right thing. Margaret was a committed Christian and spoke about right and wrong and behaved in a way which demonstrated this principle. How simple and reassuring it was to know that a clear line existed between good and bad and which side I should choose.

But one Friday evening, when I eagerly awaited *Softly, Softly*, something very unusual happened. Margaret explained that tonight she wouldn't be watching with me.

"You're going to miss Stratford Johns!" I cried. "And you won't see Inky!"

Inky was the show's police dog, handled by a character called PC Snow and, thanks to PC Snow and Inky, I was seriously thinking about becoming a police dog handler when I grew up. The only problem was that I was rather scared of dogs, all except my friend Kevin's dog, Twist.

"I've been asked out to dinner," she explained, "and I can't very well say I'd rather spend the evening watching television."

Margaret was in her twenties, not slim but pretty, with black shoulder-length hair and a ready smile which just seemed to change the light and air and molecular composition of any room, even quite a dark one. I don't think she came from Surrey but she readily made friends in the area and would discuss articles she had read in *The Guardian* with them while we swam in their pool or played with their children.

I looked at her stealthily now. I wanted to know whom she was going to dinner with. But I just could not ask. And she did not tell me.

We soon found out. George, that's who. George was a wiry, fair man with a moustache who may have been in the army; anyway, there was something rather military about him. After that, Auntie Margaret went out with him again, missing *Z-Cars*. And then, the following Friday night, Stratford Johns was sacrificed for George once more.

We children felt uneasy about George, especially when he started visiting the Lodge in the evenings, once trying to play a spontaneous approximation of cricket with us, looking awkward in his tweed jacket.

Now his presence unsettled everyone. The fact was that Auntie Margaret's social life was none of our business. We loved her like a mother but we knew that she was not our mother; she was a housemother who worked for the Borough Council. We understood that Margaret must have some other life outside us, her many-coloured family. But we didn't want her to. We wanted her to be there to look after us for ever and the thought that she might marry George and leave us induced the same sort of nausea in me as my mother's plans to take me to Jamaica.

Whenever George visited we watched the pair of them beadily. It was clear that George was madly in love with Margaret. Well, that was completely understandable. The question for us was: could she be in love with him?

She simply remained herself; entirely Margaret-like, warm, kind and firm.

"I think she laughs more when he's around," said one of the smaller boys miserably.

"She's going to marry George and have children of her own," said one of the girls. She looked at another girl and it seemed the three of them were going to burst into tears.

That was an awful thought. If Margaret had children of her own, there was a danger she would forget about her charges at the Lodge, the lost children, the children with problems, the children whose parents couldn't, or wouldn't, keep them. Us.

In fact, after a few months, to our relief, George stopped coming to the Lodge. When I felt brave enough – and there were certain things you had to be very brave about to ask Auntie Margaret – I wondered out loud if he was coming back and she said: "Oh, no, I don't have time for him, you all keep me so busy."

Which I took to mean that she loved us more than she had loved George and wouldn't leave us.

TWO

We were often visited by the local bobby, Ernie Aherne. He had a good relationship with Fairmile Hatch and the arrival of his police moped outside the Lodge seemed to create a strange fluttering among the young trainees who were helping Auntie Margaret. As for Margaret, she welcomed a police presence. And I was fascinated by him because he trained guard dogs to protect celebrities in his spare time.

This fascination may have arisen from my own fear of dogs, and it didn't take PC Aherne long to detect that fear. Kevin had a fat Border Collie, Twist, who wagged his tail so enthusiastically that his rear wiggled until he seemed to be doing the popular dance he was named after. I wasn't scared of Twist. But strange dogs, whenever I was out and about, sometimes made a beeline for me, occasionally with hackles raised and lips lifted to reveal alarmingly large teeth.

And so, one day, PC Aherne arrived with a puppy.

"No," said Margaret in her firm voice.

But, surprisingly, PC Aherne, helped by the enthusiastic trainees, managed to persuade her that a puppy was just what I needed to help overcome my fear of dogs and by the time he had put the wriggling bundle of crossbreed Terrier into my arms, I knew I was going to call him Shake and he was going to be mine.

"What about Othello?" demanded Margaret. Othello was the Lodge cat. He was big and black and his hobby was running between the wheels of moving cars. No one could understand how he had lived so long.

"Othello will adapt," said PC Aherne.

"Well, Michael will have to take full responsibility for this dog. I simply don't have time," warned Margaret.

"I will," I promised.

"That's the whole idea," said PC Aherne.

"You'll have to feed him, brush him, walk him..."

"...And train him," PC Aherne reminded me. He knew I was fascinated by the fictional Inky.

"I will," I promised, bending down to put Shake gently on the ground. He did not run off or leave my side, only pressed himself against my ankles. I already loved him.

I talked to PC Aherne a lot about how he caught crooks. I read books like *The Famous Five* as if they were training manuals. And I still watched the TV cop shows avidly. All these sources taught a keen young detective one thing: stay sharp. Keep your wits about you at all times and be aware of anything suspicious.

One day I went into the woods by Fairmile Hatch to climb trees and make dens with a couple of younger boys. We had to slip through the fence but no one tried to stop us; the woods on the other side were public and if you walked through them far enough you even reached a car park.

We were still climbing trees quite near the fence when, always at the ready, I noticed something strange. It was autumn and there were lots of fallen leaves but among them was a large, black, plastic bag. It had sunk into the ground as though it had been there for some time. But I'd played here only yesterday, and I knew there had been no plastic bag.

Someone might have simply dumped their rubbish here. So why would they have bothered to half-bury it?

This is just the kind of thing a good detective thinks. I was Stratford Johns, I was the Famous Five, I was curious. I climbed down and approached the bag. Cautiously. It was tied.

I called the others and gave the bag a tug. It had been so badly buried that it came up easily. And the weight of the bag was very interesting. Then, even more interesting, there was a clink of metal as it was released from the dark, earthy woodland compost.

My heart boomed. I loosened the tie. Whoever had buried the bag had done a poor job. Why? Was he in a hurry? Or had he perhaps been disturbed?

The thought gave me an adrenalin rush in my legs, the rush I got before school races. That was always a sign that my legs wanted to run – in this case, run away. I stopped investigating the bag and looked up. I peered between the tree trunks, through the bushes, up into the branches. The other children focused on the bag, then they saw my face and picked up my fear and all three of us began to look around us, heads jerking like birds.

No one was to be seen, so I opened the bag and peered inside. Hmmm. Something shiny in there. One last glance about and I reached in. My fingers touched cold, smooth metal. I grasped a sort of handle. I pulled. It was heavy, too heavy for one hand. I needed both.

A huge, silver trophy emerged into the light. We stared at it for a moment. The two younger ones examined it, ran their hands over it, tried to read the names engraved on the base.

"Shhh!" I said. Their piping voices fell to a whisper. I kept looking around. It was obvious the silver must be stolen. That meant that the thief would certainly be back.

He might already be back.

He might be watching us now.

Inside my legs, the tide came in and went out in an instant. My body was saying: run now and run fast.

But I had to know what else was in the bag. I pulled it open wide, wide enough to see more silver, more trophies. I was very scared and very excited at the same time. We were on constant lookout, listening for footsteps in the undergrowth, as I stuffed the trophy back in the bag and tried to lift it. It was just too heavy. Two of us were barely able to carry the thing. It sagged between us as we ran.

We ploughed through the undergrowth to the fence, scrambled beneath it and then across the playing field, constantly looking over our shoulders.

Straight to the safety of the Lodge, straight to Auntie Margaret, who was busy in the kitchen – as adults in *The Famous Five* usually are.

We dumped the sack on the floor and shrieked: "We've found buried treasure!"

I thought she'd be excited. Certainly pleased. But as we pulled out first one trophy and then another and then another, she just looked apprehensive.

Bursting with pride, we awaited her words of praise.

She said: "Oh no."

I felt the smile muscles in my face collapse.

I turned to the younger boys and said sternly: "Don't touch anything else. We mustn't leave our fingerprints everywhere."

Auntie Margaret was on her way to the hall.

I followed her.

"Do you think the thief will come back for it?" I asked, as she dialled the number of the local police.

"They'll be here in a few minutes," she said as she put the phone down.

I hoped it would be our friend PC Ernie Aherne on his moped. We waited an interminable hour, 60 minutes of excitement and terror. Supposing the thief had followed us? Seen where the silver was going? Was about to burst in, even though we had locked all the doors?

When the police car arrived, it was driven by an officer who was not PC Aherne and there was one other person in it.

The man wore a sports jacket and tie. I recognised it as the uniform that men who lived in the large houses around Cobham always wore. The police officer explained that there had been a burglary at the man's home and the trophies were almost certainly his. The man barely looked at us. He was anxious to get into the Lodge to identify his haul.

We lined up dutifully, like privates on parade, answered the police officer's questions, and then we led everyone to the place in the woods where we'd found the bag. There is no way we would have dared to return without the long arm of the law at our side. Now we looked around openly. I enjoyed doing that. I enjoyed hunting. Hunting for treasure, for signs of the thief, for footprints, for clues. My heart thumped and my whole body was on alert.

In fact, there was no sign of any further disturbance among the drying autumn leaves. I suspected the thief had driven to the car park and walked here to bury the treasure in the dark. So he didn't know that just a few yards further on was the boundary of Fairmile Hatch, from which children frequently emerged to play. Bad luck for the thief. But good luck for us.

We received half a crown each from the tweed pocket of the unsmiling owner of the treasure. The warm praise from the police officer was worth a lot more to me. In fact, I couldn't help feeling, deep down, that half a crown was rather a mean reward for such a find.

Anyway, this incident made me sure about one thing. I was going to be a police officer one day.

I told Auntie Margaret and her approval was obvious.

"You mustn't lie or cheat or steal, ever, if you want to join the police," she told me. I nodded seriously. I didn't lie or cheat or steal anyway. I had already adopted Margaret's values.

I knew which side of the line I wanted to be on. The side of right and justice. I wanted to be good. I wanted to be kind. If a child was hurt or an animal injured, I wanted to take care of it. Some of the other children at the home, children of different families in different cottages with different grown-ups looking after them, well, some were very disturbed. I knew I would never be like them.

Soon after this, I visited my father. This was always an intense experience. The throbbing reggae music, the spicy cooking, the smell of the strong rum his friends passed around, the soft clicking of dominoes, the talking which dissolved into laughter: it all, dangerously and a bit scarily, transcended the routines of the children's home and made Margaret's rules look meaningless. Bedtime? What bedtime? You simply fell asleep when you were tired.

In a strong West Indian accent, one of Dad's friends asked me what I wanted to do when I grew up. At that time Dad was working in a record pressing factory (which was one reason we had so much vinyl around – although he soon went to work in a prosthetic limb factory and he didn't bring any legs home) and I pondered whether I should say I wanted to be a vinyl presser. Because I did very much want to be like him.

But, remembering how often Margaret had told us that honesty was the best policy, and unable to restrain my pride, I announced: "I'm going to be a policeman."

They all stared at me as if I had announced I wanted to be an axe murderer. One of them choked on his rum.

Then they started to talk at once. Didn't I understand that the police were our enemy? Didn't I know how they treat black people? I doubt that anyone present in that room had been at the Notting Hill race riots but everyone knew about it. How a bunch of white youths had decided to attack the homes of West Indian immigrants and the police did so little that the immigrants were forced to defend themselves. And then the police arrested them for carrying offensive weapons instead of the white aggressors. Didn't I know about that, they demanded.

I stayed quiet, understanding little and believing not one word of it. I tried to imagine Stratford Johns arresting the wrong person. Impossible. And if Auntie Margaret was sitting here right now, I knew she would agree with me.

I looked around at their angry faces and then at my father.

He explained to me that his generation had arrived in the UK on ships, such as the *Empire Windrush*, after active recruitment in the Caribbean, to do the lowly, often dirty, jobs the British no longer wanted to do. They were shocked at the high levels of rudeness and hostility they met. It was, he said, an era when landlords put signs on their doors saying: "No Dogs, no Irish, no Blacks". And if they objected to insults, threats of violence or abuse, the police were always more likely to arrest them than the perpetrators.

The other men all agreed loudly. They hated the police for that.

I remained silent. This black/white thing which seemed to matter so much to them, it was completely outside my own personal experience. In fact, this was perhaps the first time that the existence of racial prejudice was drawn to my attention: I simply hadn't encountered it. There were about three black children in our primary school, all from the home, and there were more scattered through the nursery and various "families" at Fairmile Hatch and nobody, not the staff, not the teachers at school, not the other children, certainly not Auntie Margaret, ever seemed to see a difference between us. Indeed, I couldn't see a difference between us either.

My father poured his friends more rum, changed the record and told them that I was too young to know what I wanted to do in life, so gradually they quietened and I sat half-listening to their voices, the ebb and flow of their accents, the smell of rum in my nostrils.

It always felt like night in this room; even with the curtains open, the heavy flock wallcovering subdued the light. Here and there were a few brightly coloured ornaments. You could hardly see the men in the dark room but you knew just by listening to them, just by looking at the ornaments, that they were from some other place. Whereas I had been born in London and my accent was different and I watched *Softly, Softly*. How could the prejudice and hostility they described ever be a part of my own experience?

The next day, my father and I set off to pay Sunday visits. This did not mean going to church for us. But it did mean dressing up in our best clothes – and my father had some very impressive suits – to cross London and visit West Indian friends or distant relatives when they arrived home from church.

In the Jag, my father muttered: "Today, don't you go telling everyone you want to join the police."

"But I do!" I thought.

However, I said nothing. My father was a kind and loving man and I adored him. But his temper could be scary. If provoked, he was capable of erupting spectacularly with very little warning. Of course, he was invariably charming and from the warm, excited way people responded to our arrival, I knew they recognised that special charisma in him which I admired so much.

I loved those Sunday visits: the pressed suits of the men, the beautiful, bright dresses of the women, the smell of spicy food, the loud music. The way everyone made a fuss of me, because I was my father's son. It was a bit different from being another kid in a children's home where only Margaret could make me feel truly special. And here, music wasn't something you listened to so much as played loudly and then shouted over. The flock wallpaper, the colours, the vibrant conversations, it was all another world and it fascinated me.

And how do West Indians show their love? With food, of course – lots of it. It was considered extremely bad manners to refuse anything and every morsel was delicious. It came from a world far, far from tripe: a world of sun and spice, where there were vegetables no one at Fairmile Hatch would have heard of, let alone tried. I loved it but dutifully eating all of it was not so easy. I ate so much that my stomach ached and I thought my body was going to explode, until eventually that wonderful food made me feel ill.

And then Dad took me back to Surrey and I walked into my own world. The world of structure and regularity. Yes, it was quiet and there were rules and chores and some of the children were a bit sad, but you knew where you were with it. I went straight to Margaret and she hugged me and told me about the episode of *Z-Cars* I had missed on Saturday. I realised, to my amazement, that I hadn't even thought of turning it on at Dad's house. Which was just as well because, if I had tried to watch it with Dad's friends, I could imagine their howls of derision.

That winter was a hard one. There was plenty of snow which impeded Shake's training. Dog training was something I took much more seriously than Shake did. I studied books on the subject and took him to obedience classes but somehow Shake remained entirely impervious to the importance of training. If he felt like it, he would behave: he even won prizes for obedience. Then, at the next competition, everyone wondered how he could ever have won anything, he was so naughty. What he wanted to do really was chase rabbits and if a rabbit came his way he forgot everything he had ever learned to pursue his goal. He also liked chasing motorbikes and, whenever one whizzed past the Lodge, Shake leapt to his feet and darted out into the road behind it. Incredibly, like Othello, he was never run over.

But the snow and ice had a more serious consequence for us. The milk float got stuck in the drive and Margaret, in her big-hearted way, went out to help the milkman push it. No one quite knew how, but during this exercise she broke a leg.

Auntie Margaret had to go to hospital. The house was hushed with horror. She was in hospital when everyone knew she should have been at home in the Lodge, taking care of us. She was supposed to be invincible and no one liked it when she wasn't.

We need not have worried. Although her recuperation meant we all had more chores, me in particular as the biggest boy, and there were many more helpers, she had no intention of relinquishing the reins. She simply directed proceedings from her chair. So it was all right. She was still there for us. Although deep down inside, I don't think any of us was truly comfortable until she was darting around the kitchen again.

Something similar happened when she went on holiday. Margaret had a friend living in Tobago – a female friend, we checked to make sure – and now she was going to stay with her and her partner for a few weeks. Margaret's holiday took over the house: an enormous, invisible, anxiety-inducing presence. It was talked about endlessly, there were detailed preparations and a large map was left in the living room which showed Tobago. It seemed to be a tiny dot in a double page of blue. Each child sought frequent reassurance and was told again and again who would be looking after us. But all the same, the Lodge was strangely silent when she had gone, as if holding its breath until she came home. And of course, she did come home. Bustling, her suitcase bulging with presents, noisy, with lots of stories to tell us.

Once again, normal life resumed. But it was not to last for long.

THREE

One teatime, Margaret gave us some news. All over Fairmile Hatch, the other housemothers were giving their families the same news and it had the same effect on everyone. It threw us into disarray. Old fears surfaced, dry beds became wet, smaller children clutched their blankets, even big boys like me were stunned.

The cottages at Fairmile Hatch were closing. They housed families of older children. The nursery would remain open for now. But we were too old to stay, we would have to move.

I knew that London County Council no longer ran the home. I knew, without understanding it, that we were in the care of the Borough Council. That hadn't seemed important at all. It had made no difference to us, except that Christmas presents were perhaps a bit nicer.

However, the Borough Council had decided that the older children must move.

"Why?" we asked.

When Auntie Margaret had given us the news she had been as robust as ever. Firm and positive and strong to support us against the blow she knew she was inflicting. But now even she shrugged helplessly.

"I expect it's all to do with money. You know how people in offices sit and fret about money all day."

We were silent. I imagined a fat man in a large office with his head in his hands.

"But," she continued, "you're not to worry. Here in the Lodge, we're all staying together. We'll have a house of our own just like we do now, only in a different place. So not much is changing really."

Not much. We were only losing our school friends, the community with which the home had so carefully integrated us, our teachers, our woods and parkland and rolling play areas, our loved and familiar landscape. That's all.

I asked: "Where are we going?"

Auntie Margaret said: "Crawley."

We looked at her blankly.

"In Sussex."

Everyone tried to think of anything they knew about Sussex. But none of us was even sure where it was.

"Sussex isn't far away, it's only the next county. And Crawley has a lot of new houses, a lot of new schools... a lot of new friends waiting for you. The house we're going to is bigger than the Lodge, so you'll have more space. And, we're all staying together, that's the main thing."

So she had seen it. That sudden day off recently. All those quiet conversations on the hall phone when she got back. She had been to Crawley to see our new house without any of us guessing a thing.

Auntie Margaret started to tell us which rooms we could have, the schools we would go to, but a voice interrupted her with a single word.

"Shake!"

The voice was mine. It sounded a bit more wobbly than usual. She was ready for me.

"Of course, Shake will come too. There are lots of parks where you can walk him, Michael, and he'll have his own special room at the back. I think he'll like it there."

Parks. Well, that sounded a bit different from the gardens and woods around Fairmile Hatch. Parks meant wardens who didn't let you climb the trees. Parks meant town. Parks meant rows and rows of houses on all sides of a patch of grass.

And then I understood that we were giving up our green world for a world more like my father's, a hard world of vertical bricks and horizontal paving, where you could get lost walking mile after mile past houses which all looked alike. Whereas it was a fact that no two trees looked the same so it was quite hard to get lost in the woods.

"Where will the others from the other houses be?" asked someone.

"The other children are going in different directions to different places," Margaret said cautiously.

"Are we the *only ones* going to Crawley?"

"We don't know who's going where yet," said Margaret, "but there will be other homes with other children in Crawley not far away from our house."

"Next door?"

"No, not actually next door. Elsewhere in Crawley."

It wouldn't be the same. We wouldn't be one small family among other families scattered inside the warm embrace of Fairmile Hatch's grounds. There would be other children in other homes in a town called Crawley in a county called Sussex.

"Will we know any of the other children in the other houses?" asked someone. "What about the nursery?"

"Listen," said Margaret. "I don't know who's going where. And it may be complicated for other people but it's not going to be complicated for us. We live at the Lodge now. Soon we're all going to be together in a different house. Simple."

I had friends in the various houses in Fairmile Hatch: I'd have to say goodbye to them. And it would be difficult leaving Kevin. Since his mother ran the nursery and the nursery was staying, I assumed he and his family would remain. But Kevin said they were moving too, and they were waiting to find out where. I hoped it would be Crawley.

"It's Croydon," he said one day. "Some children's home in a place called Croydon."

Croydon, Crawley, they sounded a bit alike, so perhaps they were close.

"Croydon's not that far away," said Margaret.

"Will I be able to get there on my bike?"

"Well, it's too far for that. But I don't think it's a very long train journey."

The train. So it wouldn't be a case of going over after school, the way we wandered in and out of each other's houses at the moment.

"Will we be moving in the summer holidays?"

Margaret shook her head.

"Much sooner than that," she said.

In fact, we said goodbye to Fairmile Hatch during the Easter holidays. I took one last walk around the place. I breathed in the smell of its newly mown spring grass and fed some of it to the two donkeys one last time. I went into the nursery where I had spent my early years and looked at the rows of cots. The rocking horse at the top of the stairs. The huge, heavy curtains hanging in the great windows.

Outside the Lodge, I said goodbye to Kevin and we promised to write and to visit each other. I took a last look at my small bedroom – as the eldest boy, I had my own. A last glance at the kitchen, Margaret's chore rota for this week still on the wall. Then I walked out and did not look back. Next week I would start the summer term at a new junior school and my life in Crawley would begin.

FOUR

Crawley wasn't as bad as I'd feared. The house wasn't old like the Lodge; it was very modern and from the outside it looked exactly like the other houses. You'd never have guessed it was a children's home. The other homes were scattered anonymously throughout the town.

Crawley was a new town, which didn't just mean that the houses were new, it meant someone had designed it, with parks and cycle ways and shopping centres. It hadn't just grown up, haphazardly, over centuries, like the villages around Fairmile Hatch.

The new junior school felt huge compared to the small village school in Surrey. There were so many classrooms and so many teachers that at first it was overwhelming and I kept my world small and focused until it began to seem normal. I made friends and, in answer to his questions, tried to tell one of them, Gary, about Fairmile Hatch. How just one room in the nursery could be as big as a house, how the lawns had spilled out into the woods and I'd cycled through them or along leafy lanes to visit my friends. He looked at me with incomprehension. And soon Fairmile Hatch began to seem, even to me, like some magical place which existed on another planet. In fact, there were rumours that even the nursery was closing. I tried not to think about that.

I developed new enthusiasms: collecting coins, collecting stamps and... horses. There was a stables not far away and in return for mucking out and helping, I was given riding lessons. At school I was part of a group on TV's *Young Scientists of the Year*, without ever really understanding what the point of growing plants in magnetic fields was but liking the teacher too much to ask. And at Cubs I threw myself into my role as lead soloist in the Gang Show.

The local paper reviewed our production in the usual glowing terms. Until my performance was discussed.

"This young, coloured boy shows promise of a very good voice in the future. At the moment, he needs a little singing training in opening his mouth wider."

I read and reread those words. I was nine years old and I couldn't understand why the reviewer had mentioned this: I must have been singing through closed lips. I felt horribly embarrassed. The poor photo of the show printed above the article had turned all of us to indistinguishable shades of grey but the writer had chosen to refer to my colour. And he had criticised me. This was the first time in my life that it occurred to me the two might be connected: my skin colour and criticism made of me. The possibility made me feel hurt and embarrassed. Surely my colour had not influenced his judgement of my singing? And why on earth would someone writing about the Gang Show care about my skin colour when no one else ever had?

I suspected that Auntie Margaret agreed with me. When I showed her the article she pursed her lips in a way which meant she was displeased. But, although she looked angry, she simply said: "Well, I thought your singing was wonderful, and so did a lot of other people." How I hated being singled out from the other children or being regarded as different.

She had already made friends at the Quaker Meeting House she now attended in Crawley and some of them had even come to see me in the Gang Show and afterwards they had all praised me. However, the article still stung. I cut it out and put it in the box in my room where I kept my certificates and Cubs badges but I had no intention of looking at it again.

I got on well at school and generally tried to please and to behave. But one day a very attractive schoolmate asked me to help her in class and the teacher, hearing my voice as I explained the sum to her, immediately called me to the front.

He asked me why I was talking and, since I could not tell him without getting my friend into trouble, I stood, squirming, in awkward silence.

"I have no choice, Michael, but to give you The Slipper," he said.

Mr Muldoon was not an unkind man. He was a good teacher and a man of his time and at that time, naughty boys could expect to receive physical punishment. It's just that I couldn't see myself as a naughty boy.

The class was very still. No one moved as he crossed the room to his desk where The Slipper was always at the ready. Every child knew what was going to happen. He picked up the large, brown leather slipper, which looked as if it might have done duty at his fireside for some years. I stared at it with wide eyes. I had seen him administer The Slipper before and the very thought of it made me cringe with embarrassment for the humiliation and pain of the recipient. It had never occurred to me that I, too, would fall victim to it.

Mr Muldoon said: "Turn around, Michael. And bend over."

I turned away from him and bent at the waist, cupping my hands around my ankles for support. There was a hideous pause which seemed to last for minutes, hours: I was waiting for pain, although I wasn't sure if any physical misery Mr Muldoon could inflict would be worse than the shame I now felt, bending over to offer him my bottom in front of the whole class.

Then, some rustling, followed by displacement of the air around me as The Slipper beat through its molecules with a slight whistling sound. Next, the impact. It nearly knocked me off my feet. And finally, just a second or two later, came its tardy twin: pain. I wanted to cry out loud as a sharp sting spread across my rear, radiating outwards from the point of impact, worse than a hundred nettles, more like a fire dispersing across my back or an animal with sharp claws crawling down my legs. I did not move until the pain had completed its burning journey over my body. Maybe I hoped it would just crawl down my legs and go away. But it did not go anywhere. I stood upright.

"Take your seat, Michael, and don't let me hear you talking in class again," Mr Muldoon said sternly.

I almost ran back to my chair. My head was bent. My eyes were on the floor. I was on fire. And far worse than my burning bottom was my utter, utter humiliation. I felt as though I could never look my friends in the face again, let alone actually play with them. I would have to go home and stay in my room for ever.

The class was very quiet and well behaved for the rest of the morning. No one looked at me but during the lunch break my friends were kind, and within a short time it seemed the incident was forgotten. Except by me. Because sitting down was a painful experience and looked as if it was going to remain that way for a while.

Mr Muldoon was an outdoors man, very tall and well built. He came from the Lake District and thought that it was important for children to have lots of exercise and so he would often take the whole class – more than 30 of us – outside to run around the school perimeter. It was about half a mile long. And if you crossed the finishing line first, you were given a bar of Kendal Mint Cake.

I had a sweet tooth and wanted to win the Kendal Mint Cake but it had never occurred to me that I really could.

Usually I just ran along with my friends. But that afternoon, I determined that I would try. I focused on the finishing line and on the knots of children I would have to pass to win, a couple of them known to be very speedy. And then I ran. Really ran. I stretched my thighs forward, my arms beat through the air, and as each foot hit the ground it seemed to be pushed back up by an invisible force. I could feel my own rhythm growing faster. I passed one group and then the next. I left my surprised friends far behind. When we turned the last corner I passed the class's fastest runners and still ran hard, enjoying the smell of the mown grass, revelling in the unaccustomed stretch in my legs, the feeling of excitement as I passed the others, the sense of speed and independence this run gave me.

Mr Muldoon nodded at the finishing line. I was across it long, long before the others. He looked at his watch.

"That's a record!" he said.

As the others arrived they all clustered around him. I heard people talking about how I had overtaken them effortlessly, just glided past them, broken the record... there was a new respect for me.

That was how Mr Muldoon gave me both The Slipper and Kendal Mint Cake in one day and I still don't know if it was my humiliation at the former or hunger for the latter which enabled me to discover my competitive spirit and love of running for the first time. But after that there was no stopping me. I joined the local athletics club and running became an important part of my life. Little did I know that my ability to outpace others was going to become extremely useful in the future.

FIVE

The comprehensive school in Crawley was huge, with more than 2,000 pupils. On arriving at age 11, I was put in the second stream for almost every subject. This surprised me, as my results from the junior school had been good.

I complained to Margaret. "Is it because they know I'm in care?"

Margaret wasn't having that.

"It's no use moaning. Whatever daft ideas they have about children in care, you just prove them wrong. You should work so hard and get such good grades that they have to put you up to the top stream. I know you can, Michael."

This is exactly what happened. I was soon in the top stream for everything but maths. I had a particular interest in languages and found a French penfriend. Astonishingly, her family invited me to stay with them for a few weeks in the summer holidays.

"Shall I go?" I asked Margaret. I was only 13 and there was no way she could take time off to travel with me. I would have to organise the trip myself.

"Of course you must go," she said. She was busy mending while she played a board game with one of the boys. Even though she had pins in her mouth.

"How do I do it?" I asked.

She took the pins out and said: "You need to find the right train timetables. I'm sure you'll manage."

In that huge school there were less than a handful of other black kids and our colour said one thing about us: that we were in care. This isn't something I ever talked about or referred to. Frankly, I was a bit ashamed. I had picked up that there was a stigma about being in care. As for my colour, although now I knew that some people felt my colour must make me significantly different, for a long time I didn't view it as stigmatising. However, those suspicions I'd had when I read the nasty review of the Scouts' show in the local paper had grown.

And gradually, they became a certainty. One way I knew this was by watching television. At home, Margaret had various helpers and in the evening they sometimes watched TV with us. A very popular programme was called *Till Death Us Do Part*. It starred a white, working-class bigot called Alf Garnett.

Alf Garnett expressed views I hadn't heard before. He was opposed to any kind of immigration and hated black people, feeling they had no right to be here and were corroding white culture. He expressed his views in a very forthright way that was supposed to be funny. A lot of people laughed at it. Some of the staff never missed an episode and found Garnett hilarious.

The character would spar with his more liberal son-in-law. I seem to remember an exchange about a black man going something like this:

GARNETT: Why doesn't that wog go back to the jungle where he belongs?
SON-IN-LAW: Because he's British.
GARNETT: British people, you Scouse git, aren't that colour!
SON-IN-LAW: He was born here. He's never lived anywhere else.

GARNETT: Well, it must have been a bloody hot day
when he was born!

HOWLS OF LAUGHTER FROM THE AUDIENCE.

I watched this programme with extreme discomfort. It made
me squirm and shuffle in my seat. I didn't know how I was
supposed to react or what I should do. Laugh along? I just
couldn't. And I didn't understand why all the staff didn't share
my discomfort. How could they really think it was all right to
sit laughing at this at all, let alone when a black person was
in the room?

It must have been a bloody hot day when he was born!

There was only one person sensitive to my discomfort,
and that was Margaret. She tried to explain it was satire, that
we were supposed to laugh at Alf Garnett because he and his
views were so ridiculous. But I couldn't really see the satire.
Perhaps because I was too young. And perhaps because it
seemed to me that people were laughing with Alf Garnett,
not at him.

I decided to stop watching the programme, and Margaret
did the same. Alf Garnett was so similar to the British people
my father had often described to me that I began to wonder
whether my father might be right when he talked about prejudice. It was confusing. I liked the staff but, from my room,
doing my homework, I could hear Alf Garnett's voice raised
and the staff roaring with laughter which seemed whole-
hearted and not satirical at all.

I was just reaching an age when people did talk very openly
about race. A particular target were the Asians who had been
so callously expelled from Uganda by the dictator, Idi Amin.
They were shown on the news arriving in the UK in their
thousands. A few came to Crawley, perhaps because of our
proximity to Gatwick Airport, and attracted great hostility.

When I heard the way children talked about them, I knew they were only copying their parents, but I wondered if they talked about all dark-skinned people the same way. Behind my back. To my face, colour was discussed, but in broad, general terms. For instance, one of my classmates maintained that black people are less intelligent than white. But I was sure he didn't mean to say that I was less intelligent.

I did discuss this with Margaret.

"You can choose whether to be hurt and offended or not," she told me. "It's a choice you can make."

"How?"

"You can recognise that something's offensive without being hurt by it. Stop. Think. Decide how you want to react."

"But what can I actually do?"

"If you've thought about it and decided something's offensive, then you can take action. You can point it out to the person, because they might not have realised. Or you can complain through the right channels. There is a system, so use it. Don't take it all on your own shoulders to sort things out."

"I can't complain about the other kids in my class."

"You can stand up for yourself. But only if it's aimed at you personally. If it's not, then don't take it personally."

I did develop a piercing glare when other children were rude about Asians or black people but I stayed quiet. I was willing to adopt Margaret's soft line because I had by now seen a different response to racism: my father's. He was a raw nerve. And a very proud man. He would fly off the handle and yell mercilessly at anyone who tried to put him down. This was highly embarrassing. Whoever had provoked him always saw his fury as proof that their insults were justified: black people just did not know how to behave.

So I thought long and hard about all this and decided Margaret was right. If people said things which upset me, I wouldn't respond instantly with screaming or shouting, even if

I wanted to. I'd think hard about whether I was going to let words hurt me and then I'd decide what action I wanted to take.

At school, I was determined to show that black people did know how to behave and I worked hard, listened in lessons, was always respectful, and when the other kids locked our good-hearted maths teacher in the cupboard, it was me who let her out. Out of school, I was always busy. One of the teachers was a keen yachtsman and, although we were far from the sea, he took some of us sailing and helped us pass Royal Yachting Association exams. One teacher was restoring some vintage jeeps; at the weekends a little group of us sometimes helped him paint them. And I ran a lot. I liked cross-country but my favourite was the 800 metres. At Crawley Athletics Club there was an experienced coach who presented me with a training programme, which, alone, running around the park and in the streets, I followed.

I was cycling to the athletics club in the dark one evening when a police panda car pulled over and flashed its lights at me. I was immediately frightened. I must have done something wrong. I wasn't sure what – my lights were working – but, my heart beating fast and my mouth dry, I watched the police officer climb out of his car and walk towards me. Obviously, he was going to arrest me. I stood very still, waiting, hoping he wouldn't handcuff me.

"Sorry to stop you, son, I'm new around here. Can you tell me how to get to Lancing Close?"

He smiled and I breathed again and gave him directions.

We chatted for a while and it turned out he was our local beat bobby. He said he would call around at the house and one day he did. Margaret was pleased to meet him and a friendship between us all developed. It looked as though here was another PC Aherne, although I could see Margaret hoping that this time I wouldn't be given a dog, especially not a disobedient dog like Shake.

We met again much sooner than we expected. I was asleep in my small bedroom on the ground floor one night, just recovering from flu, when I dreamt that glass was breaking. I had taken paracetamol and my dreams were strange and felt real so I half-opened my eyes and recognised the sound and the shadow I could see as part of a feverish nightmare. I closed my eyes and tried to go back to sleep and have a nicer dream. For a few minutes.

At a sense of movement in the room, I opened my eyes again, wide this time. And what I saw made me fully alert. Someone was climbing out of the double window. I sat bolt upright. The street lamp glittered unnaturally on the floor. Glass. Shattered glass, a figure at the window and now... the figure had hit the ground and had turned at the sound of my movement. A man. He stared back into the room, stared directly at me. A pale, round face at the window, ringed by shattered glass, lit by a street lamp. Looking at me. I looked back. And in a second he was gone, the sound of his feet pounding against the pavement as he raced down the street.

This was as eerie and frightening as anything I had seen on TV, but I had no time to process my own terror. I had taken Margaret's advice to heart and was learning to stop, think and decide how to react whenever someone said something hurtful about black people in general or me in particular. What a great technique I was finding this. Gradually, I had begun to notice that I could process any powerful emotion this way. Stop, think, decide how to react. It eased any amount of pain or anger. And in this case, fear.

So I did all the right things.

I ran straight upstairs, where all the other bedrooms were, and I woke Auntie Margaret, crying: "Call the police, we've been burgled!"

While she was doing that, I went to the room at the back, where Shake had managed to slumber throughout. I let him out, hoping he would straight away smell the burglar, but he yawned and stretched and failed to see any urgency in the situation.

Auntie Margaret was looking carefully in the kitchen to see what was missing.

"Fingerprints!" I reminded her, as if this was a necessary thing to say to any TV crime aficionado.

"Now, how is it that Shake slept all the way through?" she asked. "He usually wakes up at the slightest sound." She was always kind to Shake but probably not a member of his fan club.

I looked at Shake reproachfully. Unfortunately, he decided to redeem himself when our friend the local bobby arrived very shortly afterwards. Shake went into a barking frenzy and nearly barked the house down.

"Too late, mate," said the policeman.

Oh, Shake.

The officer's presence was reassuring. He asked me to describe the man and I said I thought he was quite young, tall with dark hair. His face had been round, not hollowed out like an older person's.

"Was he white or black?" asked the officer. It hadn't occurred to me to mention his colour. Virtually everyone in Crawley was white.

The policeman went off looking for the culprit immediately while Margaret ascertained what was missing. Not much: a little money and some trivial household items. And then, I started to tremble. I had stopped, thought, processed, I had done all that. And now, suddenly, I was terrified. That face at the window, its whiteness shining, its eyes wide. I never ever wanted to see that again. A face at my window.

"Are you all right, Michael?" asked Margaret kindly. "It must have been very frightening for you."

I could not hide my distress. Auntie Margaret put an arm around me and then we went into the bedroom and began to clear up the glass which covered much of the floor.

"Don't tread here in bare feet," she instructed. "We'll sort this out properly in the morning."

"But supposing he comes back?"

Margaret and I pulled the wardrobe as far as we could in front of the window, glass crunching beneath our feet.

"He won't get past that," she said. "And in the morning we'll have it repaired."

The police officer returned, reporting that there was no sign of the young man.

"Michael's a bit nervous," said Margaret. "It must have been terrifying, knowing the man was in his room."

The policeman agreed and told me how brave I'd been.

"You don't have to worry," he reassured me. "He won't be back. Even if he tried, your dog will be on the alert this time."

I looked at Shake. He looked more like a dog that wanted to go back to his basket than a dog on the alert.

The policeman left. It was 3:30am. Shake settled down. Auntie Margaret went back upstairs. I lay in bed. Wide awake. Tense. At each tiny sound my body froze. Wild thoughts rushed through my mind. The man had seen my face and I had seen his. We had stared at each other. Maybe he would be back to kill me to prevent me giving evidence. Or perhaps he would return to go upstairs. Maybe he thought there were riches waiting there instead of just five sleeping children and Margaret. And, the wardrobe didn't really cover the smashed window. It made me feel better, but it wouldn't stop a deter- mined crook who wanted to climb in. I began to tremble uncontrollably. It was hard to stop.

At first light, I got up. I dressed quickly, stepping around the glass for my clothes. Then I woke Shake and put on his lead. It was ridiculously early for a morning walk but it was better than lying in bed sweating with terror.

There was no one around at this time. Shake seemed to have forgotten the night's drama and trotted cheerfully at my side, stopping to smell things. We went to the park, which was eerily empty.

Except for one bench. Unusually, someone lay there asleep. They must have been there all night. I had never seen that in our park before.

Shake took one look at the slumbering man and began to bark. It was his alarm bark. Angry, frantic, it was the bark he should have given last night. I stared at the man. Young, tallish. This might be the intruder. I stared harder. Black hair, round, white face. It was him.

Heart thudding, my legs rushing with adrenalin, I dragged the reluctant Shake away: he wanted to stay and bark. Amazingly, he did not wake up the man. We ran as fast as we could to the police house. After being called in the middle of the night I thought the policeman might be slow and drowsy like other people in the morning, but within a minute or two he was ready to go, just like the cops in TV shows. Always at the ready. Then, excitingly, Shake and I climbed into his police car and he drove back towards the bench.

The man was still asleep.

The bobby said to me: "I'm sure this is the man we're after. Well done, Michael. Now you go and stand back. Over there."

He radioed for more cops to come and I watched from a distance as he woke the slumbering man. Dazed and confused and not entirely happy to be woken by a police officer, the man stood up.

The bobby turned to me.

"Off you go, Michael," he said, and once again I dragged Shake away. His ears were forward and he had been watching eagerly. Shake was a police dog now.

At breakfast, the other children learned of the break-in.

"Weren't you scared?" they asked. Actually, my terror had been eased by seeing the man. I realised he was young. Shabby. A bit sad, really. Now I had seen him and watched the police dealing with him, I wasn't scared at all. And I knew it was important to reassure the other children.

"I didn't have time to be frightened," I told them. There was no way I was going to mention that haunting face at the window. "He was on his way out before I really knew he was there."

"Why didn't Shake bark?" asked another child. Good question. We all looked at Shake now, curled up and fast asleep after his busy night.

Margaret said: "You don't have to be afraid, any of you. Intruders aren't interested in us, they just want our stuff, and we don't have much of that."

When I got home from school I learned that the man had been carrying the stolen items and money and had been arrested. The window was repaired. The wardrobe was back in its right place.

A crime. A hunch. An investigation. The satisfaction of arrest. This was the justice system at work. I was already in love with it from *Z-Cars* and *Dixon of Dock Green* (we were heartbroken that *Softly, Softly* had ended), but now I had actually experienced it for myself. I knew for a fact that I wanted to join the police. That was the good thing to come out of the burglary. The bad thing was that I could not forget the face at the window. It reappeared from time to time, unexpectedly, for no apparent reason, in my dreams. Wet with sweat, shaking, I was always woken by the face. And even though I had now seen the sad young man it belonged to and knew he wasn't scary at all, the face never failed to terrify me.

SIX

I joined in lots of activities but I didn't join any particular groups. If school is divided into cliques or tribes – and at our school, tough, fighting, white skinheads were the dominant tribe – I didn't feel I belonged to any of them. I did have friends, though, and my best mate was Gary. He was very bright and he loved languages. His enthusiasm was infectious. French became my favourite subject. I especially liked the teacher, a retired army major, whose classes had everyone listening and working hard. Some of us helped him restore his old military vehicles at the weekends.

One break time a boy was handing out leaflets. I caught sight of only a sentence on this leaflet. But a sentence was enough.

"We advocate the humane repatriation of coloured immigrants and their families."

I froze. Better not to react right now. Better to think first.

Just in case any feelings showed, I didn't want people to see me reading it. I didn't even want to discuss it with Gary. I shoved it in my school bag. It lay there for the rest of the day like an unexploded bomb. When I got home I went straight to my room to read it.

The leaflet was produced by something called the National Front, and it was aimed at recruiting schoolchildren.

"Are you tired of having to endure social studies or history lessons where the teacher continually tries to run

down Britain while at the same time black kids have Black Studies lessons to give them more self-respect and black pride? And are you tired of lessons where the teachers have to go at a snail's pace to allow immigrant kids who don't speak English to keep up? We advocate the humane repatriation of coloured immigrants and their families. Schoolkids don't have much choice about whether they want to go to a school overrun by young thugs."

It is difficult to describe how it felt for the child of black immigrants to read something like that. How acutely isolating it was. How deeply hurtful to be judged, not on my hard work or achievements or behaviour, but purely on assumptions based on something outside my control. How undermining of everything I had been taught to believe in about right and wrong. How unjust to judge me by one standard and white children by another. It is difficult to describe how utterly humiliated I was by that leaflet. How demeaned. How defeated.

I remembered Margaret's words. Insults are about how you deal with them. About whether you take them personally. About whether you want to be hurt or choose not to be.

I was 13. Of course that leaflet cut me to the quick. But I was not going to let fury and pain rule me. The National Front wanted to hurt me because I was black, and so I was not going to let them. The key to defeating them was not to be offended, not to take it personally, but to recognise the highly offensive nature of the material. And to take *appropriate* action.

That night I barely slept as I planned my response. At school the next day I asked the boy who had been handing out the leaflets where they came from. It soon became obvious he hadn't really read one. That at least was a relief: an isolating factor was that no one else appeared to find the leaflet obnoxious enough to object to, not even the few other dark-skinned pupils, be they black or Asian.

The boy explained that another lad had asked him to give out the leaflets. As a detective in the making, it didn't take me long to find out where they had come from.

And that was the second shock.

My favourite teacher. The major who taught French. The coloured immigrant who should be (humanely) repatriated was one of his best pupils. With some of my mates I'd been carefully painting his old jeeps outside his house. I had felt great sympathy for him because his wife had died and he was clearly grieving for her. All in all, I had respected him and thought we liked each other. And now it emerged that he believed in my repatriation, believed I was a thug because I was black. He had brought the leaflets to school and asked pupils to distribute them because he was apparently senior in the local National Front branch and they were having a recruitment drive among the young.

It is hard to say which was more devastating, the leaflet itself or the source of it.

I went to the Head Teacher. That wasn't so easy for a pupil to do, unless you had been very naughty, because the school was vast and the head busy. Surprisingly, she agreed to see me. I handed her the leaflet and then watched her face redden as she studied it.

She promised me that she would deal with the matter at once. She would find out where these leaflets came from, take action against whomever had brought them into the school and ensure that no such literature would enter the gates again.

I was satisfied with that. Justice would be done. But I had a problem of my own now: French class.

I knew. He knew. He knew I knew. It could never be the same again, at least not for me.

The Major, however, had decided to appear oblivious to the problem. I sat out the rest of his lessons in profound discomfort, watching him, wondering how it was that I'd had no inkling of his racist views.

A few weeks later the Head assured me that the relevant staff member had been dealt with. She didn't name him, but of course I knew who it was. He kept his job, so I wasn't sure how he'd been dealt with. The following year I was given a different teacher, but I went on to win the school prize for languages (a book token, with which I bought a book called The Police Manual).

I did think to myself that, as usual, Margaret had been right. Instead of being offended and showing my anger and pain by blowing my top, the way my father would have done, I had calmly, incisively, used the channels of authority to defeat racism. It is, after all, a form of injustice and by now I had an abhorrence of injustice.

After this, I had to accept that being black meant being different and, to Margaret's bewilderment, I became very interested in black culture. I loved blaxploitation movies like Shaft and its successors, movies with black heroes. Posters of them hung on my walls. I fell in love with reggae and soul and The Jackson 5, especially Michael Jackson, who was about the same age as me. And gradually my hair became Afro. This just meant growing it, untamed, until it flew around my face and bounced when I walked. It wasn't a big statement. But it was an indication that I knew there was another tribe which I might belong to.

Margaret said nothing, although I could see this perplexed her. However, I still went to classical music concerts with her and enjoyed them. We still talked about The Beatles and occasionally played Elvis Presley. And I allowed myself to be dragged along to The Sound of Music three times in all. Greater love hath no man.

"I'm not sure," said an intense and well-meaning social worker, "that you're really black enough."

Yes, social workers, appearing at a moment's notice, writing reports, making suggestions, were still the bane of my life, although these days some of them actually talked to me. And the threat of removal, by them and by my parents, had diminished now. My mother no longer applied to take me to Jamaica; in fact, she seldom visited these days. I preferred it that way. Dad came occasionally but he no longer talked about withdrawing me to live in Balham. They both had other partners and other children now.

"No, really," said the white social worker, scraping hair to the side of her face in order to scrutinise me intensely. "You're just not steeped in black culture enough; you're not sufficiently interested in the black struggle."

I told her I liked The Jackson 5. She looked unimpressed by this offering.

A few days later, a parcel arrived addressed to me. Inside was a book about Malcolm X.

"Who's he?" I asked Margaret.

"He's dead now. He was American. A black activist who believed that violence is an acceptable way to bring about change. I preferred Dr Martin Luther King myself."

I'd heard that name before.

"He also wanted change, but he didn't think anger and violence was the right way to go about it," Margaret explained.

It sounded as though Dr Martin Luther King was my kind of man.

"You should look into all this and make up your own mind," added Margaret.

But the words activist and violence were enough to put me off Malcolm X and I knew I probably wouldn't read the book. As usual, a social worker had brought confusion and doubt into my life. There was only one way to deal with it: I put on my trainers and set off for the park.

For me, running wasn't just a competitive sport – although it certainly was that, too. It gave me time to be alone, to meditate, to sort out life's confusions, to be free, propelled forward under my own steam. Crawley Athletics Club had some distinguished runners and the coach had little time left for me, but his low-key, encouraging approach made me want to do well and on my own I followed exactly the training programme he had drawn up, demanding though it was.

Now I had become one of the best runners in the school. I'd broken school records and this brought me status and respect. I was tall but rather shy and I had hoped that excelling on the athletics field would bring girls flocking to me. But so far that was not a result.

I would not miss a training run at that time because I was representing the school in the 800 metres at the county championships soon. And I was determined to win, although I had previously been outclassed by one runner in particular and I knew my chances were slim. Experience had already taught me that setting a goal and striving for it is a good way to progress, and defeating this boy was my goal.

SEVEN

The biology teacher announced that we were going to do a project on a subject which interested us.

"You'll be researching and planning the topic and giving a talk to the class as well."

This sounded fun. I waited while each pupil was allocated a topic. I liked the biology teacher and he knew of my interest in birds and animals so I expected he'd select one for my topic: lapwings, perhaps.

The teacher said: "Self-reliance."

I looked at him in surprise.

"What's that?" I asked.

"The title of your talk."

"But..." There wasn't any kind of an animal called a self-reliance to my knowledge. "What does it mean?"

"Go and find out."

I wasn't even sure I could spell it accurately enough to look it up.

"But why that?" I asked. "Why self-reliance?"

"Because you practise it so well and the other children will benefit from hearing you talk about it."

So, self-reliance it was. For a long time I had no idea how to tackle the subject and finally, desperate for some ideas, I talked to Margaret.

She was sitting in the living room now, not doing anything in particular, which was very strange, because she was always busy. She wasn't even watching the television.

She said: "Self-reliance. Well, why not tell them about your trips to France?"

My trip to my French penfriend didn't happen just once, I had been back each summer. I couldn't see why the class would want to know about this, though. After all, the topic wasn't holidays.

"Well, how many other children in your class could get themselves to France from the age of 13? Alone? With no one helping them organise it at all?"

When I thought hard I had to admit that probably none of them could.

So I told the class about obtaining the relevant time-tables and studying them for hours to analyse the trains and connections. Buying the tickets. Packing. Finally, catching the train, then the ferry, then the train to Paris, crossing the city from the Gare du Nord to Montparnasse, catching another train towards La Rochelle and then a bus to Nalliers. I'd have a great few weeks with my tomboy penfriend Yveline and her family and then I'd come all the way back. It was always an adventure. Once, staying as sharp as ever like Shaft, I managed to outwit a gang of pickpockets in the act at Gare du Nord and return a tourist's stolen purse to her. But I didn't tell the class about that in case they thought I was boasting.

When I finished, there was silence. I hoped it wasn't because everyone was thinking about the reason I had to do all this alone: because I lived in a children's home and my housemother was far too busy to help. Or because they were remembering that the council would not pay for me to go on school trips and I had to sit the week out with the younger kids when my own class went away.

But the silence was followed by a round of applause. Probably the other children, who had annual holidays with their families, organised by their families, were genuinely surprised.

"And that," said the biology teacher, "is self-reliance."

We were getting ready for O-levels and CSEs now, which were the GCSEs of my era. Another project topic for these was chosen by me. In it I wrote:

> "At the time of writing this project, the Law Lords made a ruling that it was legal to have a colour bar in working men's clubs. This will not help the situation at all... You cannot legislate against prejudice but you can legislate against discrimination. Think how ridiculous it would be if we discriminated against people with black hair!"

My subject was immigration. In the introduction I explained that, as the son of West Indian immigrants, I had a special interest in the topic but that it was my aim to be 'factual, truthful and unbiased', although I also described the subject as 'delicate and controversial'.

> "One view put forward by people I think are prejudiced is that Negroes are less intelligent than other races. They illustrate this by looking at areas like South Africa. This view has been mentioned by members of my class at school and all I can say is: how can Negro people use the IQ they were born with if they have not had the opportunities that you have had to apply their IQ? It is totally unfair to stereotype all Negroes. There are plenty of intelligent black people."

Despite my quest for the truth, quite a few feelings did find their way into the project. I didn't see my father often but I was certainly influenced by his views, as well as by my summers in France, where my loyal penfriend instantly attacked anyone who dared to call me "le coon anglais".

> "*I noticed how friendly the French people were when I went to France… Every time we met we shook hands… the English are not so friendly. The white man and the coloured man may work quite happily together, but when they get home they will probably each go their separate ways and not mix until the next day at work…*"

That last comment certainly came from Dad, who often said that you just didn't see black and white people socialising, not even drinking at the pub together.

Margaret read the project before I handed it in, sitting at the kitchen table.

"This is good, Michael, very good. It's full of facts and figures as well as examples. I expect them to give you a very high grade."

Auntie Margaret could be counted on to encourage me. The National Front leaflet, the discussions about Asians and black people at school, although not personal, could undermine my confidence. It was Margaret, and her belief that I was clever, trustworthy, and capable of achieving anything I wanted to, that did most to counter any effects of discrimination.

But now, as she sat in the kitchen, praising my project, I noticed that she was pale. Her feet were up on a stool and she looked exceptionally tired. One of the smaller children had been adopted and we had a new child who was proving very difficult: that must be why she was so tired.

I wondered if she was too exhausted to look at the contents of an envelope I was carrying in my school bag. But she asked at once: "What's that?"

"I sent off for it."

I was still determined to join the police. I had talked to Ray about it, a police liaison officer at school, who had told me there was now a cadet training programme which you could join on leaving at 16. And I had written for information.

The pack had arrived in a big, brown envelope and, when I opened it, the first words I read were: DULL IT ISN'T. As if I needed persuading.

"Look... I could go after O-levels," I said. "It's at Hendon in north London. I'd have to live there. For two years."

We both knew there was going to be a problem next spring. I would be 16. That meant the council no longer had a duty to care for me and people told stories of children being sent out into the world as soon as the last crumbs of birthday cake were eaten. We were confident that the Borough Council would continue to fund me until I finished my exams in June. But after that I would have to leave Auntie Margaret and, since I had nowhere to go, I was already having sleepless nights.

"Would you be a policeman at the end of the cadet course?" asked Margaret, waking up a little as she, too, realised the solution the college offered.

"No, afterwards I'd have to go on the usual 16-week police officer training course. But at cadet college I could take A-levels. And look at all the things I could do: lots of sport, judo, traffic control, CID, community service... And you get to shadow real police officers and visit police stations."

Margaret flicked through the literature and then looked at me.

"It's perfect," she said. "When can you apply?"

"By the end of the month."

She smiled. I realised she hadn't smiled like that for quite a while. Maybe this new child was really too much for her. Margaret's ready smiles had been almost as important to me as meals for much of my life.

"We'll talk to John Turner about it," she said. "He'll have to write you some sort of a reference, I expect."

John Turner was our current social worker and he was not like all the others. He was the first to actually talk to me, and for some time and in some detail. With empathy. He was kind and supportive to Margaret, too.

"That's wonderful. Now I can sleep soundly," she said, getting up to go to bed.

I couldn't help noticing that she stood more slowly than usual. She was generally such a bouncy person. Was this what happened when people got old? After all, she was probably not far off 30 and that seemed very old to me.

The schools county athletics championships finally rolled around. They were held in Brighton. As we gathered for the 800m, I noticed a slight taste of sea salt in my mouth as I looked for my nemesis, the boy I had determined to beat.

There he was. Tall and blond, good-looking, a St Christopher prominent on a chain around his neck, he was always surrounded by adoring girls. And he had some very fast times, far faster than mine.

His bravado was evident well before we started the race. He was a good actor, ridiculously confident, even smiling as he looked around at the lesser mortals who were competing with him. By this time, I was beginning to understand the importance of psychology in winning a race. I knew that, however I felt, I would have to radiate confidence, even aggression, or all would be lost.

I made myself look him directly in the eye. I thought: "I've got a wonderful coach. I've trained and trained and trained for this. And I'm determined to win."

All that must have shown on my face because his golden smile faded slightly and, for a few moments, he ceased to shine. I didn't quite have the confidence to smile but I continued to look at him with an expression which said: "I'm going to beat you."

We were running the race with our faces before we were even under starter's orders. But at last we got onto the track and my body was so alive with adrenalin that I really felt I had to win. I had trained so hard, I must win.

It was a warm day and the distinctive smell of the cinder track filled my nose and then my head. There was that wait for the pistol, which feels like hanging in some time lock without a past or a future. And then, bang! A surge of energy like an electric current and a slap as my feet made contact with the ground. The stretch in my limbs as they strained forward. The shouting crowd. The sensation of speed, my own, of cutting through the salty summer air. My arms beating. My soles on springs. Running well, running steadily, keeping something back inside me.

And now, the bell rang and here we were on the final lap. The noise of the crowd grew louder. The air seemed to grow thicker. I increased my speed without pain. I approached a knot of fast runners. They accelerated but I accelerated more. I passed them. In the corner of my eye I perceived their knees and elbows working like pistons, propelling them forward, straining, their feet thumping heavily against the track.

So, here was my rival. He was ahead of the knot but not much. At the sight of him I reached inside myself and found something – an energy, a form of propulsion, a forward thrust – which pushed me closer until I was close enough to touch him. He did not turn around, but he knew I was there. The finishing line was just ahead. He tried to accelerate, but I saw him strain with an immense effort which failed to increase his speed. I did not look at him as I overtook him. My joy at passing him and the crescendo of shouting pushed me along. My lungs on fire, my heart bursting, my breath in short supply, my legs stone, I crossed the line. First. The elation. The relief. Then the effort to reclaim my body, to breathe.

I had beaten him. And that was more important even than winning, because he was my target. In those moments of joy it seemed to me, for the first time ever, that anything was possible.

EIGHT

I applied to the police cadets and went to Hendon for an interview. Then it was a question of waiting. For months and months and months. I wanted very much indeed to be accepted. A chapter in my life would be closing when I left the home in Crawley after my exams and I wanted the next chapter to be the police cadets.

One evening, after tea, when we were all at home, one of the other aunties, someone who had been helping Auntie Margaret a lot lately, asked us to come into the living room. We were surprised to find other staff members there. This was strange. We knew them, but they usually didn't all work at once.

I have been unable to retain any memory of how they broke the news which followed. I don't know how they said it or exactly what words they used. The effect on the six of us was so terrible that somehow my brain has simply filtered that out, too.

We all knew by now that Auntie Margaret was ill. There had been a few hospital stays and she was obviously very tired. I had been doing lots of extra chores until her health improved and Margaret had been allowing other people to run the house and help make decisions, which was entirely out of character. But she had nearly always been there. Yesterday she had gone to hospital again; we expected her home within the week.

There was a sort of fluttering among all the helpers in the room as we sat down, which made me feel uncomfortable. One of them got up to speak. She told us that Auntie Margaret was very ill indeed, much more so than any of us had realised. Margaret had assumed she would get better, of course. But now the doctors had told her that she would not come out of hospital again. She had a disease called ovarian cancer, which the hospital could not treat. And so she was going to die. Quite soon.

I think someone screamed. I think everyone cried. I expect it took me a while to process, as usual. I needed time for the true impact of this news to devastate me. I probably took care of the little kids while I did that. I only know it was awful. It is unbearable to recall it.

Pain and anxiety then became a constant, day-to-day fixture of our lives. I knew I should support the younger children, some of whom showed signs of falling apart. To be honest, there were times when I felt I was falling apart myself. My rock, my magnetic north, my moral compass, my everything was leaving us. She did not want to go. She could never return.

To make matters worse, no one knew what would happen to our house. As well as the fear of losing Margaret there was the fear of losing each other, because the house might now be closed and the children scattered. Some of us had been there since we had left Fairmile Hatch and really felt like family. And, because everyone knew that my time in care was coming to an end, perhaps there was a fear of losing me, too.

A husband-and-wife team arrived to deal with this emergency. God knows how Gill and Tony did it. I've chosen not to remember anything. I do recall my determination to work hard and do well in my exams for Margaret's sake. The possibility that she would not be around to receive the results was an immense, dark cloud which I simply could not bear to look at.

The shock almost knocked the police cadets out of my mind. So when an envelope arrived telling me that I had been accepted, I had to read it several times to take it in.

I knew at once what I had to do. And right now. Auntie Margaret had been hoping and praying that my application would be successful, not least because she believed that in her absence the police would look after me. I had to tell her the good news.

Telling her seemed like the most urgent, the most important thing in the world. With the letter in my pocket I leapt to my feet and ran straight to the bus stop. If it hadn't come quite soon I probably would have run all the way but the bus pulled up almost immediately. It may not even have quite stopped at the hospital before I was off it and sprinting through the grounds and then along the corridors to her ward.

I bounded to her bedside.

Last time I had visited her she could talk to me and I had detected something of her old vigour. Now she was silent. She gestured with one hand to acknowledge my arrival, which I took firmly in mine. She looked so small and frail. She was so pale, so bloodless, that she was almost blue.

"I've been accepted! They've taken me! I can move there in the summer!"

I let go of her hand and got out the letter and waved it.

She turned her head to look at me now. With great difficulty. And with even greater difficulty, she smiled.

"Good," she whispered in a faraway voice.

I believe I did see relief in her face.

As a robust woman she had embraced me so many times, ever since I was tiny. Now I was tall and gangly and nearly 16 and she was the tiny one. And there was a new sense of distance about her. She was there, but not there. I knew she was beginning a long journey alone and the thought made me feel cold and helpless. And frightened.

I could not hug her or hold her, as that would have been like hugging a tiny bird. I stroked her hand. Just once. Slowly. And said goodbye. Her eyes were closed now and I left the ward quietly. My legs had acquired a new weight. They felt so strange I had to concentrate on putting one in front of the other. A sort of darkness travelled back inside me. On the bus. In the streets. I arrived home to the news that she had died.

NINE

I do not remember anything about Margaret's funeral. So either we were not expected to go or I have simply chosen not to remember it. I recall little about the aftermath of her death in our house, except I know it was terrible. And that my way of coping was to help the smaller children and to focus on my exams. I had to do well for her.

In the circumstances, I was not asked to leave the children's home as soon as my exams were over. Gill and Tony, as the houseparents who had replaced Margaret, were adamant that I should not only stay but that when I left I was to regard the home as somewhere I was welcome to stay at any time. And, since there was a grown man about the house now, I was relieved of some chores. But, despite their kindness, grief was a heavy blanket which seemed to smother the place. I wanted to leave, I was just waiting for the day I could move to Hendon.

I was still there when my exam results came through. I had eight good O-levels.

Despite the great loss of Margaret, I had worked hard, was in the top stream for almost everything and had good mock results, so was pleased but not astonished by my grades. The school, however, could hardly believe them. They contacted me to ask me why, with O-levels like that, wasn't I staying on for A-levels? It was the first time they had ever attempted to discuss A-levels with me.

It occurred to me – and this was not a comfortable feeling – that, despite all evidence to the contrary, their expectations of me had been very low. That might be because I was in care. This stigmatising fact had always been a good explanation for almost anything – rudeness, abuse, an implied inferiority. After all, some children were in care because they'd been in trouble with the police or they'd been violent, so people were bound to expect the worst.

So it was easier for me to think that any shabby treatment I received was because I was in care rather than because I was black. But now, there were the school's unexplainably low expectations. Five years of working hard, good behaviour and excellent results and yet they were still very surprised when I did well. Surely... no, surely not? Surely the school didn't have low expectations of me because of my colour? I tried to banish the thought but once it had arrived, it wouldn't go away.

I recalled a remark I had overheard a few years ago from one of the ever-changing kaleidoscope of social workers.

"Michael's just too intelligent for his own good."

At the time I had chosen to see it as a compliment and I had wondered why Margaret reacted to this remark with something like anger. Now I wondered if she had believed that what the social worker had really meant was: "Michael's just too intelligent for a black boy." I wished I could ask her.

I couldn't help noticing that, in contrast to the low academic expectations, no one had any problem accepting that I excelled as a runner. This was entirely all right for a black person. We were acknowledged to be good at running and to dance well. But now I realised that we were not supposed to be clever.

The possibility that even the school that knew me well had judged my academic potential on the colour of my skin dented the pleasure I took in my exam results. I wanted to discuss this with Auntie Margaret. There was no one else. I had made a choice to see my mother rarely now and she was supposed to be heading back to Jamaica soon anyway. I wouldn't try talking to her about that kind of thing even if she did visit. Nor would I ask my father for an opinion when I stayed with him in Balham sometimes. If I told him that the school was surprised by my academic success, I'd be opening the door to that great incandescence inside him which was always ready to ignite at the first hint of racial discrimination.

Since Margaret wasn't there, I simply decided to guess what she'd say.

Probably something like: "Well, if their expectations were low, you proved them wrong. They'll have to change now, won't they, thanks to you. So focus on the future and let them worry about their attitude."

I shut my eyes. I could almost hear her voice, hear her saying it.

I explained to the school that I was no longer in care now I was 16 and therefore could not expect to be given any accommodation in Crawley. And that I hoped to do my A-levels as a police cadet.

Before the course started, I went to see my father again. Over the years there had been various partners. I knew there were other children in his life: sometimes I met these half-siblings although they were a part of his world and he seldom spoke of them. But now something startling had happened: he was married.

Grace was a very clever and hard-working Nigerian businesswoman with warmth and style. Dad really was in love with her. They lived in middle-aged married bliss in the Balham house with the flock wallpaper. The house hadn't changed at all over the years, except that now there were African ornaments on many of the shelves. I stared at a row of brightly coloured metallic figures, each adopting a warrior pose, then looked at Dad. He said he liked them because he only had to look at them to think of Grace if she wasn't around. I couldn't remember him talking like that about any of the other women who had been in and out of his life. Grace had no children of her own. She could never begin to replace Auntie Margaret, but still I was pleased to have this new person in my life: she was a warm, concerned and interested stepmother. She made it clear I had an open invitation to stay in Balham whenever I liked.

Dad had finally accepted that I intended to go to Hendon and then join the Metropolitan Police. But at a party his friends made one last attempt to dissuade me.

I said: "I want to put things right for people when they go wrong. I'm joining the police because I can't stand injustice."

My experience of injustice was my experience of racism. There hadn't been much, really. But when I was judged only by my colour, I felt helpless. Like a victim. Of cruelty, or crime.

Dad's friends hooted with laughter.

"You're joining the police because you hate injustice! The police ARE injustice!"

I said: "Well, if that's been your experience I want to change things!"

This made them hoot even more. A few didn't want to speak to me at all. And they weren't alone in believing I shouldn't join the police. The teachers at school in Crawley, while not actively discouraging me, had given my ambition no support. Even my own friends had suggested that it wasn't a good idea.

They said: "You're too... sort of... sensitive."

I stared at them with incomprehension.

Finally, Gary said: "Look, you might have a hard time in the police because you're black."

So the West Indians of Balham, my friends in Crawley and perhaps even my teachers were not in favour of my departure to Hendon. But I knew my plan had been blessed by the person who loved and cared about me most: I remembered the relief on Auntie Margaret's small, fading face when I told her I would be a police cadet. In addition, my GP took the time and trouble to encourage me. And so did Grace.

She and I talked about everything under the sun and where there was Grace, there was laughter. I enjoyed that last visit before I left for Hendon. I knew I had a place in London to stay, if not exactly a home there. Crawley, thanks to the open invitation Gill and Tony had extended, was more like home, although without Margaret there, I knew it never again could be.

So for now, home was a room in a high-rise block at the police training centre in north London, and from the moment I arrived, I loved the place. It may have looked like a sea of drab, grey concrete to others. To me it was full of potential.

The cadet course had been devised as a way to tempt young people into the police: at that time, the mid-1970s, pay was bad and recruitment was faltering. We were to have two years of fun – including academic training if we wanted to take A-levels. Otherwise it was a great boarding school with a lot of sport and some rudimentary policing thrown in. Then, if we decided we wanted to become police officers, we would stay at Hendon to do the normal 16-week training.

For those unaccustomed to institutions, it was hard to get used to the military style of cadet training. We bulled our boots until they shone and learned to march in time with the band. We were even taught to iron our shirts nicely. I loved every minute of it, including the ironing. After all, I had lived in an institution – albeit one which mimicked a family – all my life. Even those who did not enjoy the life knew that we were lucky to be there. How else could we have afforded to go to a boarding school at 16 which took us on Outward Bound training courses and offered endless sporting and other opportunities? My year was the first to which women cadets were admitted, and about a third of the students were female.

We all got to know each other by socialising, of course. In one lecture we were discouraged from visiting the West End. It was a den of iniquity, said the Inspector. Needless to say that was just too tempting for some and a large group of us headed down there that very evening. He had also warned us off some local bars and, of course, these were soon full of cadets, too.

There was one other black student out of the hundred or so on the course and, from the moment we started socialising, he and I both began to understand that for the next two years there would be almost continual references to our colour.

These references were without hostility: the students were white and working class and wrestled to reconcile their preconceptions of black people with the two who were in their midst. Many had never spoken to a black person before and were curious and asked questions. No one tried to be unpleasant to us because we were black. But we were defined almost entirely by our skin colour. I had grown up in a benign and colour-blind world with Margaret and I must admit this focus, even though it was friendly enough, was a culture shock.

The other black student and I dealt with this in two different ways. He became the life and soul of the party, presumably so that people would notice something about him other than his colour. I was quiet in social situations but determined to do so well at the college that people would have to define me in broader, fairer terms.

I chose to study three A-levels but I liked all the supplementary courses, like law and first aid and typing as well. And I took to the rudimentary police training like a duck to water. I had a photographic memory and only needed to read a page of the manual (which we had to learn by heart) to reproduce it in an exam the next day. But for me it wasn't just a question of reproducing words on a page: I really wanted to live it. Staying sharp was a childhood habit I had formed when I wanted to be the Famous Five or Stratford Johns and it had never really left me. So, when I went back to visit the other children in Crawley, I didn't just stand at Victoria Station waiting idly for my train: I was all eyes and ears the way I thought a police cadet should be.

Watching the departure boards with that awareness I had developed of people around me, I sensed that something odd was happening nearby. Something outside the usual concourse dynamic. I didn't turn to look but from the corner of my eye I saw that, a couple of metres away, an Asian man, who was also scanning the departure boards, had been approached by a stranger. An exceptionally tall man.

Alert now, but keen not to show my interest, I continued to stare ahead, listening hard.

The tall man didn't speak loudly. He stood close, towering over the Asian man, and said: "Give me your money. Now."

I could sense the fear in his victim's voice. I could almost smell it. He said: "I don't have any money."

"Give it to me, or you'll get this…"

Now I had to turn my head. I did so as though I was looking for a station kiosk. I was just a young man deciding whether to buy some sweets before catching his train. Except I was a police cadet witnessing a mugging. And I did see it. The flash of a blade. Almost certainly a flick knife.

"I don't have any money, I don't have any money…"

"Then you're going to get this."

The victim looked terrified. He reached into his trouser pocket and produced some notes. And, as suddenly as he had appeared, as though he had evaporated, the tall man was gone.

Now I had a choice. I could ignore the whole thing, which was not an option because… well, what would Margaret have said? Or, I could find the man and follow him.

Victoria Station's oddly-shaped concourse meant I could linger around it unobtrusively. I was tall but not as tall as the man, who was at least six feet five. That would make it easier to keep him in sight.

I saw him outside WH Smith and from that moment my eyes did not leave my target. I hoped I was so unobtrusive that he had no idea he was being followed. He moved around the station very, very slowly and, although his eyes darted to left and right, he did not look behind him. He certainly had never been a police officer.

He was not looking for a pursuer but for another victim. I wondered how he chose them. We did our strange, silent dance around Victoria Station for about 15 minutes and that gave me plenty of time to rehearse how I would describe the mugger to the police. Height. Fair, collar-length hair. Respectably dressed – or anyway, clearly not a vagrant.

A glimpse of uniform. A British Transport Police officer crossing the concourse. Now I knew I had to move fast. I must catch the officer while keeping the mugger in sight but not attract enough attention to myself for him to smell danger.

The officer was surprised to be stopped. There were a few moments when he even looked disbelieving, but as I continued my story, my eyes still on the mugger, he strode across the concourse and immediately stopped the tall man and insisted that he turn out his pockets. One flick knife. One wad of notes. I lingered at a little distance, terrified the man would run away, ready to run after him. But the officer produced a pair of handcuffs with a dexterity I had to admire and led the man away. He indicated the office to me.

Of course! The victim! As soon as the tall man was apprehended, I should have been looking for him.

I dashed back, sprinting across the concourse, threading my way through disgruntled commuters, to the place I had last seen the Asian man.

Fat chance that he would still be there. Fat chance that I would be able to find him, tell him his money had been recovered and ask him to be a witness. This last seemed the most important thing to me. I knew enough to understand that a second witness would make all the difference.

Incredibly, I found him in exactly the same spot as I had left him. One of the few still human beings at Victoria Station in the rush hour. Either his train was delayed or he was still too shocked to move.

He did not see me or hear me in that busy, noisy place at first and, when I gently attracted his attention by touching his arm, he jumped into the air and looked terrified. He was so scared that he could not understand what I was saying. When I repeated my story I saw the first sign of relief spread across his face. But when I asked him to accompany me to the British Transport Police office he began to look suspicious. Was this a trap?

"And who are you?" he asked, staring at the young black lad who was gabbling away to him about his money.

I stood up straight and said proudly: "I am a police cadet."

In the office the tall man was protesting his innocence. But now that there were two concurring witness statements, he had to admit his guilt, to my secret delight.

Much later than expected but with a good story to tell, I arrived at the house in Crawley. In a way, nothing had changed. And in a way, everything had. It seemed to me that the other children had settled down with their new houseparents, Gill and Tony, who welcomed me warmly. As for Shake the dog, his care had passed from me to a lad a few years my junior. Now he went into a frenzy of jumping, wagging and licking. Despite the fact that the children, now mostly gangly teenagers, were pleased to see me, I sensed that I reminded some of them of the past they had lost.

I'd arranged to see my friend Gary and was, of course, now very late. My visit to the home was quite brief, although I promised I'd be back soon. Secretly, I was relieved to leave. Every corner of the house shouted Margaret's name.

TEN

Hendon was a place which encouraged sporting activity and my focus was on running. The Met Athletics Club was high in the national league tables and this meant that I was now racing against the UK's fastest runners in the 800 metres and 1500 metres. At one event, I was up against the legends Steve Ovett and Sebastian Coe. Not surprisingly, I only came third.

To maintain that kind of standard you have to train hard. Pretty much every evening. Most weekends were spent at athletics events. I had a girlfriend, one of the other cadets, and she got used to waiting at the trackside; it was obvious to her how much winning mattered to me.

At the village primary school in Surrey I'd enjoyed our childish, low-key races. At the big junior school in Crawley I'd discovered how good it felt to win. Later, after joining Crawley Athletics Club and receiving some serious coaching, I'd experienced the pleasure of beating my nemesis. That may have been what finally turned me into such a highly competitive runner, but the greatest competition was with myself. To me it was about setting your own goals and then meeting them, something I'd learned from the gentle but effective coach at Crawley.

Running at national level meant that training was not just long but very serious. Sometimes it seemed my life consisted of only the smack of trainers on the ground, the pull of my leg muscles, the sound of my own breath, my mind driving my body onwards, onwards. Occasionally I thought with nostalgia of the Sussex events I'd taken part in. I remembered a misty morning on the South Downs, my lungs burning and bursting as I ran up and down the springy turf in the Seven Sisters race, the sea stretching out to the horizon on one side of us like a great, dark mirror. It had been a hard, hard event, but so exhilarating. There was nothing like that now. I ran around and around a track, the horizon composed of tall buildings, my lungs labouring in the polluted city air. And, a coach shouting at me.

This was something new. All this shouting. With its undertone of bullying, even intimidation.

The idea was to motivate me. But it was having the opposite effect. There were evenings when I didn't want to be shouted at.

The coach, however, was a small fly in my ointment. Overall, I knew I was lucky to have the chance to compete at this level and gradually it emerged there was the possibility of running for Great Britain. Some police officers did run internationally. A few won Olympic medals. If I worked very hard, I might, just might, become one of them.

But then, there would be sacrifices. And the greatest sacrifice would be a real career in the police. If you ran for the police team then you would be given lots of time off work, so you were unlikely ever to rise above the level of constable. And even the amount of time you spent on the beat would be minimal. And if you left the police, you'd have to fund yourself somehow. In the days before big sponsorship deals, this was almost impossible for someone without a family to support them.

As I progressed, it began to look like a dilemma.

The unpleasant coach spelled it out for me one day.

"You could be a world-class athlete, but you'll have to train a lot more."

A lot more than five nights a week and every weekend?

"That's what you've got to do, if you want to get on."

I agonised. I knew I was lucky to be given this sort of choice, but I just couldn't relinquish my long-held ambition of working as a police officer.

I agonised. I agonised some more. I discussed it with my long-suffering girlfriend. Then discussed it some more. What would Margaret have said? If only she was here to advise me.

Finally, the night before an important race, the coach grew tired of waiting for me.

He said: "Your lot never see things through, you just take the easiest route and give up."

Your lot.

Those words, the way he said them, cut me. But I determined they would cause me no pain, no discomfort, until I'd examined them. Scrutinised them every which way. I must not react until I had satisfied myself that he had really meant what my gut, my heart, had taken him to mean. After all, this was my coach. I may have found his attitude confrontational, but we saw each other daily and knew each other well.

Finally, I said: "My lot? What do you mean, my lot?"

The coach said: "You know what I mean."

Not your lot who are hard-working and keen to learn. Nor your lot who are getting good cadet reports, studying for A-levels and still managing to train hard. Not that lot. There was no other way of interpreting this. He meant: you black people.

And now, only now, did I allow myself to feel the blow. Judged. Again. Judged not on my merit but on the colour of my skin, judged by a series of impressions which the coach had formed over years of every person of colour he had ever known.

I felt weak, I felt helpless in the face of this injustice.

I said: "Talking to me that way isn't motivating me to follow a career in athletics."

The coach said: "It's your decision, but your lot are all the same."

For once, it did not take long to process the insult. And to know that I wasn't helpless. Those feet which ran so well, they could also walk away.

I turned around. It had started to rain, turning everything grey. Beside us was the shabby, metal spectator stand where I had left my kit. I leaned into the stand now, grabbed my sports bag and walked off across the athletics field. The rain worsened. It stung my cheeks as the evening breeze threw it into my face. I did not look back – I knew this man could not coach me again.

I spent a long time processing all this. At first I thought that now I would run on my own terms, without his training. I did this, but it wasn't the same. My decision was made and it was made by the attitude of that coach. I was going to keep running, but I was not going to be an athlete. I was going to be a police officer as I had always intended.

My girlfriend was pleased. I ran a bit less in the evening and I went to fewer athletics events so she spent less time watching me and more time actually with me. I was still training hard enough and running often enough to win a few races but the pressure to excel was off. I began to recognise, from this comparative distance, the pressure racing creates. The pressure to train, the pressure to win, the pressure to hold onto your title. Now it was a relief to feel that pressure lift.

With more time together, we grew closer, this girlfriend and I. Did I mention that she was white? I can't see what importance that has but for some reason it seemed very important to other people. She came from Lee in south-east London, which turned out to be full of people who had watched too many episodes of *Till Death Us Do Part*. Or maybe they were in it. Anyway, a white girl with a black man in Lee at that time had to face a lot of very unpleasant abuse. We both did. Her family never asked me not to visit but they weren't at all sure about me. They were concerned that she could be attacked because of the relationship. As our time in the cadets came to a close, I felt us falter and I knew we would not continue together.

In the two years I spent as a cadet in Hendon, I had journeyed through all the stages of grief for Margaret. Her absence became as unassailable a fact of life as her presence had once been. When I passed out of the Cadets, I felt this acutely. She should have been there, sobbing at the sight of me marching in uniform. More even than she had sobbed at *The Sound of Music*. And she would have been so proud of that bit of sleuthing at Victoria Station (I'd been too shy to tell anyone about it, but the British Transport Police wrote to Hendon to commend me), which had won me the Dix Trophy for Outstanding Policemanship. Margaret would have loved that, too. And she might hardly have believed that, after my A-level results were released, I was awarded a police scholarship to go to university in a year's time.

My mother had a new family and we had almost lost touch. I certainly would not have thought of asking her to watch me pass out of the cadets, and she could not have come anyway. I had heard, through my father, that she had now returned to Jamaica. I could invite two people so I invited Dad and Grace, fearing Dad would refuse to come, even though, realising it was useless, he had entirely given up his opposition to my joining the police by now. I knew that walking through the gates at Hendon, a place throbbing with police officers, would be for him like putting his head in the jaws of the lion. All the same, he and Grace did come. When we all marched past and he saw his son, the tall one at the back, the only black face among many white faces, well, there is an old video of him almost bursting with pride and wearing an ear-to-ear smile. As for me, I was now staying on at Hendon to do basic police training and to join the Met after two happy, although grief-filled, years as a cadet. Dull, it wasn't.

ELEVEN

So this was it. I'd been waiting for this since I sat watching *Dixon of Dock Green* at Fairmile Hatch when we children were all so small that six of us could fit on one sofa, and Margaret as well. And now it had happened: I was a copper.

To prove it, I had a little black wallet. It was my proudest possession. On the front, stamped in important gold letters was:

Metropolitan Police Warrant Card.

Inside, signed by no lesser person than the Commissioner of the Met himself, the card said:

This is to certify that
Michael Fuller
holds the rank of Constable in the Metropolitan Police.
This is his warrant and authority for executing
the duties of his office.
Signed
Sir Robert Mark
Commissioner of Police of the Metropolis

My shirt was ironed and very white. My shoes were shiny and very black. My uniform felt stiff and new and correct. It was my first day on the beat.

I didn't have to go alone. As a new probationer I was always sent out with an older colleague. Joe and I maintained an even pace as we turned into the North End Road. I tried to walk normally, as if I wasn't self-conscious.

"Does everyone think people are staring at them when they first go out?" I asked Joe.

"Yep," he said. "It was a long time ago but I remember. You feel as though the whole street's looking."

That made me feel better.

"But," he added, "in your case, they are."

Suddenly I didn't feel better at all.

He said: "You can't blame them, most people haven't seen a spade in uniform before. Or only a bus conductor's uniform."

Fulham Police Station had been a shock for me. It was a busy place in a very mixed area – some of Fulham was as upmarket as its reputation but there were also huge housing estates where there was a lot of poverty as well as a very high crime rate. I was pleased to be here and eager to get on with the job. But what should I, what could I, say in response to my colleagues' widespread use of the words spade, wog, coon or sometimes even nigger?

Such language was thrown about routinely and often in a derogatory way to refer in general to any black person but usually a black person who was under arrest, that being the only contact most white police officers had with black people. And old-timers like Joe thought there was nothing wrong with referring to me that way. This felt personal, although I knew no insult was actually intended. Is an insult still an insult if it is only perceived and not intended? I had been pondering this eternal question since I arrived, and I sometimes think I have been pondering it ever since.

I also knew that as a young probationer there was no point in my challenging this language outright. I would have to learn to tolerate it while I worked out what, if anything, I could do about it. It was vital not to alienate anyone on my shift because the teamwork and mutual support was, literally at times, necessary to keep you alive. So the most important thing, for now, was not to react to the word 'spade' even if it wounded me.

We walked on in silence.

In less than an hour, I'd been stopped three times.

First, a couple of young black men walked past us on the street, did a double take, and then one of them ran back and stood in front of me, forcing me to break my stride.

He said: "What you doing, man? What you *doing*?"

Taken aback, I said: "I'm doing my job."

"You don't have no place with Babylon," he informed me. "Fiyah bun Babylon, they hate us, you shouldn't be with them, traitor, so why di bumborass you wearing that uniform, you should—"

I opened and closed my mouth as though to interrupt but perhaps it was just as well that he showed no sign of stopping because I really didn't know what to say. I hadn't anticipated this sort of confrontation and had no response ready.

He was older than me, perhaps in his early twenties, and because he spoke in English and patois, slipping seamlessly between the two, I could not understand all that he said. I'd heard Dad's friends using a few of the insults but I did not know what they meant. Nor did I want to.

He finally finished his tirade. Sucking his lips, he said: "You fassy hole!" I knew enough to know that was a bad one. "You should be ashamed of yourself."

He spat on the ground and then returned to his mate and they walked on. For some time I could hear their receding voices, loud, derisive.

"You all right?" asked Joe, who had tried, with no success at all, to silence the man and move him aside.

Was I all right? Something in the man's eyes, something in his disgust and disdain, had drawn blood in a way that all the talk about wogs and coons back at the police station never could. It was a deep cut.

I had thought the black community might welcome the very rare sight of a black officer. Now I told myself this was just an unfortunate, one-off act of aggression. I tried not to show how shaken I was as we walked on.

Suddenly, a battered car screeched to a halt beside us. An elderly black woman eased her large body out of the passenger seat.

"Well, just look at you! I said to Winston: 'Winston, you just look at that, you stop this car now, now I say, I have to talk to him!'"

The driver climbed out and followed her.

"God bless you, may God bless you," he said to me, shaking my hand energetically.

A discussion ensued, me nodding frequently and Joe trying to bring things to a close.

"I never thought I'd see this day, I never thought it would come; you're making history, that's what you're doing. Why I've never even liked the police but I see you and I think to myself, there's a sign things are changing."

"God bless you," Winston repeated, still clasping my hand.

I smiled at them. Now this was more the sort of reaction I'd hoped for, although I hadn't guessed that people would be quite so emotional.

"... and what you are, you're a sign of hope, that's what you are! I congratulate you, young man, and welcome you to this community. We'll do everything we can to support you, won't we do that, Winston?"

"God bless you!"

Eventually, they got back into the car. They were partially blocking the road and a small, honking traffic jam had accumulated behind them. The other drivers probably thought there was an emergency or anyway that something extraordinary had happened, for two elderly folk to abandon their vehicle and be gesticulating and talking so excitedly to the police. It crossed my mind that perhaps the sight of me really was something extraordinary. I hoped I was wrong.

"They were nice," I said.

Joe raised his eyebrows. "Spades nearly always have an out-of-date tax disc on the car and I doubt those two were any exception. But I decided not to look too closely in the circumstances. The way they left their vehicle also constituted a traffic hazard, and I decided to let that one go, too."

We continued on the beat and when we got to the market the white traders stared at me in disbelief. Some fell silent and busied themselves about their stalls. Others put their hands on their hips and did not respond to my greeting, although they responded to Joe's. A few of them muttered under their breath if they thought Joe could not hear. Once, when Joe lingered to talk to someone and I wandered a few yards ahead, a trader, head barely visible behind lines of mops and dishcloths, hissed at me. This stopped me in my tracks. He sounded like an angry snake. I braced myself for the abuse which must follow but Joe arrived at my side. However, I was sure that another man, bulky, with thinning red hair, barely visible behind his wares, said to the hisser, in a low voice, loud enough for only me to hear: "It must have been bloody hot when he was born."

Joe and I proceeded. As a kid, in my play police uniform, I had pretended I was on the beat. I had strolled around the grounds of Fairmile Hatch knowing how I must be. Alert. Sensitive to everything going on around me so that I could spot anything suspicious. And ready. Always ready, to rush off at a moment's notice to an emergency. Somehow my belief that it would be that way had never left me. Until now. Nothing much seemed to be happening in Fulham that day except the sight of a black man in police uniform.

I can't remember how many more times my colour was remarked on before we returned to the station or how many heads swivelled in my direction, although I was certainly not the Met's only black officer. Norwell Roberts was the first and he had been quite a media figure when I was a boy. After reading about him in the newspaper, I had made him my hero and role model. One article I saw said that there were times when it was so hard to be a black officer that he could hardly stop himself going into a quiet room by himself to cry. I had read that but had somehow managed to forget it. Until now. I didn't cry, but I could understand why you might want to.

As time went on, people in Fulham grew used to the sight of me and there were fewer comments. I began to love going to work on the beat because anything could happen or nothing might happen – you never knew what to expect. But I knew that after six weeks of being accompanied by a "tutor" constable, I would be out there on my own. That was a bit daunting.

"Ready for it, lad?" asked my probationary sergeant. I swallowed and nodded. He started to chat to me – about my long-standing interest in the police, about my schooldays.

"So… where were you actually brought up?" he asked.

I had learned to field questions about my background. In general, I didn't really want people to know I had been in care, and specifically, I did not want my police colleagues to know. I had already heard them referring to people they arrested as Barnardo's boys in a certain tone. That tone suggested an inevitable association between care and crime.

Not many people asked me about my past but if they asked where my family lived I could fob them off with: "South London." Most didn't enquire further, so the discrepancy between my dad in London and my life in Crawley went unnoticed. But not by this sergeant.

"So… your dad lives in London. Did you live with your mum in Sussex then?"

"Sort of."

"What does that mean?"

"I lived with a different family."

"Foster?"

"No, not really."

He stepped back a bit to scrutinise me better. I avoided his eye.

He said: "Don't be ashamed, lad, if you were brought up in care."

I stared at him. How on earth did he know?

He said: "I'm a Barnardo's boy myself."

That's how.

He asked me more questions and I found myself telling him about Auntie Margaret, what an amazing mother she had been to me and how we lived as one family with her.

"That's quite something. And it was the old London County Council too. Well, I never! Barnardo's wasn't like that. Not at all."

He told me about his home, the rows of iron beds in large dormitories, the constant fear of bigger boys, the indifference of some key staff members. And that may have been the first time I realised that other children's homes were not at all like mine.

I could be sure of one thing: the Sergeant would not tell anyone else that I had been brought up in care. We knew, without even conferring on it, that it was something we just didn't talk about.

TWELVE

It was important to stay on good terms with the rest of my shift because, when we were out there working, we relied on each other. I was determined to learn not to take to heart some of their language and assumptions about black people. Their jokes could be funny and offensive at the same time, and it was important to laugh at the humour and not examine the assumptions behind those jokes.

"No offence, Michael, but..." their racist jokes began. So they were inviting me to join in and not to take personally what they were saying. I did try to do this, but I was often hurt by the jokes. They were made at the expense of people who looked like me and the assumption was that we were all both stupid and primitive. I tried not to show that this upset me. Sometimes I did become very withdrawn. If people noticed, they would say: "Come on, don't be oversensitive."

One officer, who was a nice man, put on a horrendously bad West Indian accent whenever he spoke to me and threw in all the Jamaican slang he knew. This caused uproar. I tried to laugh, too. How else could I belong? And the fact was, as I got to know the team, I came to like them more and more despite the pain this could cause. It would, I reasoned, be more painful not to be one of them. So I joined in as much socialising at the pub and at Dino's restaurant as time allowed.

I also socialised with friends in the hostel where I now lived. The section house was on a busy road in Hammersmith and housed about a hundred police officers. There was a porter on the door and a canteen where the staff warmly greeted the arrival of a black face on the other side of the serving hatch. Black staff served white diners and this was an entirely usual dynamic for London institutions at that time. It meant that many white people only had contact with black people in servile positions, although of course the police officers in the section house also encountered black people when they were arresting them.

My tiny room was upstairs near the shared showers. I'd got used to drab rooms of basic necessity at Hendon so the section house had felt like home since I had arrived with my suitcase and hardware of the era: an alarm clock, a small portable TV and, most importantly, a cassette player. On a summer's day, music wafted from poor-quality cassettes through every window. The music reflected popular taste: Earth Wind & Fire, Marvin Gaye, George Benson, Stevie Wonder. I played soul but I also wanted to listen to the music Auntie Margaret and I had enjoyed together. But her eternal absence sometimes made her favourite Mozart pieces too hard to bear. She had left me her record collection in her will and, along with other stuff of mine, this was stored for me in the house in Crawley. Gill and Tony had said I could keep it there as long as I liked.

For the first six weeks of my probationary period my colleagues did their best to protect me from the confrontations which, to my horror, were guaranteed to arise almost every time I showed my face on the beat. White people did sometimes make offensive remarks, even unknowingly – ("Your English is so good, where do you come from?" "London." "No, really, where from?" "London!") – but they were much more likely to appear indifferent. The same could not be said for members of the black community. Whether it was positive or negative, response was assured.

So the first day I went on the beat with no officer by my side, I was fearful. I was dreading the North End Road market most of all.

As soon as they saw me, the stallholders stopped what they were doing. When they were sure no other officer was around, they glared and whispered from behind their French apples and their hardware sundries. They nudged each other. This escalated into catcalls, mutterings and peals of unkind laughter. No one actually shouted abuse, they just whispered and intimated it.

I tried to ignore them, but the words I caught scalded me inside. The fat, red-haired Alf Garnett was there of course, trying to belittle me. I'd already decided that he was the ring-leader and that where he went, the others followed.

It was important not to let them make me feel small or inferior. I couldn't let them win. So I dodged behind the stalls to the area where they parked their vans. I walked up the line, looking hard at each vehicle, each windscreen. The noise from the traders dropped a little.

It didn't take me long to spot a suspect tax disc. One glance told me that it had been taken from a different vehicle and the number inexpertly inked over. I stared at it for a long time and, as I did so, the muttering and laughter behind me faded out completely.

I asked whose van it was, and it belonged to the red-haired bully. I just couldn't believe my luck. I requested that he open the door and then I grabbed the disc before he could snatch it away and destroy the evidence.

Politely, I said: "I'll take care of that, sir."

In fact, although I was doing my best to sound as though I was in control, I was almost totally green at this. I even had to radio the Sergeant and double-check that displaying a fraudulent tax disc was an arrestable offence. He assured me it was, and an area car arrived almost immediately with, to my relief, Andy on board. Andy was an older cop who tried to help me and watch over me. Now he supported me while I made my first arrest.

My hands shook as I cuffed the market trader, and my voice wavered as I said, for the very first time: "You are not obliged to say anything unless you wish to do so, but what you do say may be put into writing and given in evidence."

Yes, of course I enjoyed it.

Back at the station, I had to search him and do all the paperwork. Andy helped, telling me two things which did not surprise me about my prisoner. He had a record of violent offending. And he was an active member of the National Front.

After that, he and his fellow traders quietened down. In fact, people all along the beat became less hostile as they got to know me. Except those angry young black lads. Some were very young. A typical scenario occurred one day as I walked with Joe through a tunnel and into a group of about ten lads, who howled with anger and derision at the sight of me.

"Come on now, boys, let us pass," said Joe, who was very good at crowd calming.

"Uncle Tom!" shouted one. "You Uncle Tom!"

"You're disgusting!" jeered another.

I tried not to react, but they wouldn't have noticed. They were all yelling at once.

"What you think you're doing? Why you in those clothes, man, you going to a party? You're not really in Babylon, are you? What you doing mixing with them? You know how they treat us, you going to treat us that way, too? They only arrest black people around here, they let white people do what they like, but if you're black…"

They had been born in this country but knew West Indian insults, which punctuated their speech.

"Just keep on walking," said Joe.

I did this. But the boys bounced and yelled all around me. After some months on the job, I had found that the best strategy was to keep moving. I did not look the youths in the eye and showed no reaction to their words. But it was very hard indeed not to take their insults personally. I tried to tell myself it was the helmet, the uniform, the shiny buttons, their own histories with the police that they were protesting against, not me. But in this situation it wasn't so easy not to feel the insults. Each one of them cut me a little. Like a paper cut. Surprising that something so small can hurt so much. Invisible. But deep.

Eventually, Joe and I could not keep walking. The youths had me surrounded and their tone was increasingly aggressive.

"You know how many times they stopped my brother last weekend? Three! Three times! And they didn't find *nothing*!"

"My dad got stopped just going home from his night shift!"

"I got searched twice yesterday!"

"How many white people you stop, eh? Or do they tell you just to stop black people?"

I decided to try my other strategy: reason. By now I had a few arguments ready.

"Listen, you hate the police because of the way you've been treated, but if there were more black officers, that would change…"

I could just about hear my own voice. Small. Measured. Rational. And no match for all the shouting. Of course, no one listened, they only shouted louder.

Joe decided to intervene.

"Now that's enough of this, you coons! Just piss off and leave the lad alone or I'll have to arrest you!"

He spoke into a lull and unfortunately, everyone heard him. I looked at him, crestfallen, and the words simply inflamed the youths into another round of abuse, which I secretly thought might be justified this time.

Fury does eventually abate, particularly if it falls on barren ground. I stopped trying to argue back and just stood there while it rained insults. I knew the rain had to stop some time and, after a few more minutes, it did. We were able to proceed with our dignity just about intact.

As soon as we were out of earshot, I could not help myself.

"Oh Joe, what did you say that for?"

"Say what?"

"Well, they're complaining that the police are racist and you started calling them..." I hesitated. I could hardly say it. "...coons."

"Oh, come on!" he protested.

"But it could have turned really nasty." There was always the threat of escalation in these incidents, the threat to our personal safety.

Joe shook his head. "Now, you're not going to get upset about a little thing like that, are you?"

Careful now, Michael. One false word and you could turn the whole shift against you.

"To them it might not be a little thing," I said softly.

"Michael, I know you're a clever boy and you're off to university this autumn, but will you take a piece of advice from an old-timer?"

Joe was one of many who didn't really approve of university. He thought police officers could learn all they needed to know on the beat, not in the classroom.

He said: "Don't be oversensitive. You'll never get anywhere in this game if you're upset every five minutes."

Oversensitive. This wasn't my first, very tentative, attempt to draw my colleagues' language to their attention and the response had always drawn an accusation of oversensitivity. It was the same old problem: officers thought that if they meant no harm then they did no harm. Plus, as they pointed out, they were only speaking in exactly the same way civilians spoke.

Over time, the insults from the black community did ease. People just got to know me, and perhaps I also came to understand their anger better.

Black youths (and often their parents and grandparents) regarded the police as racists, not because of their language but because they were so often stopped and poorly treated by them, thanks to the so-called 'sus' laws. Under the sus laws, we were empowered to stop, search and arrest any person who was 'suspected'. And it was evident to most of the black community that they could be 'suspected' just because of the colour of their skin.

It took me a while to understand that misuse of the sus laws was doing immense damage to relationships with the police. In fact, I don't think I fully saw that until I carried out my own sus arrest.

One night on the beat around midnight, I heard, or perhaps sensed, that something was going on. A shuffling noise. A dark figure advancing along the street, moving differently from the way people move when they're going somewhere. Whatever it was that alerted me, I stopped dead and waited. Catching crooks was something I was good at and really enjoyed and now it felt as though one was coming my way.

A man, almost certainly the worse for drink, was shuffling unsteadily around a car, trying one door and then the next.

I had learned that the only way to be inconspicuous at night was to turn off my radio and take off my hat. I did this now, and crept slowly towards him.

He was walking from the back of the car to the front. I waited for him to start pulling aggressively and determinedly at the driver's door. Then I put my hat back on and stepped out into the glow of a street lamp.

"You're under arrest."

He jumped a foot in the air. His face wore that combination of shock, guilt and horror which I was just learning to recognise as the look of someone caught in the act. It never failed to please me.

He cursed a lot as I took him back to the station. The Sergeant had to alert the CID (because every crime had to be investigated) so I was sent up to their office.

I said: "There's a bloke downstairs I've arrested for sus."

The CID officers all wore plain clothes but their choice of similar pinstriped suits made this another uniform of sorts. One of them looked up and said: "Sus? Did he upset you, then?"

I shook my head. "No, not at all."

"Sus?" repeated the man.

I said: "He was trying to break into a car and I watched him do it."

By now, more heads were looking up from their work. They all seemed to be waiting for me to say something. I couldn't imagine what. I looked at them helplessly.

Finally, one of them asked: "Mate, what colour is he?"

I said: "White. Why?"

They stared at me and all burst out laughing. At every desk a man in wide lapels and a broad, striped tie was clutching his sides or falling off his chair. I watched them with total incomprehension.

Finally, one of them explained to me that the sus laws were a device for white officers to arrest black people who had pissed them off. Word got around the station that I had arrested a white man for sus and that seemed to tickle pretty much everyone. As for me, I gritted my teeth and pressed ahead with the paperwork. I understood the joke only too well, but I didn't find it funny. No wonder black people were becoming so angry and abusive if there was a law which was being applied only to them.

It was always a relief, when I felt marginalised, to go to the barber. There is no point in a black man going to a white barber – the result is simply butchery. Our hair has a special texture of its own which the barber has to understand and now I had found a good black barber in Fulham.

Mac's was a busy place. The first time I went there I waited a long time and realised that people who had arrived after me were being taken in front of me. That's when I realised that this was no normal queueing system, it was Mac's system, and he took people in the order he liked or respected them.

I was off-duty and Mac didn't ask me what I did for a living and when my turn came, we got along just fine. Mac was soon busy with his clippers while I sat in his chair listening to all the talk around me. Because black men talk at the barber's. They talk about everything, they talk in loud voices, they argue with perfect strangers, they debate heatedly or they chat laconically; all strata of society can be found at the barber's and it didn't take me long to know I liked this place and felt at home here surrounded by black men. Work, with its racist language and jokes, seemed far away. Sitting in Mac's chair and laughing along with the others, the shop warm, the chat friendly, it felt like family of sorts.

When I left, I hadn't just lost a lot of hair, I had lost a lot of the anger and hurt I sometimes carried around with me. It was like resetting my compass. I knew who I was again: a black man who was accepted among black men. I decided never to tell them I was a police officer – I was sure that would soon get me thrown out.

THIRTEEN

It was a relief to step away from the moral complexities of race relations and do what I liked doing best: catching criminals. For me, this was the heart of the job. Crime always creates a victim and I had a deep need to bring justice to that victim whatever colour they were.

I was on the night shift, patrolling alone and on foot around a local housing estate. It was about three in the morning and all was quiet. In fact, the only sign of movement was the occasional police car, driven by my mates from my shift.

I looked up in time to see Nick and Geoff approaching. The police car slowed, the passenger window came down and I saw a water bomb hurtling in my direction. I dodged into an alleyway and then laughed as the water bomb exploded on the pavement just behind me.

"Missed!" I yelled.

"Next time!" shouted Nick in the departing car. I could hear Geoff laughing as they pulled away.

The alleyway I was in led to a row of shops and a housing estate so I continued. When the car was gone, silence fell. I walked quietly. I'd developed that silent walk for the night shift.

Then I heard something. I paused. What was it? I waited. Then I heard it again: the sound of splintering wood.

My heart beat faster, because I knew something was about to happen. I immediately turned down my radio and took off my helmet. I waited.

Movement overhead. Shuffling. I looked up. A wall, about two and a half metres high. And a figure directly above me, with a black bag over one shoulder.

He hadn't seen me. He was hesitating, deciding on the best way down. And as he moved into the arc of a street lamp, something glinted in his right hand.

This must certainly be a burglar. I wondered what was in the bag.

Now he was steeling himself to jump. As he did so, I stepped out of the shadows in front of him. He froze for a moment and then ran further along the top of the wall. I ran beneath him. The burglar ran back. So did I. It had the makings of a *Tom and Jerry* cartoon. Except for that glint in his hand. It must be a knife.

A knife.

I remembered the voice of my instructor at Hendon as though he was standing right there. A knife meant I was supposed to radio for help.

I broke out of our silent dance. *"Urgent assistance. 152."*

A request for urgent assistance means that every officer nearby converges on the caller. Modern radios have an emergency button that when activated give the officer's location automatically. But back then my training hadn't yet been backed up by experience and I'd forgotten to say where I was.

Now the burglar was on the move again, away from the alley. I set off in pursuit and then launched myself at the wall. My fingertips scrabbled at the soft brickwork, could find no purchase and slithered back down in a shower of dust.

Try again.

I ran at the wall and flung my body up, up, the way I'd flung it into the air during high-jump training. And this time my hands managed to grasp the coping stones and I hauled myself to the top.

The dark figure ahead of me sprang onto the back roof of one of the shops, but I was hot on his heels. He clambered up to the next level, a flat area about five metres from the ground.

All he cared about now was getting away. He dropped the bag and dashed towards the shop fronts, where his only possible means of escape was a running leap into the road. From a height that must have been close to the height of a double-decker bus.

I managed a sort of rugby tackle which brought him down. For a moment, I felt that I'd won. I'd stopped him. But he had other ideas. He kicked and wriggled and the weapon got dangerously close to my body. I could feel it, hard against my side, without seeing it. I was in no doubt that he would, without hesitation, plunge it into my body if I let him.

I twisted his arm and heard the clatter of the falling weapon. But he fought on.

I felt his teeth in my hand and his fingernails in my chest as he clawed at my uniform, tearing off the buttons, ripping open my shirt. I was determined not to let him go. But as his teeth sank deeper and deeper into my flesh, I thought: *How much pain can I stand?* I soon discovered the answer to that one. I heard myself roaring in agony and released my grip. The burglar wriggled free.

I could have pounced again. But I hesitated. He was poised on the edge of the parapet. If any action from me prompted him to jump, he might be killed or seriously injured.

I watched him. Not moving. Just waiting. Gulping air back into my lungs.

He jumped.

I ran to the edge and found there was a shop roof immediately below. He was standing there. I dropped down onto it and stepped towards him.

And he jumped again. This time to the ground.

A long pause and then a thud.

I moved forward cautiously. I saw a motionless body sprawled in the road, lying face down. Hurt? Stunned? Dead? Or faking? Would he suddenly leap to his feet and run away?

I knew I had to go after him.

My adrenalin was pumping again, but I did stop to consider: *Is this a risk worth taking? Should I climb down the way I came up and run around to the body?* And the answer was no. Because he might get away.

I jumped.

The landing sent rods of pain up through my legs. I staggered but managed to hold the ninja stance I'd learned in gymnastics as a police cadet. Gradually, I straightened. Feet. Check. Legs. Check. Back. Check.

A police car screeched to a halt, perilously close to the prostrate burglar. Nick and Geoff, water bombers extraordinaires, leapt out and onto him. I joined them.

He turned out not to be injured at all. He fought ferociously, kicking, punching and struggling. But, thankfully, not biting. Finally, we had him handcuffed. A van arrived to take him back to the station while I checked out the shopping parade.

I could see where he'd broken into a clothes shop. And I knew how he'd done it a few minutes later when I found the knife – which turned out to be a particularly sharp chisel. The damage he could have done if it had made contact with my skin. I tried not to think about that.

I retrieved the black bag and discovered what he'd taken: a pile of new jeans, the then very fashionable Levi 501s. The adrenalin was draining out of me now. I realised we both could have died for a few pairs of jeans.

A sleek car pulled up. A dark blue Jaguar, shining under the street lamps.

"Er, excuse me," said a plummy voice. A woman got out of the car. It was nearly four in the morning and she was wearing a long, elegant dress and looked as if she was just off to a ball. You might think that Fulham consisted almost entirely of people like this but they were in fact in the minority, greatly outnumbered by the poor.

"Officer, I'd like a word with you," she said.

This was getting surreal. I was holding my helmet. My uniform was in tatters. I was covered in dirt. And she was...?

"Lost, I'm completely lost, Officer. I'm looking for The Boltons. Am I anywhere near The Boltons?"

No. You are driving around a tough west London housing estate, which is socially and geographically quite far from The Boltons.

"Not really, Madam," I said. "But I can point you in the right direction."

"That would be awfully sweet of you."

She did not seem to notice the state I was in, let alone ask if I was all right. So I told her the way to Chelsea and she thanked me and her Jag melted into the night, leaving me standing there alone in my ripped uniform.

"You're fucking lucky!" Geoff said later. "You didn't give us your location. If it hadn't been for our water-bombing mission, we wouldn't have known where you were."

Saved by a water bomb.

I promised myself I'd never make that mistake again. And I promised myself that in future, when dealing with any potentially violent suspect, I'd go straight for the hands before they could reach for that gun, that flick knife, that chisel.

I was tired but triumphant, because catching someone while they're actually committing a crime happens very seldom in any police officer's career. My supervising sergeant slapped me on the back. Even the CID congratulated me. The only disappointing thing was that the burglar himself, although stocky, strong and violent, looked alarmingly young beneath the harsh lights of the police station. He turned out to be under 18. We called his horrified parents, who arrived to find him in his cell.

They were furious with him. They seemed to me good-hearted people who were at their wits' end with their difficult son. He was sulky and maintained a teenage silence. Another angry black kid. We kept him in overnight, not because of the burglary but because of the serious assault on me. And that assault had shaken me. As usual, it had taken me a while to process what had happened but now I was drained of adrenalin and felt weak with a fear I had not felt at the time. Our fight had been very violent and at height, making it doubly dangerous. And I was sure that, if I had not got the chisel away from him, he would have stabbed me with it.

I wrote my statement, did the paperwork and left a tired detective to interview the young burglar while I went back to the section house. It was only when I lay down to sleep that I felt shocked. I shut my eyes and the lad, the way he held his chisel, appeared inside my head. His expression was clear: he wanted to kill me.

I kept my eyes shut but for a while sleep would not come. Now that I was safe, I was swamped by fear for what had so nearly happened. I fell into a light, fitful sleep.

Later that night, I woke up sweating. I had dreamed, not about the jeans burglar or his chisel, but that face at the window again, the face of the thief back in Crawley who had broken into my boyhood bedroom. Pale, haunting, he stared at me through the shattered glass, half lit by the street lamp, until I was terrified into waking. It was the first time I had dreamt about him for a year or so.

I waited patiently for the fear to pass and sleep to return.

The jeans burglar was bailed to go to the next juvenile court, which was only a week later. The detective who was giving evidence – a sample of the stolen jeans, my statement, photos and the doctor's statement about my injuries – was there. I was there as a witness too, of course. We waited all day. Finally, we were told that the court had been so busy with other cases that it had run out of time. The case was adjourned for a fortnight.

So a fortnight later the detective and I arrived at the juvenile court as arranged and once again we waited all day and once again the court ran out of time and adjourned the case to the next court.

On the third attempt to hear the case, the magistrates decided that it really must be dealt with today. Unfortunately, this time the detective did not turn up with the evidence. I rang my sergeant. He rang the CID. Nothing happened. I rang the Inspector and he rang the CID. Then I rang the CID. Everyone rang the CID. But no one could locate the missing detective. I waited anxiously as the time of our case neared. No detective.

The magistrate said that, since no evidence was presented, the case must be thrown out. This did not seem to me like justice at work. And, unfortunately, there was no prosecuting barrister to agree with me: the case had been considered so clear-cut it was thought that the detective could handle it, so there was no one to argue for the prosecution at all.

Outraged, I found the Court Inspector to ask for his advice. He is a police inspector who works at the court.

He frowned at me.

"No, you won't get this case adjourned. The magistrates have clearly said it must be heard today, so there's no point arguing."

"But the detective hasn't shown up and they're going to drop it!"

"Well, the kid can't be prosecuted if there's no evidence."

"He tried to kill me. It was a serious assault, it can't just be thrown out."

The Inspector shook his head.

"All you can do is speak to his lawyer. You could try a bit of plea bargaining."

Plea bargaining? Isn't that what one lawyer did with another? But, of course, the prosecution had no lawyer.

I said: "Why would the lawyer bargain with me? He can just do nothing and his client will be free!"

"That's my only suggestion," said the Inspector, who had evidently seen this sort of absurdity so often that he had grown used to it.

So I found the youth's lawyer. He looked sorry for me.

"You haven't been in the police long, have you?" he said.

"Well... no. But what's that got to do with it?"

"If you had, you'd know I've got you over a barrel."

"This isn't about letting your client walk out of here. It's about the fact that he attacked me and could have killed me and needs to see that there's some sort of justice system or he'll just go and do it again."

The lawyer looked serious. I hoped he'd become a barrister because he had a belief in justice.

Finally, he said: "Look, I don't have to bargain with you, but I will. I'll advise my client to plead guilty to theft."

"But the assault..."

"That's the bargain I'm offering, and in the circumstances it's more than fair. Guilty to theft, if assault charges are dropped."

The kid had been listening to all this and now was smiling. His lawyer looked at him and he nodded happily. At his side, his parents exchanged confused glances. They had probably been hoping the court would teach their son a stern lesson: a reasonable expectation. But this was hardly likely when his charge sheet looked as if he had been caught doing a bit of shoplifting on a Saturday afternoon.

I walked away. Injustice. I had thought I was joining the police to right wrongs, not to drop charges because of administrative errors.

Finally, I was called to the witness stand to give a summary of the evidence. I was halfway through my oath when the courtroom door flew open. Before anyone could do anything about it, before anyone had registered their presence, two young lads ran into the room. They were about 12 years old, one black, one white, and they streaked in, screamed a few obscene words, ran in a circle and then ran out. This was so sudden and so quick that no one even chased after them. They were nothing to do with the court or its proceedings. They were little kids who had run in from the street to be naughty, perhaps for a dare. And what was there to stop them? Not fear, not respect, not even a security barrier. It was a further mockery of justice.

When they had gone there was a silence and everyone looked at everyone else. Perhaps we were waiting for the kids to run back in. But they didn't. And so after a moment we restarted my oath.

I gave the juvenile court a brief and factual account of what had happened on the rooftops that night. I could not help describing the assault, although I knew there were no assault charges. The defendant did not look at me. He did not look at anyone; he sat staring around the court without interest as if the proceedings were nothing to do with him. I was happy to see that his parents seemed highly embarrassed.

Since it was my case I was allowed to step down from the witness box and stay in the court to hear the outcome. The defendant was given a conditional discharge. A trivial sentence. He looked at me now. Grinning. Afterwards, when the court had emptied and I was expressing my feelings bitterly to the Police Inspector, the magistrates passed on their way out. They asked, in a rather suspicious way, why on earth, when I had been victim to such a serious assault, I had been happy to see the charges dropped?

I was beginning to feel that justice was a strange beast and one on which I could not rely. I hoped that my degree course might help me to understand more about how the system of justice worked, as well as other systems and other people. After agonising over where to go and what to study for my scholarship, I had decided that Social Psychology was the most useful course for a police officer. The University of Sussex in Brighton was close to Crawley and, if I had any roots at all, that's where they were. I determined to work as hard as I could and learn what I could at the police station and then try to make sense of it all when I got to university in the autumn.

FOURTEEN

I went back to the station from the juvenile courtroom and told the others how, after wasting three days in court waiting to give evidence, I had watched the kid who assaulted me so viciously receive a conditional discharge because the detective hadn't come to court with the evidence. My sergeant, who had spent much of his day trying to locate the missing detective, was speechless with rage.

"A conditional discharge! He attacked you with a chisel, they should have locked him up!"

Everyone on my shift was livid.

"Well, there's a kid who's going to do it again because he thinks there's no penalties!"

"Which copper is he going to assault next time? One of us?"

"That kid is heading for a life of crime."

"If he's not in jail now, he soon will be!"

The Inspector came out of his office to hear the story and then, with gritted teeth, headed over to the CID.

He complained bitterly. To no avail. Back then, there was huge antagonism between those of us in uniform and the detectives, who were not. Detectives were regarded as sharp-suited, Cortina-driving work dodgers. For us, the failure to appear in court was a real breach of duty. However, the detectives didn't take it seriously at all and the man who hadn't appeared was never really disciplined.

In fact, corruption was rife in the CID and everyone knew it. It was a problem throughout the Met – low pay plus journalists or crooks with wads of cash on offer proved too much of a temptation for many – but the CID had a reputation for being particularly corrupt. A popular TV show of the time was *The Sweeney*, which showed detectives bending the rules because they were so dedicated to their cases. It seemed to uniformed police officers that there was a lot of rule-bending in the CID but not so much dedication. However, *The Sweeney* seemed to set sartorial standards which all detectives aspired to. They were instantly recognisable from their feathered haircuts, wide ties, tailored suits and roaring engines as they zoomed importantly out of the car park.

Uniformed officers knew what was going on but we were expected to work around this – or collude with it. One morning, I ran up the stairs to the CID offices with some urgent piece of paperwork – and found the whole place empty. Deserted.

I thought that at the very least there must be one person around and assumed that person must be in the Gents. I went to check my theory and as I opened the door, I heard whispering. I entered cautiously, using that quiet walk I had learned for catching crooks. The whispering came from a cubicle at the end. Under the door I could see five pairs of feet. I left as rapidly as I could. Unbeknown to me, the officers had been sharing out bribes in the cubicle.

A few days later the station was alive with gossip. One detective at Fulham had turned Queen's evidence: in other words, he had shopped his colleagues and avoided prosecution himself. The result was that there had been a handful of arrests and some members of the CID had been charged with corruption.

When a temporary inspector took charge of my shift and we were told he came from the Flying Squad (the elite detective branch, in which *The Sweeney* was actually set), we were

a bit apprehensive. Why had he left the Flying Squad to super-
vise a bunch of uniformed, front-line coppers?

The first time I saw him was on parade. We constables
always went on parade at the start of every shift. We were
expected to show our "appointments" – whistle, truncheon,
notebook, handcuffs – for inspection. Our shoes had to be
shiny, our uniform smart.

We milled about waiting for him, talking or looking at the
"Wanted" posters on the wall. There were other posters on
the canteen wall, too. For the National Front. No one else
seemed to find this offensive. Has my imagination supplied
this or was there really an invitation to join a NF meeting enti-
tled "Immigrants, their Diseases and the Burden they Place on
our Health Service"?

The new boss appeared and we got into line. Something
about the stiff way he walked suggested that it was many
years since he'd been in uniform and right now he would
prefer a suit.

He made a few comments and when he reached the end of
the line, he nodded at us. "Right, you're all set. Go out there
and get to work. Lots of stops. And make sure they're black."

And make sure…? Did he just say…? Surely he can't have
said: "*And make sure they're black?*"

I felt the way the only person who's just seen a ghost must
feel, because the others now filed out as if they simply hadn't
heard him.

I stood there, stunned, until only two of us were left: me
and the Inspector. I stared at him in disbelief. He acted as if he
didn't care at all what I thought, although he couldn't quite
meet my eye.

He was the boss, and I was the lowest of the low. What
could I do? Demand to know exactly what he meant? If I
challenged him, I'd be starting a battle I would certainly lose.
He obviously believed that it was acceptable, in our working

climate, to say those things, to think those things. And apparently, he was right. Because no one had challenged him.

While I debated with myself what to do, the moment to protest passed. He had turned on his heel. I was left standing there alone. Seething with impotent rage.

Somehow the rage turned into something which made me feel very small and demoralised as I joined my colleagues. I longed to discuss with them what had just been said and how it had made me feel. Talking about it would have reduced it – I would have felt less isolated. But drawing attention to my colour and to my sensitivity in such a way was totally, utterly out of the question.

I didn't see much more of that inspector for a few weeks, to my relief. But he'd left an ugly taste in my mouth, like something rotting. Only a trip to the barber's could help.

"How you doing, Michael?" asked Mac. I was a regular now and Mac liked me and picked me out of the queue quite quickly.

"Fine," I said, listening to the man in the next chair telling everyone about a police raid on his neighbour's house. How the police were bumbling idiots. I didn't care what he said. I liked it here. The men, laughing and chatting in one big group, were like a salve in the wound the Inspector had made.

Mac's son, Winston, was working that day and he looked at me closely in the mirror.

"What do you do for a living?" he asked.

I paused.

I couldn't say it. Nothing would be the same at Mac's if I told the truth.

"I'm applying to go to university at the moment," I said. A few people looked at me askance but the police debate was more interesting and they rapidly returned to it.

Soon afterwards, I was on my way to work and driving over Wandsworth Bridge when I saw a black man being attacked. He was trying to get away from the two white skinheads who were punching and kicking him. If he managed to flee a few paces, they chased him and brought him down.

I knew I couldn't tackle this alone. I had no radio, of course, and this was long before anyone carried mobile phones. There was only one way to call for help in those days: a telephone box. I slowed, looking for one. The skinheads saw me and perhaps guessed what I was doing. Or maybe it was the colour of my skin which made one of them grab something lying nearby and hurl it towards me.

This missile appeared, startlingly, in front of my windscreen. Almost instantly there was a loud crack, and a split appeared right across my line of sight. Then the windscreen shattered spectacularly. It was like peering out from the inside of a glacier.

I pulled over. My car was a treasured Triumph Dolomite Sprint and it was, in fact, my pride and joy so there was no way a skinhead was going to get away with this. I was livid and no processing time was required to know that. Not when someone had damaged the Sprint.

I got out. A brick lay in the road. I marched over to the skinheads. At this point their victim managed to escape but they did not care: they were much more interested in making a victim of me.

"That brick could have killed me," I said. They looked as if they thought that would have been no bad thing.

I was in half blues: that is, police tie, white shirt and black trousers, ready to put the rest of my uniform on at work.

"I'm a police officer," I told them, showing them my warrant card, "and I'm phoning my colleagues now. You'll be arrested."

For a few moments, I saw panic in their eyes. They turned to run and I turned too, to find that phone box. In my experience a working telephone box was seldom to be found where you wanted one but today, amazingly, a box was at hand and I opened its heavy door and stepped into its small world.

Although bounded only by a metal frame and thick glass panes, telephone boxes could give a sense of safety, which now, as so often, was an illusion, because the two skinheads had doubled back on themselves and were standing up against it. They were both large and one of them, the one who had thrown the brick, was huge. Their great round faces pressed against the glass and there was an eerie moment when I was transported back to that night years ago in Crawley. The night of the intruder. The pale face, staring at me through the window. I began to sweat now.

The skinheads jeered and threatened me, straining their faces against the glass into strange, ugly shapes.

"This is being recorded!" I informed them, waving the phone at the end of its lead. But their threats only got louder. I was enveloped by skinheads, and with just glass between us. They began to tug at the metal handle of the box. On the inside, I pulled with all my might to keep the door shut.

"The police are on their way!" I yelled through the glass, hoping they would get here soon.

At that point I felt the handle of the phone box, which was too shallow to allow a deep grip, ripped from my fingers. The door opened. The two skinheads loomed before me. Massive. Their heads shaven. Their faces twisted with hatred.

"Black bastard!" roared the biggest one.

Most criminals did that. It wasn't enough to call me a bastard. My colour was an important part of their hatred and always had to be named.

"Attack me and you'll be in even more trouble! And I'll tell you something: I won't forget your face. Ever!" I shouted at him.

I doubt it was my words which made them turn and run: it was more likely to be the sound of a police siren, approaching fast. They disappeared at speed over the bridge and the telephone box felt bright again without their oppressive presence. I stepped outside and was glad to leave its stale air behind. I might have chased them in my car if it had been drivable – but this was impossible with a smashed windscreen, which made me really despondent. The Sprint was a fast car and her windscreen was made of reinforced glass with a green tint – it would cost a lot to repair.

The siren was deafening now and a police car screeched to a halt by me. We searched high and low for the skinheads but there was no sign of them.

I did not want to give up, I hated crooks getting away. But the two officers in the car shook their heads and declared the search over.

"They're probably in Wandsworth by now," said one.

However, I was determined to catch the skinheads, or at least the enormous brick-thrower. There was a pub near Wandsworth Bridge which was known for the gangs of National Front skinheads which congregated there and my partner and I regularly crossed the bridge to check faces. But the man had really disappeared.

A few weeks later, I was on duty in uniform at Stamford Bridge for a Chelsea game. I was standing outside as fans trooped into the ground when a huge group of skinheads marched past. There were at least 60 of them, all together. I watched them. One stood out: he was broader and taller than the others. And I recognised his face.

The skinhead saw me staring at him. There was a moment of recognition. Then he tried to melt into the crowd, although he was a bit big to disappear. I saw him checking all around, trying to see how many coppers were on duty there.

There was just me and one other. He probably thought that meant he was safe. But I turned to my colleague.

"That big one, he's wanted and I'm going to arrest him."

My colleague surveyed the massive crowd of marching skinheads.

"Are you sure about that?" he said.

I was sure. I waded into the crowd, through the hordes of shaven heads. They were so surprised that they actually gave way to me. I grabbed the one I wanted by his massive arm.

"I recognise you," I told him. "This way."

He did not try to stop me, nor did he try to inflame the situation by setting his mates on me. He was considerably bigger than me but offered no resistance. Instead, he allowed me to lead him, lamb-like, outside the flow of people.

I said: "You're under arrest, and you know why. You attacked a man and then caused criminal damage to my car."

He showed no surprise. It was almost as if he had been waiting for me.

That afternoon I completed the arrest and associated paperwork. I'd missed the game but that was a small price to pay for the considerable satisfaction of catching him at last.

The very next week I was back at Stamford Bridge. Behind me, the crowd chanted and yelled, a huge sea of people swaying this way and that. In the distance I could see the inspector in charge of us. It was the temporary inspector from the Flying Squad: I hadn't seen him since parade that day.

I was stationed by myself at The Shed end of the ground, where a fight was guaranteed. And, sure enough, one broke out and spread across the terraces like fire, igniting a huge group of fans until the numbers involved were so great there was no way I could tackle this alone with the stewards.

So I went straight off to find the Inspector.

I said: "We'll need a lot more people."

It was hard to talk to him as if that incident had never occurred, as if I didn't know he was a racist. I stood tall and looked him in the eye. But he was not the arrogant man who had told us to stop as many black people as possible. He seemed troubled. And distracted. He barely heard what I said and did not glance at the fight, which was beginning to look spectacular.

He just shrugged. "Yeah, well, go and sort it out, Mick."

I got hold of the Sergeant and we called in some back-up.

The Sergeant shouted: "Sticks out!" and suddenly we were in the middle of the noisy, sweaty, beery crowd, dragging warring groups apart. Some wouldn't stop pounding their opponents, and we had to remind them of our presence with our truncheons. I am non-aggressive and I did not fight at school as a boy or later as a man so I hated this. But it worked. Since the fans were more interested in attacking each other than the police, it wasn't difficult to disperse them, although fights resumed later at the pubs around the ground.

Afterwards I did think once or twice about the Inspector's troubled face. How it had looked as though he had bigger worries than a hundred Chelsea supporters fighting with the away team's fans. I soon found out what those worries were.

A few days later he was arrested and later found guilty of corruption, dating back to his Flying Squad days. He was jailed and I never saw him again.

From the reaction to me when I was on the beat, you might have the impression that I was the first and only black officer in Fulham. In fact, there was one other, but he was in plain clothes and so did not elicit the same response as a uniformed black officer.

Jacob Venus was a snappy dresser who was as bald as a coot and managed to make that look enviable, too. He was handsome, a lot of fun and immensely popular with everyone, especially women. I looked up to him. One day, he and I were both in the uncomfortable position of policing a National Front demonstration together. Ironically, it was our job to keep the anti-fascist protesters away from the Front (who were sheltering beneath a forest of placards bearing the catchy rhyme "Defend Rights for Whites!").

As I listened to them rant about people like me being an inferior race, I was a schoolboy again, reading the Major's leaflet. But now I had learned to master my emotions. I never allowed my anger or hurt to show these days. Not when the other officers bandied words like coon or nigger around. Not when black kids catcalled me in the street. Not when I was effectively defending the right of the Front to demonstrate. I reminded myself that I was simply there to keep the peace: I had to be impartial, however I felt inside.

Then, in one of those lulls which sometimes occur during marches or demonstrations – during any gathering, in fact – a voice said: "Well, you know, really the National Front is right."

The voice did not belong to a demonstrator, it belonged to a police officer.

No one reacted. Certainly not me. No one argued. Except for Jacob Venus. He exploded. And I mean *exploded*. In a way I could never, ever let myself. His bald head creasing as his face contorted in fury, he told the white officer to shut up. But the white officer, ginger hair bristling, wasn't going to allow a black cop to tell *him* what to do. Many other cops could hear him and the whole incident would have ended then and there if they had simply told him to keep quiet. But no one did.

Jacob Venus was saying: "This is disgusting! You're not supposed to be political! You're not supposed to get involved in this."

But the ginger-haired officer droned on and on: "Well, they're right. It's a fact. They're right."

Jacob was getting so angry that if someone hadn't stood between them they might have come to blows.

After the demonstration, there had to be a review into why dissent in the police ranks had been as great as the dissent between demonstrators and protesters. I feared Jacob would be disciplined for reacting towards his colleague so aggressively. They'd say the white officer had been inoffensive and fall back on the usual charge of oversensitivity.

However, Jacob was so popular that nobody played that card. The groundswell of opinion among all the cops was that the white officer shouldn't have been expressing political views at a demonstration. The inquiry was informal and I don't think anyone went so far as to say that the white officer's words had been inappropriate (certainly, no one else had tried to stop him speaking at the demonstration itself). But Jacob Venus wasn't actually disciplined, and clearly, most people supported him. And that was a victory of sorts.

I was very happy about the outcome. It made me wonder if I should speak up more often when, for example, my colleagues used racist language. But that could only create divisions, and I had spent the year trying to fit in with my shift, laughing and joking with them and not calling them to account.

Jokes were an important part of police life: for probationers, the most common hoax was to get them to the hospital mortuary to help identify a body. As they approached the shape beneath the sheet, it would move, being a fellow officer. Happily, they didn't try that one on me but I was asked to participate in a trick on a young woman probationer. The Sergeant suggested I play the part of a mugger. They set up a "crime", located the "criminal" and ordered her to give chase as I escaped.

I was selected to be the mugger because I'm black. Because criminality is so common in the black community. Right?

Later, I looked back and cursed myself for reinforcing the stereotyping of black men as criminals. At the time, I simply did it. I was a good sport. I ran fast and led the young officer a merry dance, causing hysteria in the rest of the shift.

"Bugger's just grinned at me!" she roared furiously into her radio, puffing hard, as I zoomed past her. A lot of white people think black people all look the same, so it didn't occur to her that the criminal was me. Afterwards we all had a drink together and the joke was on her and I felt like one of the gang. I was prepared to sacrifice a lot to belong.

FIFTEEN

In that first year I was taken through all the situations in which a copper might find himself. And, inevitably, these did involve encounters with the dead.

We had to learn how to deal with death, how to behave at a murder scene, how to break bad news and how to treat the relatives of the deceased.

The first dead person I saw was an elderly woman. She lay on the floor in the centre of the living room, between the sofa and the armchair. For a few moments, I looked at anything but the body. I noted that there were no obvious signs of violence, that the house was clean and tidy. I noted its sparseness and simplicity, something I had begun to associate with the very old.

The woman's husband had let us in but had not joined us in the living room.

"I'm no pathologist, lad, but even I can tell she's been dead for some time. She's as stiff as a board," said the Sergeant. "So I'm asking myself: why didn't he call an ambulance a lot sooner? He says he's been here all along and she wasn't known to be ill."

I could not avoid it any longer. I had to look at the woman now.

I felt a bit scared as I surveyed her frail body, her wrinkled face, her closed eyes and open mouth, her still, veiny hands.

So this was death. She was there only not. In fact, the most notable thing about the body that lay on the carpet was the complete absence of its owner.

"Right, now what's the first thing we do?" the Sergeant asked me.

Since we probationers had learned the entire police manual by heart, it was easy to give the answer and a lot less easy to actually do it.

"Inspect the body."

I wasn't looking forward to that.

"Good, and what are you looking for?"

"Er... obvious signs of violence."

"Right. And so...?"

Wait. Hadn't I forgotten something?

"Don't I have to make absolutely sure she's really dead? In case I need to do first aid."

"That's true enough but there's no doubt at all in this case, lad. So, we already start asking ourselves how she died and we look for any signs of violence..."

I stared at the woman again. Since I'd started this job I'd spent time with old people and noticed that lots of them had so many areas of skin discoloration that they looked like paintboxes. Maybe that could be bruising on the old lady, but maybe not.

"... I think we can both agree that there's no knife in her chest so next, we need to ascertain that there's not one in her back either."

There was no blood on the floor. It was hard to believe the old lady might be lying there bloodlessly with a knife in her back but the Sergeant showed me the correct procedure anyway, lifting at the shoulder and turning the body just enough to see whether there were any stab wounds.

The husband shuffled in. He was wearing carpet slippers which were so old and loose they were a tripping hazard. He must have been at least 80 and the dead woman was probably a similar age.

"Tea for two? How do you take it?" he asked cheerfully. This smiling man was the husband of the body on the floor. Strange. The Sergeant looked at me and raised his eyebrows as the old man shuffled out again.

"We'll look at her head carefully now, to see if there are any marks there. If she happened to fall and knock herself, or if she's been hit."

But there were no marks on the woman's head.

"I think we'll have to regard this as a suspicious death because of the husband's failure to phone promptly for the police or an ambulance. I reckon she could have been here a day like this, perhaps two."

"Maybe he's just shocked," I suggested.

"True, people do all sorts of funny things after a sudden death. But let's say she was having a heart attack and collapsed. If the pathologist says that the husband could have saved her if he'd called an ambulance, then we're looking at charging him. And that's just one possibility."

"You don't think he killed her!"

"We can't rule it out at this stage."

The old man shuffled in with the tea on a tray, slopping it over the sides of the cups. It would be hard to find anyone who looked less like a murderer.

"Sorry," he said. "Hands not very steady today for some reason."

The Sergeant asked him questions about his wife's health and whether she had complained of feeling ill and how long he had known she was on the floor. His answers were confused.

"Why didn't you call an ambulance, sir?"

"Well... I don't know. Except I didn't want to waste every-one's time because I... I could see she had died. Although, she, you know, she always gets up if she falls, and never a word of complaint…"

I felt sorry for him. He didn't seem clear-thinking enough to plan and carry out a homicide. And he didn't look like someone who would murder his wife in a fit of rage, certainly not without leaving an obvious mark on her.

The coroner's officer arrived, then the police doctor (otherwise known as the FME, or Forensic Medical Examiner) appeared to certify death. He examined the body and, realising I was a probationer, rather frighteningly invited me to examine it with him.

"Now, touch her head just here…"

I did everything he asked. But gingerly.

Finally, he authorised the removal of the body to the mortuary for post-mortem. The coroner's officer had already called an undertaker and the men had been waiting respectfully in the hallway. I went into the cramped kitchen. The husband was sitting down.

"My turn to make you a cup of tea," I suggested.

"No, thank you. I feel odd today. As if this is all happening to someone else and I'm watching," he confided.

I was sure that he was in shock. And I could hardly believe he'd had anything to do with her death. The next day, word came through from the mortuary that the pathologist had determined natural causes. He said that the woman's heart had failed and there was nothing her husband could have done to save her, even if he had instantly called an ambulance.

I knew I had crossed an invisible line. I had seen and touched a dead body and from now on I would be able to do so without the fear of the unknown.

The next test was the death message. That is what we called delivering the news that someone had died. Until the arrival of mobile phones and social media, giving bad news was something the police had to do often.

There is a textbook example of the right way to do this but relatives of the dead have a habit of not behaving like the people in the police instruction manual. When I arrived with Joe at the home of a middle-aged woman to give her news of her father's death, she simply would not follow the script.

I went through the first few steps: "Is your name Mrs Jane Wilde? Are you the daughter of Mr Thomas Booker?"

So far so good. Now I was supposed to persuade her to ask us in so that we could make her a cup of tea and sit down with her. But this woman continued to block the door.

"Tell me now. Just tell me!"

"We'd rather not talk on the doorstep—"

"I want to know now!"

She started to shake.

"Just tell me."

"Could we come in to make you a cup of tea?"

"No!"

I turned helplessly to the experienced Joe.

He said: "I've got some very sad news for you. Your father died this morning."

Of course, from my first question, identifying her as Mr Booker's daughter, she had sort of known what was coming next. But Mrs Wilde obviously hadn't read the manual. She jumped a few questions ahead.

"What happened to him?"

"Well, sadly he's passed away."

"How, how, oh, he wasn't all by himself, was he?"

That's the sort of information we didn't have.

"Madam—"

"Tell me if he was alone!"

"We have a number for you to ring and—"

She snatched it from my hand. We were supposed to make sure she was all right before we left but it wasn't at all clear how to do that when she just wanted us gone so that she could phone the number. She practically slammed the door in our faces.

Joe looked at me.

"They're all different," he said. "And some are easier than others. That was an easy one."

We returned to our respective beats. These had been assigned to us that morning at parade by the Sergeant, and each usually covered about one square mile of Fulham. You were expected to patrol your area for eight hours, taking one hour for refreshment, and in that time you were entirely responsible for anything which happened there. I hated the possibility that I might miss something and was constantly alert even when I took my break.

For the same reason, I would never leave my beat unless called away. Some cops got bored or even lonely walking their beat all day, and it wasn't unusual for two to walk together. But of course that always left one beat unmanned. Meaning both that you might miss something and that the Sergeant could get so annoyed that he'd discipline you.

You could, however, be taken off your beat for an incident: calls would come in and officers would volunteer or be sent out in ones or twos to deal with domestics, sudden deaths, fights – anything could happen in a day, and that's what made the job so exciting.

A call came through asking for an officer to accompany a detective to a school where a juvenile had been threatening a teacher with a knife. The school was now holding the child. There didn't seem to be much happening on my beat, so I volunteered.

The detective drove us to the school, which was a huge secondary. Lunch break was over and all the pupils were in their classes. The female plain clothes officer parked the car and we were discreetly ushered in: no school wants the public to see the police on site.

"Here's the knife," said the teacher who greeted us. She gingerly handed me a large kitchen knife, which I took as evidence. We were being quick-marched along an echoing corridor, inhaling that school smell of polish and rubber and sweat and disinfectant. There was a sense of urgency. They wanted us gone, especially me in my uniform, and the boy too.

"We've had a lot of trouble with this pupil," the woman explained. "Sulky one minute, shouting the next. In History class his teacher asked him for his homework and he started that yelling thing again. Mr Wilson told him to calm down and he jumped up and pulled out a knife."

The teacher was opening a classroom door now. Inside sat two people: Mr Wilson and the pupil.

I said: "Oh no! Not you again."

It was the jeans burglar, the kid who had nearly killed me in the middle of the night for a few pairs of jeans. He stared at me and the sulk, the arrogance, the look he had been preparing for the entrance of the police went right out of him when he recognised me. His face became sheepish.

All criminals look different when you know them. They thrive on anonymity. Once you know their names, where they live, something about them and even their parents, it is much harder for them to maintain their hard criminal face and the human behind it is revealed. Don't mistake those words for compassion – I feel none. I don't care how disadvantaged a criminal has been, I doubt he had a worse start than I did. My feelings are entirely, 100 per cent, for their victims. And, since I had very nearly been a victim of this big, angry kid myself, I regarded him now with total disdain.

I asked the teacher, Mr Wilson, to tell me in front of the youth what had happened. He described how, when asked for his homework, the boy had leapt up in class and wielded the knife. Mr Wilson had persuaded him to put the knife down and had then called the police. He was a teacher doing his best in an inner city school and he was perhaps used to threats of violence. But not knife violence. He relayed his story with sadness.

I asked the jeans burglar if he agreed with this version of events. He nodded.

I said: "We can't interview you here: because of your age we need an independent adult present. I'll have to arrest you and take you in for interview."

He nodded again.

I arrested and cautioned him for threatening behaviour and possession of an offensive weapon and, as I handcuffed him, he very briefly looked smaller and younger.

There is something we call a teachable moment: it's the moment when young people (or anyone, in fact) realise they wish this wasn't happening and that they don't want to be like this. In that moment, a criminal's life can change. But, if the jeans burglar had a teachable moment, it passed quickly. He shrugged and rolled his eyes to show that he felt no remorse.

I said: "The way you're going, you'll end up killing someone and then you'll spend your whole life in prison."

He did not look at me. His face was a blank. I felt there was no hope at all for him: he had chosen his path and his future would be a pattern of criminal violence and jail for the rest of his life.

"What happens now?" his mother asked when she arrived at the police station. She was crying.

"He won't escape a detention centre this time," I said.

"I want to shout at him, but I can't stop crying," she confided, as I led her to the interview room. It was the last I saw of her.

SIXTEEN

I left the jeans burglar to the detectives, completed my paper-work (and any arrest generated a lot of that) and went back to my beat. As I walked along, I became aware that a nearby car was behaving oddly. It revved madly for 50 metres and then the brakes were slammed on noisily. This happened three times.

I sauntered over to the driver. He was a young black man and by now I had learned to brace myself for such encounters: abuse levels had dropped as people got used to seeing my face but young, black males remained by far the most aggressive demographic towards me.

"What are you doing?" I asked. Apart from anything else, I was curious.

"Testing the brakes. I'm from the garage behind the arches."

"Ah. Well, look, can you test them somewhere it won't drive all the residents crazy? Maybe around the gas works? All that revving and squealing's really noisy for the people who live here."

"Yeah, all right."

"Which garage did you say?"

He told me. We said goodbye and, since it had been quite a friendly encounter, the next time I was passing, I dropped in at the garage. It was run entirely by churchgoing black guys and they showed me around.

"You're not like the other police, you're actually friendly!" they said as we got to know each other. Of course, I always had my Dolomite Sprint serviced there after that.

I began to feel this was an important part of my job: just being a friendly presence in communities with a traditional hostility to the police. And perhaps acting as a role model. Personally, I thought I was doing young people a favour if I arrested them for carrying an offensive weapon when I found a knife on them. Most carried knives for self-defence with no intention of using them and I was trying to show them that if they carry a weapon, they're at risk of killing someone with it. But it didn't make me popular and was something else which isolated me from the communities I was trying to include.

We were often called to arbitrate in serious rows and silly ones too. I once had to resolve a dispute between landlord and tenant which had turned nasty because the tenant would neither pay her rent nor get out of bed. That was easy: I told her not to be so silly and to pay what she could now and the rest later. Disputes between husband and wife were usually the worst and hated by most cops because, when we walked into a room full of anger, that anger could be very rapidly deflected by all sides on to us. I didn't mind mediating between warring factions, although it felt a bit strange sometimes telling a posh, middle-aged, professional couple in a large, expensive house to behave themselves. Both partners would try to win me over to their point of view, usually by accusing each other of something. I'd listen carefully to them and look for evidence of injury. Then I had to decide whether there should be an arrest or a warning. And the main reason most officers hated domestics? If you made an arrest, you could expect to do a lot of paperwork for nothing. The complex emotional nature of domestic abuse meant that, no matter how badly hurt, the chances were in those days that the victim would withdraw charges and evidence within 24 hours.

For a treat, if I'd worked hard and done well, I was given a perk. I was taken off the beat for a month and assigned to a patrol car. Specifically, a response car. With a blue light. As a kid, I wouldn't have been able to imagine anything more exciting than this. And I hadn't changed much.

An emergency call from the public would go to Scotland Yard, who would then pass it to Fulham, who would then call us. My job was to take the calls and the details and the driver's job was to get us there.

Problem: the two people in the car were at opposite ends of their policing careers. I was a young probationer, keen as mustard and anxious to get to every emergency in double-quick time. Jason was nearing retirement, had worked in Fulham for years, knew both the crooks and the streets like the back of his hand and was sure it was not worth hurrying for every emergency. Especially if he fancied a cup of tea.

My frustration was acute as, while adrenalin rushed up and down my legs like a swarm of mad bees, Jason serenely sipped his tea and nibbled his Bakewell tart. The radio had to be manned constantly. The words "Foxtrot One, Foxtrot One" sent the bees swarming again as I grabbed it. Only for Jason to say: "Nope, we're not answering that. Not until I've had my tea."

Within a few minutes, the control room at Scotland Yard, who were like gods to me, would phone the local station complaining that Foxtrot One had not responded.

"Let them moan!" said Jason, tucking into his Bakewell tart, apparently oblivious to my agony.

Police recruitment was poor so we were understaffed, and there were many emergencies to respond to, often as many as 20 in a shift. Although Jason wouldn't always rush, we usually did manage to respond quickly. Blue light flashing, siren blaring, dodging in and out of the traffic, we'd dart from emergency to emergency – a fight, a stabbing, an alarm signalling a burglary – and the day would fly past in a haze of blue light and Incident Report books. It was heaven. Even the paperwork wasn't a burden, although it involved a lot of logging by me. Logging which, no matter how I dressed it up, gave away our response rate and exposed Jason's impromptu tea breaks. When nothing much was happening – and this was rare – something usually happened. That was because Jason knew his patch and the criminals on it so well that he was always screeching to a halt.

"There's John Trinder. Stop him, have a look in the bag and arrest him, lad. He's wanted."

"But… why?"

"Non-appearance. John's a legendary burglar round here. See him hurrying along with a big bag and you know whatever's in it isn't his." He wound down the window. "Hey, John, what've you been up to?"

I leapt out and asked to look in the bag and sure enough… Jason was never wrong and countless criminals were caught purely because he had the knowledge. He and the other area car drivers were the high-status cops, with their fast driving and blue lights. Unfortunately, soon afterwards, a limit was introduced on the amount of time an officer could stay in one area. The Inter-District Transfer scheme was designed to prevent corruption but officers like honest Jason, whose invaluable local knowledge had been built up over years, were caught in the rip tide. Once they were moved around, the intelligence they provided was never replaced and the number of crimes solved inevitably decreased.

My job as a young constable measured up to everything I'd ever hoped it would be. Each day was so different: I could be sent to resolve disputes, rush to a shooting, direct traffic, clear up after a road accident, break up a fight, search and arrest, deliver a death message, take statements from witnesses… I enjoyed it all. And I liked crime investigation the most. In fact, Fulham crime was difficult to police because there were so many gangsters on the patch. We called them "career criminals" or C11s and we were all expected to know their names and what they looked like. They tended to resolve their own disputes before we could by beating up rivals, running them over or shooting them.

Soon, something became clear to me: if I wanted to specialise in crime investigation, I'd have to become a detective as soon as possible when I had completed my two years' probation. But my probationary period was about to be interrupted. In October, I was to start three years away from policing.

"Come and see us before you go off to that university!" said Grace.

"On Sunday afternoon!" agreed Dad. "Ossie and Marigold are coming."

I was delighted. Ossie and Marigold were our most prominent family members and when they came over from Jamaica it was like a royal visit. My parents' generation – sometimes called the *Windrush* generation because so many arrived on the ship of that name – generally seemed to come not just from a different place but a different era. They spoke with strong Jamaican accents and they worked very hard at one or sometimes two or three low-paid jobs. Marigold was my father's sister, so she was of that same generation. But Ossie and Marigold were different from the rest.

Ossie was upper class, highly educated and cultured. He was a high-profile lawyer as well as a politician in the Jamaican Labour Party and Marigold was a woman who was as striking as any model and perfectly poised in any social situation. When they arrived at my father's terraced house it was as if two large and exotic butterflies had just flown in. They were interesting and interested. They talked to me about my job as if they really wanted to hear about the police, which was not entirely normal in my father's house.

"You must come to Jamaica," said Marigold.

"You need to see where you're from," agreed Ossie.

"We'll take care of you. There's so much art, so much culture that people just don't know about," she insisted.

Dad nodded.

"You should go," he agreed.

I couldn't see how I would ever afford a trip to Jamaica but Ossie and Marigold, whenever they came, convinced me that there must be more to the old country than I had realised and that some of the people there were quite different from my parents. Nothing my father or my mother had told me had made me want to visit, but Ossie and Marigold were ambassadors.

At work, when I heard the way cops referred to black people as ignorant and uneducated I always bristled, but especially when I thought of Ossie and Marigold. It seemed to me that when it came to language or culture or education, they would shame most of the cops I knew.

"Good luck at university," they said.

"Work hard and take all you can from it," Ossie advised me. "But I know you, Michael, and I know you'll do just that."

SEVENTEEN

The University of Sussex had a reputation for being radical. It was modern, sprawling and vast and it seemed to me that anyone could do anything they wanted there. From the moment I arrived and was handed a leaflet asking me to join a demonstration, I knew this was an entirely different world from Fulham, from Hendon. Demonstrations weren't something I had ever been invited to join before; they had simply been a policing challenge.

I was better off than most, having a police scholarship which paid my fees and effectively a low monthly wage rather than the grant which students generally had to live on. This represented quite a reversal of the previous reality and I could just about afford to run my car. My own background was poor and in the Met I had witnessed extreme poverty and shocking social conditions, while most of the students now struggling to manage on a grant were raised in well-heeled, middle-class families. The car park was full of cars their parents had bought them. Although many actively campaigned against poverty and social injustice, few had witnessed it, let alone experienced it.

At Sussex, for the first time in my life, I found that being black was considered rather cool. Those same white, middle-class students had great empathy for the black community, without ever having really encountered it, and many wanted to be warm and friendly. However, police officers were the opposite of cool, so as a black cop, I was an enigma. A good proportion of the friends I made thought it was their duty to explain to me why I should not stay in the police, and the most dedicated did their duty diligently for the entire three years I was there. I enjoyed the company of these sometimes wealthy, always highly political students, who believed the world was very badly run and that they could do better and make it a fairer place. I enjoyed debating with them and partying with them – they understood and respected my position enough to ensure that no one used drugs when I was around.

My student friends were disappointed when I didn't take part in protests, strike action or demonstrations. But I had no political bias at all and, despite a keen interest in politics and a willingness to learn more, I just could not commit to any party or philosophy. That might sound like the easy option, but being non-committal wasn't easy when there were some students who were prepared to disrupt exams, occupy the Vice-Chancellor's office or organise buses to London protest marches and who tended to treat anyone who didn't as ripe for conversion. But even some of the most politically passionate began to give up on me when, during the General Election of 1979, the campus was in ferment at the possibility that right-wing Margaret Thatcher might become prime minister and I didn't even vote.

In fact, the students who really broadened my mind came from overseas. My subject, Social Psychology, was taught in AFRAS, the university's School of African and Asian Studies, and the place smouldered with political debate. Here, for the first time in my life, I was not in a black minority. But I was still in a minority, because almost no one else was black and British.

In fact, the social consequences of skin colour are different in every country; I discovered this the more I travelled. And how I travelled. My meagre wage meant that I could work for part of the holidays and travel the rest of the time and, independently and alone, I saw as much of the world as I could. But nowhere were racial politics more baffling than in the US.

I was visiting a student friend in St. Louis and, arriving in her area a bit early, I decided to go to a nearby bar. As I walked in, the place fell silent. I thought the total hush which had descended was very odd but I assumed my arrival happened to coincide with one of those strange lulls that can sometimes descend in any crowded place.

I ordered a drink. It was soon obvious to me that the bartender was very nervous. He served me, but he was the only person in the place who moved.

I stood at the bar. The room remained frozen and silent, as if the clients had been turned to stone. I felt everyone was looking at me but I did not want to scan the room to check. That was the most unpleasant orange juice I've ever had. I was determined to finish it, not just gulp it down and run out. I didn't know why, but I knew I had to drink it in a slow and dignified way.

But I felt awkward. Hot, despite the air conditioning. Attacked. Although not a hand was raised.

Finally, I put the drink down for the last time on the bar, turned, and tried to walk tall. As I went through the door, I sensed that, as though someone had flicked a switch, they had all come back to life. I did not look back to check this theory.

When I met up with my friend, I told her about my uncomfortable experience.

"You went in *which* bar? Oh no!"

"What's wrong with it?"

"Oh, Michael! That's a white bar."

A white bar. Where were we, South Africa?

"Didn't you understand? They were freezing you out."

"But... isn't that against the law?"

"Nothing's written down. It's not actually stated."

"So, how do black people know they'll be treated that way if they go in there?"

"They just do!"

This and other experiences in the US introduced me to the strange world of America's racial politics. Black people have been in the US in large numbers far longer than they have in the UK and yet, I suppose thanks to slavery, their integration seemed a century behind the UK's.

At university, I was mixing with activists from all over the world, particularly anti-apartheid campaigners from South Africa, both black and white. On the whole, the overseas students were older, whereas the bulk of white British students had come straight from school. It was with these older, international students that the really stimulating, challenging debate took place. When I heard about their political activities, how their own countries worked and how some had challenged this, how their way of life and thought had been so different from my own, it didn't take me long to realise that my world had been very narrow until now.

Their experiences in their own countries persuaded me that I should look at the police in a more detached, analytical way instead of, deep down inside, still buying into the *Softly, Softly* narrative which I had enjoyed so much. I saw that, for many people, the police really were the enemy. Not just for left-wing white students who had little knowledge or experience of police activity, but for people from overseas who had seen how their police acted as oppressive agents of oppressive governments. I tried to understand how different other people's experiences of the police were. And one day, this was made all too easy for me.

I was proud as ever of my treasured Triumph Dolomite Sprint and on this occasion I was taking it for a service. Looking for the garage, I signalled left but then realised this was the wrong road. So I carried straight on and took the next left instead. Most drivers can tell when someone's lost, and they are tolerant of this. But the one behind me wasn't. He saw me signal and change my mind, then he saw me take a different turning. He saw my cool Afro haircut (I was proud of that, too) and he almost certainly saw the colour of my skin.

A black man, driving a Sprint.

I was aware of the police car following me. Its blue lights and siren sparked up as I turned into the side street, but it was a moment before I realised that they were pulling me over. I drew in and they drove up so close behind that they almost touched the Sprint's bumper.

I got out and so did the officer in the passenger seat. His door slammed behind him and he walked right up to me and that's when I saw his expression, distorted by a loathing I had done nothing to provoke.

"Right," he snarled. He was standing close, too close, close enough to spit on me as he spoke. "Right, where have you nicked it from?"

I knew what he was really saying: no black man can possibly own this car.

My awkward laughter made the white lines on the cop's white face deepen with fury.

I said: "I'm a police officer."

He snarled again, this time with disbelief.

I pulled out my warrant card and showed it to him and he took a step back to scrutinise it. He changed position and looked harder. Then he held it up to his eyes like a mirror and stared harder still, his face folding along different lines: lines of incredulity.

He looked from me to the card and the card to me.

"Right," he muttered. "Right. So… that's okay then."

He walked back to his vehicle and as they drove away, he was telling his mate that they'd just pulled over a copper. I could still see his look of disbelief as they drove off.

Back in my car, I did my best to rationalise what had happened. Of course, none of it was because I was black. I was obviously a student and most students don't drive beautiful little beasts like the Sprint, if they drive at all. So no wonder they thought it was stolen.

I resolved that, when I went back on the beat, I would never, ever talk to anyone like that, not students, not anyone. I would always be firm and respectful, never angry or sarcastic or supercilious. I would learn from this incident.

I did have one other encounter with the police as a student, and I learned still more from that.

I had not stopped running, but now it was mostly for pleasure, although I did run competitively for the university too. One hot day I ran through Stanmer Park, a huge green area near the university. It was several kilometres in length with woods and wild places as well as more manicured areas. Students used it a lot for walking and picnicking and today, of course, they were sunbathing.

I ran right past a man who was hidden in the grass. He was lying on his stomach and staring at the sunbathing girls through binoculars.

I stopped, turned back, and asked him what he was doing.

He said he was a member of the university security team. There had been a series of rape attacks and he was carrying out observations. He was middle-aged, tall and fair with glasses. He didn't seem like a student or lecturer, so I had no reason to disbelieve his story, especially as he spoke with such confidence. In fact, a few years ago I might have simply believed him and run on. But a year on the beat in Fulham had sharpened my instincts – or my suspicions anyway.

I continued my run. Straight to the university security office.

In their small room, the security staff looked as hot and enervated as everyone else. They were unexcited by my information. Yes, there had been rape attacks. No, they did not have anyone out doing observations. And anyway, plain clothes observations were not their style.

"He's probably just a Peeping Tom," said a large, red-faced man, fanning himself with his newspaper.

"If we investigated every bloke who had his binoculars out when the girls are lying around half-naked, we'd never do anything else," said his colleague.

"It was a bit odd," I said. "First, he knew about these rapes…"

They shrugged.

"And then he lied and said he was on your staff. I think you'd better call the police."

The men were reluctant but when I explained that I was a police officer they exchanged looks and then agreed to do so.

I went home, hoping that a detective would find me and take a statement, but none did. I was sufficiently concerned to tell a friend who was also on a police scholarship and he agreed with me, even if the security staff didn't, that the Peeping Tom could be a threat to students. He came running with me in the park, but we did not see the man again.

Since I'd heard nothing, a week later I went back to the security office. And there, on the wall, hanging right above the head of the red-faced man, was a picture of someone I instantly recognised.

"That's him!" I cried, involuntarily. It was a police poster and I was looking at a very good photofit picture of the suspected rapist.

So now a detective did visit me. But the interview did not go well. It was obvious from the start that he did not take me seriously at all.

"How long have you been in the police, son? Five minutes?"

"Well, I was at Fulham for almost a year and before that at Hendon for—"

"You haven't even finished your probation, then. Keen, aren't you? Well, you can learn from this because the fact is, you're just not a good witness. You see a man with binoculars looking at the girls. That doesn't mean a lot, does it?"

I was silent as he told me that the latest rape victim was Scandinavian and had now returned to her own country.

"So, we'll probably be closing the file on this one," he concluded.

I was horrified.

"But... what about all the other students? I mean, he could strike again. I'm sure the man I saw was the man in the photofit."

The detective did not look me in the eye.

"If you see him again you can call us, all right? But don't you try arresting him. Don't you go near him."

The detective was against me, the system was against me. I knew from experience how irritating the police find persistent members of the public who keep reading much more into things than they do. I knew I would soon be regarded as a problem if I persisted. In fact, more of a problem than the rapist.

EIGHTEEN

University wasn't all soul-searching and political debate. It did involve a lot of partying. I loved dancing, especially to reggae and soul music. My favourite disco was called the Crypt. Discos of that era were full of coloured lights and smoke, because smoking was still acceptable in public places. A blue, red and green smoke haze over the dark room made it strange and beautiful, like another planet. The Crypt seemed to trap smells, and as I danced, I inhaled the scent of that era: a perfume that girls liked called Charlie, Brut aftershave, as well as sweat, nicotine and beer.

A lot of African and Caribbean students went to the Crypt. A fact which was evidently widely known because one evening 15 white men suddenly appeared in the doorway. There was fighting and yelling as they forced their way into the packed room. Everyone stopped whatever they were doing. Dancing, drinking, talking, flirting, no one could do anything but stare at these big, angry men, who were massing with threatening gestures at the threshold. If anyone had thought of escape, it would be impossible.

I watched the men's gullets contract and their mouths widen until they took up half their faces. And then they started to scream at us.

"National Front! National Front! National Front!"

They were moving towards us all now, looking for a fight.

After an astonished pause, a group of students reacted. They started throwing bottles and chairs and shouting back at the roaring men.

"Get out!"

"National Front, National Front!"

The onslaught on them continued and it took less than 30 seconds for everyone in the room, the National Front supporters included, to see that they were seriously outnumbered. I don't think anyone has ever claimed National Front members are intelligent.

Now, after their belligerent entrance, the only thing for them to do was turn and run. Which they did. Followed by about 50 angry students, many of them black.

I rushed out behind them in time to see one of the National Front supporters trip over something and fall to the ground. Most of the furious mob ran on, others surrounded him, and within moments a Middle Eastern student I half knew had grabbed a pointed wooden fence stake from somewhere and was standing over the wriggling National Front supporter, who was held down by another student. To my disbelief, I saw he was about to thrust it into the white man's chest.

There was no doubt in my mind that this could only result in serious injury or, more likely, death. I didn't stop to think about how much I disliked the National Front, or how aggressive and stupid they had been to appear at the disco, I just rushed forward and grabbed at the stake. The Arab guy was so surprised that he let it go and whoever was holding down the Front man let him go too and he ran off. I doubt he realised that his life had just been saved by a black police officer.

The Arab guy was enraged. I tried to persuade him that he really didn't want a life sentence for homicide, not even if his victim was a member of the National Front, but he remained livid. The other students returned now and headed back into the Crypt. I invited the Arab guy to join us but, although he was calming down, he was still too annoyed to forgive me.

It would have been good to carry on dancing but broken chairs and broken glass littered the floor. The evening had been ruined. The whole incident was uncomfortable, uncomfortable because of the Front's behaviour, the angry reaction of the students but most of all the fury of the student whom I had stopped from killing someone. It was all a bit like policing those National Front marches where I had to hold back the protesters so that the marchers could exercise their democratic right to wave banners saying 'Blacks Go Home'.

I did return to work sometimes in the holidays, or to give evidence in court cases; often enough, anyway, to keep my room in the section house. Whenever I went back, it was good to meet up with my shift again, like putting on familiar, comfortable clothes or eating a favourite meal. University was so full of different people from different places and I met so many more when I travelled that when I sat down in Dino's with my shift, I really felt sometimes that here was a sort of family. I looked different from them and my life had been very different from theirs but we had enough experiences in common now for me to feel I was one of them. I certainly could never be one of the radicals on campus. And as a police officer and an agent of the state, I didn't fit in with the black overseas students. Working and socialising with my colleagues began to feel like the best fit I could hope for. If only they wouldn't keep making those frequent and disparaging references to wogs and coons.

When I went to my father's house soon afterwards, I remembered those references and felt angry in retrospect, as if it just was not safe to allow myself to take offence for at least five days. Dad, Grace and I went Sunday afternoon visiting, of course, and the music, the voices and the warmth of the welcome made me feel at home, as if I had been visiting

Jamaican families every Sunday of my life instead of just occasionally. There were a few people who tried not to speak to me, who couldn't forgive me for joining the police. But they were family too, and they deserved respect for their opinions. How could my colleagues talk so dismissively of these people, of my family? There were some in this community I greatly admired, especially Ossie and Marigold. How could police officers reduce them to jokes about bananas because they were black?

Of course, when I was in London I went to Mac's the barber's. Now he greeted me like an old friend.

"Michael, tell me about all your book learning at university," he said, taking me straight out of the queue. "Oh, look at this Afro hair! I'll have to stop with my clippers now and start with the shears."

I sat in the big, comfortable chair while Mac worked and everyone discussed politics. I closed my eyes and the mixture of London, African and Jamaican accents surrounded me like a warm blanket. Maybe this was where I belonged.

But it was back to Sussex for my final year now. I was determined to study hard. Sport was my antidote to academic demands and I still ran as often as I could. I hadn't forgotten the man I suspected of rape: neither had my friend. Looking out for him was a habit while out running for both of us now.

Then one day, I saw him.

I was at the sports centre, getting ready for a karate class, when he swung into the changing room with his kit. I stared at him. It was like seeing a 'Wanted' poster walk right in. He noticed me at once, turned and dived out.

I followed the detective's instructions and did not chase after him. But this encounter told me he was part of the university, perhaps a staff member, although he might have been a mature student. Needless to say, when I told the police, they were not interested.

After this I became even more convinced that I would come across him sooner or later. My friend and I continued to look for him whether we were in bars, in the canteen, in Stanmer Park or in the gym, convinced that there would be reports of further rapes.

After some months, we had heard nothing more and had not seen him either. My friend dropped round at the house I shared and we made coffee and sat down in the living room. He winced when I put on some Mozart. By now I had moved my stuff here from Crawley and Auntie Margaret's vinyl, that had been left to me in her will, was stacked by the record player.

"We probably aren't going to see the suspect now," said my friend. This was true. It was cold, so we were unlikely to stumble across him when running.

I said: "But if I do, I'll arrest him."

"They told you not to."

"Whatever the detective told me, I'm arresting him. I've decided."

"Shame you didn't decide that when you saw him in the changing room," said my friend.

We discussed what we could learn from it all. As a member of the public dealing with the police, it hadn't been a good experience. In fact, I felt like a doctor who had just become a patient and gained a completely new perspective on his practice. We agreed that if someone was trying to tell us something in future, we'd never treat them in such an arrogantly dismissive way as the detective had dealt with me.

He left and I knew that I would keep an eye out for the suspected rapist for the rest of my time here at Sussex. I was in the habit of vigilance and I couldn't just drop it now.

I sat back down to work at my student digs. The phone rang. I ignored it. Then it rang again. That suggested some urgency. I picked up the receiver.

Immediately, there was my father's voice. This was uncharacteristic: generally, I phoned him, not the other way around. He sounded strange, too. Loud then soft, and sort of cracked, as if his words were struggling to find their way through his West Indian accent. I could hardly understand him.

"Grace what?" I asked. "Grace is where? What?"

Eventually, I extracted the information that my stepmother had been critically injured in a car crash and probably had only a very short time to live. My father, knowing how fond I was of her, thought I might want to see her before she died. And she might want to see me, too.

I rushed up to London. Grace was conscious but heavily drugged in those last hours of her life. She held my hand. Our parting was affectionate. But the smell of the hospital, the smallness and stillness of the once vibrant woman in the bed, it brought me unbearably close to Margaret's death again. Now, I felt a double loss. I was so numbed that, try as I might, afterwards I had no memory of driving home. She died a few hours later, leaving my father devastated and bitter. At last he had found a woman to marry and stay with and she had left him.

Grace's death was shocking and I dealt with it as I had dealt with Margaret's. Both preceded important exams. Once again, I threw myself into studying. It was going to be books, not grief, for me. Only when I shut my eyes at the end of a long day did sadness engulf me, like some animal which has been waiting patiently for hours to pounce. Sometimes, once asleep, I was woken by the face at the window. It still haunted my dreams and when it appeared, it never failed to wake me.

NINETEEN

In April, not so long before my final exam, riots erupted in south London. I watched them on the TV with incredulity. The racial nature of the riots – black people against white police – seemed uncomfortably like some of the scenarios my overseas friends had described in their own countries. Or even something angry African-Americans might well do if they were frozen out every time they walked into bars that white people wanted to keep for themselves. But what I could not believe was that this was happening in the UK.

When the call came to work, I responded. Partly from a sense of duty, but curiosity also drove me. That morning, I went straight from undergraduate book chaos in Brighton to a minimalist police hostel in Hammersmith. I was looking forward to seeing my mates again, but the place was deserted. A ghost town. No friendly catering staff even, because the Met had practically moved into Brixton.

I was soon sent to Fulham and that's where I got on the big, green bus. I didn't know any of the other officers on board. I'd probably worked with a couple of them a few years ago, before I went to university, but now I sat on the bus feeling like a stranger. Of course, the others were all white.

We drove through south London and then the coach pulled over, the engine was switched off and we waited. And waited. We were waiting for orders.

At the front of the bus sat the Inspector. He was in charge but now he was engrossed in *The Daily Telegraph* crossword puzzle. The Sergeant, behind him, was deep in his *Daily Mirror*. Some groups were playing cards. I wasn't playing cards; I never do.

Outside there were a few people milling around. Mostly young black men. Like me. I could feel them staring in through the windows. I closed my eyes.

The Inspector's radio traffic was incessant. A frisson of alarm cut through the babble.

"Urgent assistance…"

"Ambulance required…"

But mostly the radio was drowned out by the coppers who were sitting closest to it. They were talking about football, about women.

"Get a load of that!"

I opened my eyes.

"What's her problem?"

I saw the woman they were talking about: a white woman with a black man.

"Going with a coon!"

"Must be desperate."

"No white lad would touch her."

"So she plays hide and seek with an ape."

The two cops were giving everyone who walked past the same treatment. The slow, menacing young men, the old folk who leaned on each other's arms, the middle-aged woman with her shopping.

"Get back to the fucking jungle!"

"What about her then? Been feeding her too many bananas!"

"They should all go home. We know they can leg it. Why don't they leg it back where they came from?"

And so on.

I didn't want to hear them and I tried not to. I wanted to be like everyone else on the bus: deaf. But I couldn't be. No matter how hard I tried, their words grated and now they were starting to wind me up.

I stared at the street. And for the first time that day I asked myself: should I be there, with those people who share my colour? Instead of in here, pinned to my seat?

Don't take it personally. That's what I was taught to believe. Don't take it personally. Just sit tight and complain through the official channels. The Inspector was still engrossed in his crossword. He was the official channel. But was he – was anyone here – really going to leap to these people's defence when the differences were so clear? Black/white, civilians/police, angry/indifferent.

When things get really nasty, you need a tribe. Your tribe takes care of you and comes to your aid if others threaten to overwhelm you. Tribes mean safety. With a tribe, you're never alone. But which tribe was mine?

The two racists were big men, heavyweights. I feared that if I alienated them, they might abandon me out there, and then, if I were in need of support... However much their prejudice made me curl in on myself with anger and with pain, right now I was trapped into silence by the fact that I could need their help.

The mood outside was turning ugly. I could sense it from the way people were moving, standing closer together as their numbers swelled. Their voices were getting louder; some had started shouting abuse. No one shouts abuse at you when you just sit quietly in a police car, so here on the bus something new and scary was happening. I caught sight of their faces and one or two were strangely contorted. With something which looked like hatred.

It was important to remember the mantra that Margaret had been the first to teach me: I was not being personally insulted, so I should not take this personally. But I knew she could never have imagined a situation like this.

An old woman, walking by with a big, young man, perhaps her grandson, looked up at me from the street below and her face curled. I could see her lips forming words. I knew from her face that these words must be full of anger and disgust. I drew back. The last time I had seen an expression like that was on the face of the white cop in Brighton who had pulled me over because he thought I must have stolen my car. He had no evidence, but he regarded the colour of my skin as evidence. I had witnessed his assumptions. His attitude. His behaviour towards me. And I had simply rationalised this, told myself it was a trivial incident, a check on a student.

Now, sitting on the bus in Brixton, I knew that the incident wasn't so trivial and shouldn't have been so easy to rationalise. Anyone in Brixton would have known what it had really been about. The hatred I saw on their faces was racial hatred and it was happening on both sides of the glass.

"Coons! Wogs! Sooties!"

The cops' voices grew louder. I knew that was because they were scared. Scratch the surface of their racism and you'd probably find terror. I couldn't forgive it, but it helped a bit to explain it.

And they were right to feel scared. The 30 or so on this bus would normally have been a big police presence. But there was nothing normal about today, and 30 could feel like a very small number indeed if the tension grew. I remembered reports on the news yesterday that police buses were set on fire. I heard another request for urgent assistance on the Inspector's radio. Then another. I sat straighter in my seat and remembered how, if you feel frightened, people will pick on you. And if you think like a victim, you'll become one.

We all knew that on board the bus. We tried to look strong but everyone, no matter how engrossed they pretended to be in their crossword, their newspaper, their card game, was aware of the growing threat. In fact, there would be no shame in leaving at this point. Moving out of danger and finding a new strategy is an entirely acceptable policing option. And something about the Inspector's studied nonchalance, about the way the men were talking to each other, something suggested that policing a potential riot was outside anyone's experience. But, it wasn't our job to think about options: we were the front line.

Suddenly the radio's babble, which had been sounding like some foreign language, broke into the clearest English.

"Serial 451."

Serials like us were working all over Brixton, delivered in green buses like this one. We were Serial 451.

Everyone stopped talking. The Inspector, wearing the radio, sat up and sat still. We looked at him. We couldn't hear the instruction clearly so we watched the back of his head until he got to his feet and swung around to face us.

"It's all going to rat shit out there. We'll be creating a cordon across Railton Road. Our job is to stop people moving up…"

Slowly, putting on our jackets, stretching, reaching for truncheons, we got to our feet. This was something new, something unknown. Which made it exciting. And terrifying.

When we had arrived there was a lot more pavement than people. Now, at the edge of Railton Road, I could hardly see the pavement. As soon as we got to our feet, anyone outside became wholly focused on the bus. The young men instinctively stood closer together, straighter, taller. They stared at us as we climbed out. Some shouted.

I overheard the Inspector telling the Sergeant, "I didn't join to do this."

He was an old sweat, close to retirement, with years of the *Telegraph* crossword stretching ahead of him. He didn't want to lead his men into a riot, and we all knew it.

We were off the bus. Now what?

Nothing. No instructions. We milled about aimlessly. Where was the Inspector? I caught sight of him, wandering off, his ear pressed to his radio. So we were in one of London's radio black spots. A black spot, Brixton's that all right. I was seized by a nervous urge to chuckle as the Inspector disappeared in search of better reception.

When I looked back at the crowd again, it had swelled. We were law and order, alarmingly outnumbered by the mob. We didn't want to look scared, but we were. Some people, grim-jawed, mouths fixed, were preparing themselves for a fight.

"There's 30,000 of us," they told each other. Trying not to feel intimidated because in fact, at this moment, here, now, there were only 30 of us.

A few kids were baiting us, shouting things, and a constable stepped forward. From his accent I could tell that he had been brought up as a member of the ruling classes. Maybe he had come in through graduate entry. But there was no time to think about that; he was stepping forward to reason with a group of mouthy troublemakers. They simply pushed him through a shop window.

Astonishingly, he picked himself up and walked out through the hole he had made on his way in. He must have been hurt. He had just been assaulted. It was our job to call an ambulance and arrest the suspects.

But we didn't.

Instead, incredibly, some cops laughed. Nervous, inappropriate laughter, because they had understood that arresting someone now, when we were heavily outnumbered, could get us into serious trouble. Could be the tipping point we all instinctively feared.

So while the posh copper, staggering a bit, was led off towards the medics, we were sent to the bus to retrieve our shields.

I enjoyed the protection of the bus for a few seconds. I half wished we were still on board. Out here, our presence was aggravating the situation.

Gradually, instinctively, without anyone telling us to, we arranged ourselves into a ragged line. The black people we were supposed to cordon, perhaps mirroring our movements, also formed a line of sorts. So now we were facing each other and, before we knew it, we had battle lines.

The size of the mob intimidated me. The nearest were about six metres away, close enough for me to see the expressions on their faces, and I was shocked by them. We were the police but they were staring us out as if we were an occupying army.

"Babylon! Get out of Brixton!"

Our shields went up, not in response to missiles but like a signal to the crowd to start throwing them. And there were plenty of missiles available. This was a run-down area of London with building sites everywhere, so it was easy for youths to pick up bricks, wood and metal debris.

And then, as if a spotlight had suddenly picked me out, as if all the people were one person, the crowd noticed my black face.

"Oi! You! Yes, you! Coconut!"

Coconut. A familiar enough insult from my days on the beat. Coconut said I'm brown on the outside but white inside. A traitor to my community. It always cut me a bit, but there were more insults to follow. I didn't really know exactly what they meant but I knew they were Jamaican and they were especially for me. Rasclot! Bumbaclot!

So they had singled me out.

A strange lull and then suddenly a single cry rose from inside the crowd.

"Kill the black one first!"

There was a roar. Guttural, like laughter, like fury, the fury of the mob.

My eye met the eye of a huge Rasta. He shook his head at me, dreadlocks bouncing.

And now they were picking up those bricks.

An adrenalin rush in my legs, in the blood vessels, as though the tide's just come in and gone out in one moment. That sensation I got before a big race, stalking a burglar, breaking up a pub fight: my heart rate rose, I sweated. So now I knew just how scared I was. My legs were telling me I should run. But I had to stay put and hold this ragged travesty of a cordon.

As the first brick flew through the air.

Towards me.

My shield must intercept its slow, graceful trajectory and I got behind it. The brick thudded and bounced off, sending small shockwaves up my arm. The thud of hatred. Followed by others. Many others. A barrage of broken bricks. The noise was deafening. We stood there, receiving the hatred. Thud, thud, thud, each thud causing tremors of pain up my arm.

After the brick barrage had continued for five, perhaps ten minutes – for time has a strange irrelevance when each moment is so intense – came an unexpected pause. I was relieved to breathe normally again, and I even allowed myself to hope that it was all over.

Glass smashed nearby. What was that? A beer glass? A bottle? No time to think because something was splitting the air close to my head. What was it?

My face was hot, it was burning. I wanted to put a hand to my cheek but I was distracted by the cop next to me.

"Jesus Christ!" he yelled.

My head filled with fumes. Petrol vapour, the smell of it, the essence of it, inside my ears and my mouth, my nose and my brain. I couldn't breathe. There were flames reaching all around my neighbour's shield, licking beneath it and shooting up his body. Somewhere, inside the smell of petrol, I smelled burning, and I turned, dreading to find him on fire.

Only his beard was singed. Other cops were running in all directions but my neighbour and I instinctively linked shields. I saw they had blackened at the base.

So that was a bomb, a petrol bomb. I believed it was aimed at me. It could have burned someone alive. It had been thrown with exactly that intention.

And then there were more bottles breaking, more fumes, more flames. The shock of the attack was almost worse than the attack itself. So was the knowledge that we were completely unprepared for this. We had shields that darkened in flames and cut visibility, and we weren't using them properly anyway. We should have held them together but we held them ineffectively and too high, so the flames just crawled underneath, leaving a thick, black shadow in their path. Our cordon had broken as we scattered. We were incapable of organising ourselves into a strong, defensive line. We were untrained and ill-equipped for this level of hatred, for this baying anger. It was terrifying.

And some cops were angry too. The comments they were making on the bus, the buzz since we had formed a cordon, the abuse and attacks we had taken, it had all turned some of them into hornets and they were yelling now, psyching each other up to fight back.

When the petrol bombs eased, the Sergeant led us forward. Instead of standing here taking missiles, we were going to try to disperse the crowd. This was tribal warfare and now I heard the sound of 30 tribal drums.

Well, 29.

I hastily reached for my wooden truncheon with my right hand to bang it against my shield. We were supposed to be frightening the crowd as we advanced, intimidating them into moving. But some coppers were moving forward with a fierce determination which said they wanted to go into combat. I hoped they wouldn't. Because we would certainly have lost against a crowd this size.

Our ragged cordon progressed. I hardly banged on my shield. I hate that sort of aggression. And, to my relief, the crowd scattered. People darted away from us like a shoal of fish. And at last we paused. Ahead of us, the centre of the street was clear.

Surreally, a middle-aged black woman walked down the road with her shopping bag, looking straight ahead of her, unseeing, refusing to acknowledge what was going on all around her. She walked past smashed windows and groups of angry men, right through the scattered members of her community. And on, on, through the police lines. As if her world wasn't on fire. As if it wasn't happening.

Within minutes we saw that the crowd was gradually coming together again, right in front of us, drawn by a mysterious, invisible magnetic force. But this time there were more of them. And more. And more. The order came to withdraw. The crowd surged towards us. When we reached the road junction, the Sergeant led us on once again. The crowd retreated.

We achieved nothing. We were the tide, and the crowd was like water too, swirling and dispersing but always re-forming through sheer weight of numbers, always moving, quiet one moment, noisy the next, its moods unpredictable, its direction uncertain. And through it all came the occasional old man or woman, walking past the broken windows, the bricks, the petrol bomb debris, the angry crowds, as if they were invisible.

Night fell and after three hours of ebb and flow we hadn't moved far from the bus. And then it ended. The crowds wandered off, the street was relatively quiet and everyone knew that it was over just here.

We were told to wait.

And wait.

And wait.

We stood listening to the Inspector's radio in the city half-light, realising our crowd had joined others and that a huge weight of aggression was pressurising other serials.

"Serial 663. Urgent assistance. We have officers seriously injured and we urgently need—"

Before one finished, another cut in.

"Serial 110. We need urgent assistance, urgent assistance..."

I could hear the utter weariness, the shock, the devastation in the voices of officers calling for aid.

Some of us asked: "Why are we standing here, why can't we go and help?"

The Inspector put on his close-to-retirement face. "We've been told to stay here and we're staying here."

Eventually, we were ordered back on the bus. There were still a few kids around, watching us wearily climb the steps.

"Fuck off!" they shouted. "Get the fuck out; go back to where you came from."

As if there had been a battle and they'd won.

I could see my colleagues by the dim inner light, without their helmets, sinking into their seats, tired, red-faced, dirty. The bus smelled of sweat. I stank of petrol and this enclosed space intensified the smell until it filled my head again.

We drove out through the half-lit streets, past wrecked shops, debris all over the roads, smashed windows, cars burned out and overturned, houses scarred. Armageddon.

I heard a few cops muttering about the black people we passed.

"Bloody animals, look!"

Then another said, with infinite relief: "We're going home now."

I stared out of the window at the mess and thought: "These people aren't *going* home. This *is* their home."

The war-torn landscape moved me deeply. Its desolation filled me with sadness and doubt. Doubt about who I was and what I was doing. I joined the police because I hate injustice. But judging someone by their colour is injustice and, instead of dealing with it, some of my fellow officers perpetuated it.

I had to ask myself: could the police ever change? And, had I been deluding myself that I was one of them? Because perhaps I could never be.

What about the mob I witnessed in Brixton? Could they ever change? Today I had seen them, with uncontrolled anger, wrecking homes, businesses and property. Could they ever stop feeling that raw, undiluted hatred? I had policed lots of demonstrations. I had walked alongside protesters, watching their emotions with benign detachment. But today the emotions had been turned against me. Me! Although I was a police officer and here to protect them. To keep the peace.

I knew which side I wanted to be on. The side which puts wrongs right. That had always been my side. That is the role of the police in society. However uncomfortable some of my colleagues made me feel, I believed that if it hadn't been for the police, for the serials working in busloads like ours all over Brixton, the place could have turned into a burnt-out, lawless no-go area. The rioters might have seen police treatment of the black community as the cause of the problem, and I understood their frustrations, but I could also see that police were necessary there.

That day left me wholly confused and miserable. I had looked into black faces and they had looked back at me with a deep hatred I hadn't seen before, deeper than anything I'd encountered on the beat. I wanted to help, not hurt them. But the uniform I was wearing meant they couldn't see me as anything but their enemy. I had thought policing was my calling.

I went to the barber's before I returned to Sussex. As I sat in Mac's chair, debate and comment on the riots ripped through the room. Everyone supported the rioters and was outraged by the police behaviour, which they believed had prompted it. I said nothing.

"What did you say you do?" asked Mac's son Winston suddenly, looking at me in the mirror.

"I'm a student," I reminded him.

Somehow the place did not give me the sense of belonging that it usually did.

When I got back to university, I didn't tell the other students where I'd been. I didn't want to talk about the riots. I had to focus on my finals and ignore the question which invaded my sleep, stole my revision time, robbed me of the pleasure the first summer sun brought.

Did I want to be a police officer after all?

I knew who I wanted to discuss this with. I knew who would bring moral clarity and wisdom to the problem, whose advice would be given simply and generously. Someone who loved me as a mother and whom I would never see again.

Of course, as I drove up to Crawley I knew very well that Margaret wasn't there. I'd visited Gill and Tony often enough over the years to know they'd made the place well and truly theirs. Shake had died. All the children who had been in the home with me had left now and been replaced by a new, ever-changing, multi-coloured family. My stuff had been taken down from the loft and installed in Brighton.

They told me all the news. Now everyone had grown up, most had jobs and stable relationships. I drove home recognising that we were all different adults from the children we had been in care. My life had been broadened, my ideas challenged, my assumptions undermined by all that had happened since. Students on police scholarships were notorious for not returning to the police force after university: they often became teachers. So, who did I want to be now?

TWENTY

Back at Fulham, back in the same room in the section house, the only thing to have changed was the music which wafted from the other men's windows. Now it was The Specials, Adam and the Ants and, of course, The Police.

My indecision over my future had ended when I bumped into a member of my old shift and joined them at Dino's again. Of course. I belonged with them: we ate, drank and worked together and I was one of them. Whatever had happened with a bunch of unknown cops in the Brixton riots, these were my people. I asked to go back to that same shift and was welcomed unequivocally.

But the riots had been a bruising experience. Lord Scarman held an inquiry and when his report was published I read it avidly. It said: "Institutional racism does not exist in Britain: but racial disadvantage and its nasty associate, racial discrimination, have not yet been eliminated. They poison minds and attitudes: they are and, so long as they remain, will continue to be, a potent factor of unrest."

The report was the lead story in every newspaper and I read them all. Many recognised that the black population was disadvantaged. They recognised this disadvantage because it was now beginning to look dangerous to white people. The *Mirror* said: "Bloody race riots threaten to destroy our society if blacks are not given a chance." *The*

Sun talked about "The Hatred that is Poisoning Britain", the *Telegraph* said: "Scarman tells of 'Disease Threatening our Society'" and the *Star* said: "We Must Cure This Disease: the sickness will become incurable unless immediate measures are taken."

But the newspapers were complimentary about the policing. The *Mail* said: "The police of Brixton: alone they faced the threat to law and order." *The Times* editorial said: "Lord Scarman does not believe that the police dealt with the riots badly. He praises their courage." Actually, I did not find that Lord Scarman was so full of praise for the police. He pointed out, among other causes of the riots, heavy-handed policing, loss of confidence in the police and the Met's failure to work with communities. I wondered how the Met would be addressing these issues, if at all.

It soon began to seem as though I'd never been away. I simply picked up where I'd left off and that meant finding myself exposed daily to friendly but racist banter.

After so much politics at Sussex it was even harder now for me to listen to this. Whereas before I hadn't wanted to admit I was offended because I wanted acceptance, now there were occasions when I couldn't or wouldn't hide my feelings.

"Present company excepted!" a colleague would say, glancing at me before launching into something crude. Little black Sambo. How black people love bananas because they're really all apes. How it must have been a bloody hot day when they were born.

If I didn't laugh, people occasionally did look embarrassed. Or, collectively, they would josh with me.

"Come on, man up, Mick, we all have to take a ribbing here," the older cops said. It was so confusing. Earlier today, a group of black kids had shouted at me:

"Coconut!"

"Traitor!"

Those same older cops had been kind and supportive. They'd said: "Don't take it to heart, Mickey." And now they were telling me to man up if my own shift attacked me.

When the continual barrage wore me down and I couldn't ignore it any more, I went running. The rhythm of my body propelling me forward, the sound of my feet hitting the pavement, the joy of being alone, it all brought relief. The irony wasn't lost on me, though. How I could only come to terms with the way I had to behave in company by being alone.

I couldn't forget my decision, when I'd left for university, to become a detective. Now I knew I had to make a certain number of crime arrests and impress the bosses a lot. I did this and, one day, I went to work out of uniform. What a relief! It wasn't just that I was sure I would love detective work. Now it would be much harder for members of the black community to pick me out for abuse.

I was still a police constable and as lowly as ever but now I was, with sadness, leaving my shift behind. I was a member of the crime squad. No more road accidents to clear up, no more domestic quarrels to referee, no more traffic offences to deal with. My focus now would be crime. And my vehicle would be… a bicycle.

With a plain clothes partner, I patrolled Fulham on two wheels. We wore jeans and casual sweaters and no one knew we were police officers – except for the local criminals. We had all learned to recognise each other when I'd been in uniform and it didn't take long for them to spot me on my bike. Sometimes I spotted them first. Down that side street there was a known burglar, marching off with a suspicious-looking bag. I'd cycle over, stop him and ask him to open the bag and, if it was full of burglary tools, he'd know the game was up. Criminals hated our bikes. We were swift and silent and could appear without them even knowing we were around. We must have cycled many miles every week. And, to our immense satisfaction, I think we caught someone committing a crime almost every day.

The main aim was to respond rapidly to a call about a burglary and to catch the burglar in the act. So, a neighbour might ring 999 and report some suspicious activity. This would go to the control room at Scotland Yard and then, within a couple of minutes, to Fulham. My partner and I would zoom on our bikes to the address and uniformed officers would be called. We would invariably arrive when the burglar was still inside the property: there were few who could finish the job in much less than ten minutes.

There is nothing so exciting as catching an intruder red-handed. We'd surround the house. The burglar was almost always terrified. He had planned a simple, straight-forward burglary, ensuring a way in and a separate way out, nothing too ambitious, and the worst event he had anticipated was that the homeowner might come back. In which case, at the sound of the key in the lock, he would expect to hop out of the window.

Instead of that, police officers were all around the house and there was no escape.

When they heard us coming in, burglars found all sorts of places to hide. In water tanks in the roof, behind cupboards, in children's toy boxes. Any nook or cranny which would shelter the desperate. And if the burglar was scared, I have to admit that going in, armed only with a truncheon, was also very nerve-wracking for us. Not knowing where he was hidden. If he was armed. Whether he might jump out from his hiding place. We really preferred to send a police dog in, if one could be found in time.

The sound of the police van, followed by the bark of a big German Shepherd and the call of his handler, was guaranteed to strike horror into the heart of any hiding burglar. Sometimes you didn't need the nose of a dog to locate him:

everyone could smell the burglar's terror. We would find him inside the bath panel covered in his own faeces, or up in the attic, damp with urine. Occasionally he decided the lesser of two evils would be to jump out of a window. In which case it was important to run faster than he did. But the most likely means of escape – and very few did escape – was from the loft of one house into the loft of another and then another, because many lofts were joined together in those days.

On one occasion we were sent to fetch not a burglar but a sailor who had gone absent without leave. He had locked himself in a room and was hurling insults at us, the gist of which was that he wouldn't come out.

Finally, the Sergeant, perhaps because he had been so roundly insulted, decided to send in an anti-terrorist dog. While other dogs are trained to stand off and bark at a suspect, an anti-terrorist dog is trained to attack. The dog was a German Shepherd and he was huge. His handler told us: "Whatever you do, stay behind me. Make sure you don't stand in front of me or the dog."

He didn't need to tell us. There was no way we were getting in front of that monster.

Instead, we lined up on the stairs behind the dog while the handler sent him in. But the dog did not succeed in securing the sailor between its mighty jaws because the man, who was quite an athlete, simply disappeared out of the window.

This tormented the dog, which, teeth bared and hackles up, immediately turned to rush down the stairs in order to maul the sailor when he hit the ground. The line of terrified police officers was forced to turn and run, with the dog close behind. Many attained a speed previously unknown to them. As soon as we were outside, the dog ignored us and rushed around the house to his prey. But to his disappointment, the sailor had not jumped to the ground but climbed up onto the roof and was now protesting loudly.

And there he remained, swearing horribly at us, despite all our attempts to talk him down. Finally, a naval provost team arrived and the Sergeant, who had two broken front teeth, gave him a look and the sailor meekly joined them on the ground.

The most exciting thing that could happen to an aspiring detective in plain clothes was secondment to the murder squad. And finally, feeling very young among all those hardened homicide investigators, my secondment came.

My first murder victim had multiple stab wounds and, explained the Investigating Officer, there was only one helpful piece of information. The victim's video recorder had been stolen. And it was a Betamax. At this time, it was clear that Betamax had just about lost its war against VHS for the home video market. Almost every family in the land had gone to VHS. So if the murderer decided to try to sell the stolen video recorder, he would not just be pushing his luck, he would also stand out like a sore thumb. It seemed to me that all we had to do was find a bloke selling a Betamax video recorder in this area and we might be lucky.

The Senior Investigating Officer was one of those rare men – and it was especially rare for an investigating officer – who listened to the people working for him, no matter how junior, pushing them for their thoughts and ideas.

"Er…" I began.

Every grizzled head turned towards me. They were already getting ready to laugh.

"Why not put it on *Police 5*?" I asked.

The entire room guffawed. Some of them even gave a sort of howl, the sound of poorly suppressed laughter.

But the Senior Investigating Officer said: "Go on."

I said: "Well, we could ask people to contact us if someone's tried to sell them a Betamax recorder."

That did it. All the old sweats started laughing openly. I could feel embarrassment creeping up my neck and across my face. I thought: *Just learn to keep your mouth shut, Michael.*

But they stopped laughing when the Senior Investigating Officer said: "That's a good idea. We'll do it."

Police 5 was a five-minute TV programme through which the police appealed for help or information and it was rumoured that it played a role in solving about a third of the cases it featured. It was presented by Shaw Taylor, whose catchphrase was: "Keep 'em peeled!"

So we asked for anyone who'd been approached by a man selling a Betamax.

"Keep 'em peeled!" said Shaw Taylor and, amazingly, there was a call straight away from south London.

"I've got a bloke coming round in an hour with a Betamax recorder he's selling. Thought I'd let you know."

Some colleagues rushed to the buyer's address and were waiting for the seller when he arrived. They apprehended him and took his Betamax, which turned out to be the one stolen from the murder victim. And, in fact, he later confessed to the murder. I went from zero to hero overnight and stayed with that investigating officer in that squad for as long as I could.

If there had been any doubt, now I was sure that I wanted to become a detective. This was the obvious next step because solving crime was what I really enjoyed. Progress in the police depends on passing exams and I soon found myself on the junior CID course. I loved it, and I especially loved learning about criminal law and the investigation of murder and serious crime.

We were given a series of cold cases to apply ourselves to. We were encouraged to offer new ideas and think of new lines of inquiry – unusual at a time when senior detectives were gods who did not ask for help. Although we never actually solved a cold case on the course, it seemed to me then that any file which had been left open should be regularly revisited. I felt that the police should never give up.

Once I was a detective, I decided to try something interesting and a bit different. I applied to work in Special Branch.

TWENTY-ONE

Special Branch was a secretive department which dealt with sensitive cases if national security was involved. It was concerned with intelligence and counter-terrorism, so anyone who wanted to work there was carefully vetted. I thought that personal protection work would be interesting, probably because I watched too much James Bond.

There was an exam to enter Special Branch. After university, exams did not cause me anxiety. I had discovered that leaving formal education didn't mean you had to stop studying. It just meant you could study anything which interested you. For me, that meant evening classes in political philosophy and then a diploma in wine. My girlfriend would buy different wines and we'd try them and then I'd attempt to identify them and guess the price. I've never been much of a boozer, and I'm certainly not a beer drinker. If I went out with the crime squad, I preferred wine and this was regarded as odd – even a bit feminine. It made me different. But I had learnt not to care about being different.

For Special Branch there was no uniform, no jeans, no bicycle but, instead, a smart new suit. Not that I would stay behind a desk. I was to be given firearms training, and then armed. I took the Tube to Westminster then walked past the Houses of Parliament, its towers high against a blue sky. Past the great white buildings of the mandarins in Whitehall to Scotland Yard.

My new boss was tall and bald and unsmiling. He looked at me across the table and knitted his fingers together.

Then he said: "You're very fortunate to be accepted to work in Special Branch. We don't usually take coloured officers."

I stared at him. I had a horrible feeling this was meant as a compliment. It seemed to me that I had applied in the usual way and passed the exams just like everyone else and the possibility that I had been accepted in spite of the colour of my skin did not feel like a compliment to me.

As usual, I needed to think about this one, process it, before I decided whether this was a racist remark and what I should do about it. Processing did mean I avoided a hot-headed response. But it also meant that, if I decided I should respond, it was invariably too late. Like now. The boss was dismissing me, taking me out to the office to meet my new colleagues, and I didn't know how I could object at this point. Or perhaps at any point.

But as I met colleagues, learned where to get a cup of tea and familiarised myself with my new desk, I thought about his remark. Of course, he suspected that I was only here because I was young and ambitious and using Special Branch as a shortcut up the Met's greasy pole: some people did that. He had wanted me to know that working here was a privilege, not a shortcut to promotion. His comment had been less about race than it had about ruthless ambition. Hadn't it? Well, perhaps it was racist. But calling out my new boss on my first day wouldn't be a good move. And anyway, we might warm to each other as we got to know each other better.

I may have worn a suit to work but deep in my heart I was still in uniform. That meant, as the girlfriend who later became my wife found, I was never really off-duty. I'm still not sure if some instinct of mine meant I kept stumbling across crime when I wasn't at work, or if this happens to everyone. Anyway, somehow front-line policing stayed in my life even when my world was based around armed protection work and desk work.

We'd been out in central London and were driving home very late one night when I put my foot on the brake. We had just passed a pub and right outside it was a ghastly sight: a man beating up a woman. Specifically, he was kicking her head. I leapt out to restrain the man, which, although he was very big, wasn't that difficult because he was so drunk. So was the woman, who turned out to be his wife. My girlfriend, meanwhile, was stuck in a dark phone box on a dark corner, dialling 999. The whole incident felt normal to me. A late night. A nearby pub. The lights of passing cars. The smell of alcohol and cigarettes. A noisy, staggering drunk abusing me while his victim lay on the London pavement awaiting an ambulance. It was horrible for my girlfriend. For me, well, it was my life.

While we waited for the police and ambulance, the woman half sat up, clutching her side. She moaned with pain but managed to grab my leg.

"What's going to happen to him?" she asked.

"He'll be arrested," I said. "Look at the state of you."

She had lost a few teeth, her face was covered in blood, she was black and blue and she held her ribs tightly with one arm. The other hung, oddly limp and disengaged, at her side. The arm was broken, I was sure, and a lot more.

She said: "Don't let them arrest him. Let him go. Please, love."

I said: "No way! I saw him assault you and he needs to learn that's against the law."

The woman started clawing pitifully against my leg.

"I love him! I love him, let him go."

This set the husband off again and he began fighting me while she pulled at me from the ground. For a moment I thought they would topple me over, but I regained control by pushing the man back against the wall.

"He's hurt you very badly," I told the woman, trying to shake her off my leg.

"I love him, don't arrest him."

Finally, she moaned and lay back down and the drunken husband slumped against a wall and closed his eyes and we were a strange but tranquil trio for long enough to enable me to look around. I checked my girlfriend was okay first. Yes, she was getting back in the car, looking unamused. I turned the other way to see if a police car was in sight. And realised, for the first time, that one was already there. It had not arrived in the last few minutes. It must have been there all along.

The husband slid down the wall then fell asleep on the pavement, his head on his knees. I walked over to the police car and showed them my warrant card.

"Why didn't you deal with this?" I demanded.

They shrugged.

"Because we were dealing with a bloke here who's just been mugged."

"Did you call an ambulance?"

"Nah, we decided he was okay and sent him on his way."

"But didn't you see what was going on over there? That woman has been beaten up. She has broken bones!"

They shrugged again.

The driver said: "We saw there was a bit of a scrap going on."

"Surely you should have prioritised her," I protested.

Most police officers hate domestics and would have argued in those days that intervention between husband and wife was invading private, personal space. Plus, it was considered a waste of time since the women would always drop the charges. So these two had preferred sitting in their car.

I said: "I witnessed it and that's all the evidence the Judge will need. Arrest him, please."

The ambulance arrived to pick up the wife. I waited while the paramedics examined her. The angry husband woke up. He was arrested and led away, issuing drunken threats.

"Right, we're taking her in," said the ambulance driver, looking up. "Reckon she's got at least three fractures and probably internal injuries."

I went back to the car and we drove home.

"It's a bit depressing," I told my girlfriend, "when the perpetrator and the victim both attack you. I mean, I was trying to help her and she wasn't helping herself at all."

Back at work the next day, and trying not to yawn, I was leaving for my lunch hour when I noticed the boss glaring at me. We had not, in fact, warmed to each other. I was sure he was a bully and I'd already worked with a lot of those. My instincts told me, although I wasn't completely sure, that he was a racist bully. He certainly made me feel uncomfortable sometimes.

"I sincerely hope you're not going studying..." he said. I had a book in my hand and, actually, yes, I was. In fact, my sports bag was full of police law promotion study books and I was taking them into St James's Park with me. I was still a humble constable and I was now studying for my sergeants' exams. I chucked the book in the bag and zipped it up. I thought he must be joking.

So I joked back.

"Not me, I'm off to the gym!"

As I walked out, I saw the surprised faces of others in the office. They had looked up from their promotion studying and were staring at the boss. I didn't know why. I still thought he must have been joking.

It was quite a while before I found out that this was no joke and that when I wasn't present he talked openly to colleagues, many of them much more senior than me, about stopping me from taking any police exams which would further my career.

In fact, he was determined that I should not rise any further in the Met at all, because he was one of those men who thought that black people should always stay at the bottom of the pile.

Someone, not me, reported him. He had made the mistake of assuming that he was in the company of other racists who agreed with him. And he was wrong. In fact, working at Special Branch had been an entirely different experience for me from working in the regular police force. It wasn't just the suits. Or that everyone was generally well educated. There wasn't the banter that I'd previously experienced and that meant I didn't have to hear people talking every day in a derogatory way about wogs, coons and niggers. Even the boss wasn't racist to my face.

When he was dealt with, I was called in and told so. I wondered what on earth was going on. My colleagues told me they had reported him for what he'd been saying about me in my absence. I was shocked: I was a victim and I hadn't even realised it in that polite world of the back-stabbing middle classes.

The boss was frosty with me after that. I tried to be indifferent. After all, I was taking my exams and he couldn't stop me.

I kept tabs on the case of the drunken man who had been beating his wife up outside the pub. He had inflicted a lot more injuries on her than the obvious ones that night: in fact, the list of fractures and internal injuries was shocking. She had not wanted to press charges but he had previous convictions for assaulting her and was finally persuaded to plead guilty, so there was no trial and I did not have to give evidence. I was glad when he received a hefty jail sentence for GBH. It was important to show that, whatever the victim felt, society disapproved of his behaviour.

When I passed my sergeants' exams, my boss made no comment. For me, the exams are memorable for just one reason. On the front of the exam paper were some notes in bold and one of them was baffling. It said that anybody putting Masonic signs on their answer sheet would be immediately disqualified. I hadn't really heard of or encountered the Freemasons at that stage and thought this was very strange.

Passing my sergeants' exams was a cue to start looking outside Special Branch for my next job. Protection work had turned out to be boring. Looking after VIPs has a lot of kudos, but unlike James Bond, you spend most of your time simply hanging around for hours with a gun outside meeting rooms, waiting for foreign dignitaries to emerge. I had soon realised it wasn't as glamorous as I had imagined.

At about this time, I discovered something I didn't know I had. Ambition. It must have been hiding all this time, because all I had wanted for those first few years was just to be the best police officer I could. Now it occurred to me that I could actually climb higher in the ranks. I knew some very bright people who were competing for places on something known colloquially as 'The Special Course'. This particular course had been redesigned and was a new and extremely innovative course which offered accelerated promotion to people whom the Met thought might become high-flyers. It was considered a fast route to the top and until now the top was somewhere I hadn't thought of going.

That bad experience with the boss had, ironically, made me more determined and ambitious. All my reports were good, I had done well in exams and proved myself a capable police officer. I was now a graduate so why shouldn't I aim higher? Suddenly, my expectations changed. The bright, white ambitious people I knew who were applying for the special course had been instilled with ambition during their upbringing. I had been brought up without entitlement and with low expectations but now my confidence was growing. And I did not intend to let my colour hold me back. Just as I did not intend to let people think – as they clearly often did – that standards had been lowered for me because I was black.

After an exhaustive three-day interview process, I was accepted for the accelerated promotion course. I left Special Branch and returned to mainstream policing as a sergeant, taking the special course on block release over the next few years. This course was radical for the Met: it was based on experiential learning and even involved an exercise which felt like a very serious version of the games we used to play in the woods back at Fairmile Hatch: escape and evasion survival in the Brecon Beacons with paratroopers in hot pursuit.

I passed another milestone when I finally moved out of the section house. My father, who was still grieving angrily for Grace, helped me look for a home, my colleagues gave me lots of advice about mortgages and one day I collected the keys to a tiny two-up, two-down terraced house which I could proudly call my own.

The last family had lived there for 40 years and others may have sniffed at the pink, flowery wallpaper and potting shed which masqueraded as a conservatory. I loved every inch of it. There were no other black homeowners in this leafy area and the neighbours' favoured reading was the *Church Times*. I think some of them were shocked to meet me. But their assumptions imploded when they found I was a police officer. After that, they were entirely welcoming. This was the only place I had lived in since birth where I felt totally secure: it really was my first home. A few months after moving in, my girlfriend joined me.

When we married, our first big holiday was to Jamaica. It was time to take Ossie and Marigold up on their invitation to discover my heritage. For so long my roots had been firmly embedded in a children's home with Margaret but now, in my mid-twenties, as my colour was so often noticed and commented upon, I developed a desire to learn more about who I really was and where my family had come from. And it wasn't just the thought of discovering Jamaica which attracted me: I wanted to get to know that inspirational couple, Ossie and Marigold. They stood for everything which so many white British people seemed to think black people lacked: culture, education, charm and elegance. I wanted a little of their stardust to fall on me.

Did I feel, in my heart, that this trip to Jamaica might be some sort of homecoming? That the plane would land and I would look at the green landscape and feel that I belonged?

I didn't. Instead, I was daunted.

I could hardly understand a word people said. I had got used to West Indian patois in London, especially the insults, but here the patois sounded completely different. People seemed loud and brash and aggressive and it took me a few days to see that this was just their natural exuberance.

Ossie and Marigold were very welcoming. They lived in palatial surroundings, with a swimming pool, and when we were brought ackee and salt fish for breakfast, I said: "Thanks, but I don't like fish."

Ossie shook his head.

"That's the British in you," he said. "You're in Jamaica now."

He was keen for me to experience everything the country had to offer: its history, its rich, vibrant culture, its tasty food and its people. He really believed that by rejecting fish, I was rejecting Jamaica and so, reluctantly, I agreed to try it. Eventually I grew to love ackee and salt fish, along with fruits, jerk chicken, curried goat... I even developed a taste for Red Stripe beer and Appleton Estate rum.

When we left Kingston we found that Jamaica is a stunning and leafy country. Exotic trees, their leaves immense, cloaked the mountainsides. Waterfalls plunged over precipices, beaches stretched for miles. But for me it wasn't about admiring the scenery, it was about visiting relatives. This was a mixture of duty and curiosity.

Relatives, in Jamaica, are legion. Families are vast, sprawling and complicated. Some of my relatives were very rich, but some so poor that I was shocked. Others were buried in the back gardens of the living in Portland, where my parents came from, and I heard stories which went back many years, to the days when both my mother's and father's families were landowners.

Portland is a slow-paced rural area, lush and green. It was then largely undeveloped and much of it was accessible only by bumpy and meandering dirt roads. Here, I met my grandfather in his small shack amid the banana trees. He had been the village tailor and my father was one of his nine children. Born in 1905, he was of the generation to keep all the money he made in a paper bag hidden in the ceiling. One morning, he noticed that the floor was covered in small papery debris. Rats. They had used all his money to make their nests. So from then on, it was the bank for Stanley Fuller.

He was 80 when I met him and a great storyteller. He credited his long life to a daily intake of aloe vera and a home brew called Portland Bush. I tried some. Reluctantly, because it was the colour of dirty water and did not smell good. Never again: I thought I'd rather die young than drink it every day.

It was inevitable that, because I was seeing so many relatives, I would have to visit my mother. I did not really want to. So many people in Jamaica are brought up by relatives that the mother-child relationship is not romanticised as it is in the UK, so no one expected me to adore her. But they certainly expected me to see her.

I found her in a small, pretty village. Everyone knew I was coming because everyone was related to someone who knew someone who was related to me and the telephone lines were busy. There were some large houses lining the dirt track but I was led around one of these to a shack at the back surrounded by big green leaves. It was the size of a large garden shed. Wooden. With a corrugated tin roof. A balustraded porch. Inside was one room which contained a toilet, sink, stove, a bed partitioned off from the rest... and my mother.

She lived here alone and was treated as an old woman by everyone now, although in fact she was only in her forties. We smiled politely at each other. She was dignified and perhaps a little cold, but she was obviously pleased to see me. We struggled for things to say to each other. If she was still angry, she did not show it. She did not light a cigarette. She did not ask for my pocket money. But I gave her some anyway. It was expected. After less than an hour, I left.

I spent those few weeks immersing myself in the history of Jamaica and the history of my own family. When people in the UK asked me where I was from, I knew they were suggesting that, as a black person, I could not really be British. I had always assured them I was entirely British. And visiting Jamaica confirmed that. I had never really doubted it but maybe some deep down part of me wondered, if so many British citizens didn't think I was one of them, might I not be more Jamaican? But my bearing, my accent, my very thought processes meant that, while I might be accepted there, I could only be regarded as British.

I smiled on the plane back. The British regarded me as Jamaican. The Jamaicans regarded me as British. Did that mean I was forever trapped on some long-haul flight between the two?

The UK felt small and dark and a bit confined after the sunny excesses of Jamaica, but it also felt like home. For the next few years, work alternated with blocks of time away on the accelerated promotion course. Passing this meant that I leapt up the ranks. I was now a police inspector. Married. Even a homeowner.

TWENTY-TWO

Another first day. This time, my first day as a police inspector at Vine Street Police Station. I admit it, I was nervous, so nervous that I was early. I was due for a 2:00pm shift but was arriving at about midday, to get any formalities out of the way. I took the Tube in my half blues: police shirt, tie, trousers. I carried the rest of my uniform in a sports bag.

Vine Street is in Mayfair, just off Piccadilly, one of London's most upmarket areas. I walked down Piccadilly wondering if I wasn't really too early. An elderly couple were waiting to cross the road at the pelican crossing. I was watching them but not watching, my mind far away, but my eyes registering the way this old pair pushed the button and then waited.

The green man appeared, always walking, always beeping, and they started their slow progress across the road. I saw a taxi approaching. It seemed to me he was leaving it a bit late to slow down. Very late. And then it was too late. He sailed through the red light, passing just centimetres in front of the old folk. They jumped back. The taxi encountered a trail of traffic just after the light, and stopped.

The old man walked up to him, banged on the roof and said: "Oi! You've just gone through a red light! You can't do that, you nearly killed us!"

The traffic ahead of the taxi moved on; the taxi could have moved on, too. But it didn't. Instead, the driver jumped out, ran around his cab and punched the old man in the face.

The victim, who must have been in his late seventies and perhaps older, crumpled like paper. He staggered, then fell backwards and hit his head on the kerb, his body left sprawling in the road, arms out, head bloody.

I was about 30 metres away, just about to cross Piccadilly myself. I ran over to the driver, who by now was back in his cab and turning the key in the ignition, and said: "You're not going anywhere."

He looked at me but continued to start the taxi.

I said: "I'm a police officer and I saw what you did. You're going to be arrested, you're not driving off."

Except he was. As the taxi moved forward there was an ungainly struggle around the ignition for its key and, as we fought for control of the cab, I felt my back twist and a string of pain wind itself around my spine. All the time the taxi driver was shouting and yelling. Not at me. Not at anyone. At the world in general. And I was sure that here was someone who had lost the plot.

I still don't know how I managed to extract the key. But, once the taxi had stopped and I had the key safely in my hand, I said: "Right, get out."

At midday, Piccadilly is dense with people and by now they had stopped pretending to walk by or look in shop windows: they were thronging the pavement and openly staring at us. A small crowd had gathered around the old man, who still lay in the road. And the traffic had halted on both sides of Piccadilly. Behind the immediate vehicles, there was some hooting and calling.

The taxi driver stared at me but made no move.

"Come on," I said. "Get out, I'm arresting you." I then cautioned him.

The taxi driver hesitated. He was silent now. Then, slowly, he got out of the cab. He stood by his door meekly, making no attempt to speak or run off, his head hung.

An ambulance arrived for the old man. His wife stood beside his prostrate form, tears falling silently down her cheeks as the paramedics surrounded him. She made no attempt to brush the tears away.

A police officer approached me.

"What exactly's going on, sir?" That tone the police use with the public. But, I wasn't the public and, seeing my half blues, he realised this at once.

"I've arrested this man for assault; take him back to the station please," I said. And then added: "I'm the new inspector at Vine Street."

And that was how I met my colleagues. At the station, everyone was welcoming and very helpful. And a bit incredulous, it being rare for an inspector to make a hands-on arrest.

"What a thing to happen on your first day!" they all said, as they helped with the paperwork which the arrest created.

I checked to see if the taxi driver had previous convictions. There were three: one for criminal damage to another car and two for threatening behaviour. I was astonished that, with a record like that, he could have become a black cab driver.

I was so busy that it was time to start my shift before I'd even finished my sandwich. But as I was leaving the office I shared with the other inspectors, in walked a sergeant carrying his jacket.

"Sorry, guv. Sorry to do this to you on your first day. But I've got to show you this. I've just been to my locker and look what I found."

He handed me the jacket and I examined it. The buttons had been ripped off; in fact, the jacket itself had been ripped.

"And look in the pocket, sir. Someone's left some white powder in there."

I looked at the clock: it wasn't quite two o'clock. My back was throbbing from my fight for the keys of the escaping taxi and I hadn't even started work yet. This was going to be an eventful job.

"There must be a story behind this," I said. "Do you have a vendetta with anyone?"

"Only the ex-wife, sir, and I don't think she could get into my locker here."

I knew that this was something to do with the personal dynamics of the shift and that he was being bullied. Or perhaps it was retaliation because he himself was a bully. I asked: "Have you any idea who did this?"

"None at all. I think I get on all right with everyone."

I shook my head. "Well, I'm not putting up with this on my shift. I want the locker fingerprinted and please get me the name of anyone who's been in the locker room."

Hundreds of people had quite legitimately been into the locker room. The results of the fingerprinting were inconclusive. The white powder turned out to be talc. And no one had seen anything suspicious. Of course. Before I even asked one of the detectives to treat it like a real case, I knew there would be no resolution. But I wanted everyone to see my approach. Here was some bullying for God only knew what reason and the men who worked for me needed to recognise that I had every intention of going after the culprit and charging him if I found him. So, I took it seriously, the detective took it seriously and, although no perpetrator of this malicious act was ever identified, the bullying stopped right there.

As usual, each team was known as a shift, no matter what their working hours, and my shift consisted of 20 to 30 constables, sometimes even more. As inspector, I was in overall charge of them, with two sergeants beneath me. The shift worked together at all times, although the pattern changed – we could be on a rota from 10:00pm until 6:00am or 6:00am until 2:00pm or 2:00pm until 10:00pm. There were lots of shifts at Vine Street and each shift had its own inspector.

That locker room incident which happened on my first day told me all I needed to know about my shift. Morale was low. There was some bullying. And evidently also lots of complicated inter-personal relationships.

I resolved to be a no-nonsense sort of inspector, who would not indulge malcontents but could be relied upon to be even-handed with everyone, even the most difficult members of the team.

TWENTY-THREE

I wanted to spend more time on the front line but inspector was a managerial position. I was lucky with my shift: I liked everyone I managed. The team was as varied as the area and Mayfair was an area of extremes. On our patch lived the extremely rich and the extremely poor, on our streets were business people in a hurry amid a high density of strolling tourists and scores of lingering prostitutes. The buildings were mostly historic but sometimes starkly modern and they included nightclubs, hotels, galleries, the best restaurants...

When a shift went out and when it came back, there was always parade. The officers going out had to look smart and alert. As I entered the room they stood to attention and I inspected them while the Sergeant told them where they were going today.

"Tony, John, you're doing the Piccadilly beat, Dinah, you're doing Mayfair..."

Uniformed officers on the beat are not really about crime investigation but my shifts made a lot of arrests. Shoplifting, illegal gambling, drunkenness, fighting, drug dealing... there was always something going on in our very special neck of the woods. At the heart of the West End, amid all the bustle and wealth, was loneliness. We encountered it every day. The young child who had run away from Wales and somehow found his way to a doorway in Mayfair. The man who stood on Piccadilly Tower at 2:00am wondering whether to jump, urged on by the crowd which had gathered beneath him, perhaps assuaging their own loneliness with this cruelty. The prostitutes who had sold themselves not just to their clients but their ruthless pimps. The addicts who had escaped from who knew what to shelter with their drug of choice. What were they all looking for? Love? Acceptance? Contentment?

The great sadness of the streets of central London could be hard to cope with every day and, for an escape and a team-building exercise, I organised a weekend for my shift by the sea in Eastbourne. We paid for it ourselves and spent the days doing whatever we wanted, then got together in a relaxed way in the evenings to eat, talk and dance. This gave everyone a chance to get to know the new inspector. We became cohesive as a group, while all the time my distance, as the boss, was respected. And now I found I liked that distance. As a member of the shift, I would undoubtedly be subjected to the same racist jokes and patter I had been at Fulham. As the boss, I didn't have to listen to it.

I heard the old jokes ("Present company excepted, of course!") among the inspectors sometimes, but less and less often. Many of them had only known black people as criminals and having a black man as an equal colleague was shifting perceptions. I was even invited to join the Freemasons. I knew a lot of Freemasons and liked many of them very much. All the same, I had tried to maintain my ignorance of this organisation. I hated the idea of it. The secrets and the signs and the symbols. And I knew there was an inspector who had been moved because he kept observation outside the lodge and took notes on who was going in and out to prove that a promotion board had been biased.

"I don't often join clubs," I said.

My colleague told me the Masons were much more than a club, that they do extremely good works.

"But who else is in your lodge?" I asked.

"Some are only for police. Others take all sorts," he said. "That's what makes it so interesting."

"Like who?"

"Police, judges, a few criminals…"

I didn't like the sound of this.

"You mean police and judges and criminals all sit and eat together?"

He said: "It's not like that. Some people have done time, that's all."

I said: "I don't think we should be in the same club as criminals. I try to catch them, I don't want to be mates with them."

No one excluded me from the Freemasons. I excluded myself. I watched many senior officers finish their duties and go straight to the lodge. I saw that here was a huge group, bound by friendship and something even deeper. I was sure that some people joined for advancement, others because they supported the Masons' good works or some because they simply wanted to belong to a tribe. But I knew this could never be *my* tribe. It was too exclusive, too full of secrets. Its members were favoured for promotion by other members and that was wrong. I didn't like secretive organisations which looked after their own; they hid too much. I did not want to join.

Despite this decision, I enjoyed the camaraderie at Vine Street. As the casual, day-to-day racism which had dominated so much of my police career lessened, I began to wonder if it was something which might be endemic only in the lower ranks. Maybe as I became more senior it might just evaporate.

It didn't.

At Christmas, season of goodwill, pickpockets, pub fights, GBH and prostitution, there was a staff social. A top comedian had been hired for the evening and he was well into his patter when I walked into the room. By then he had clearly warmed up his audience and they were in a mood to laugh at anything. He noticed my arrival, paused and interrupted himself to say: "Oh ho! A spear chucker's just walked in!"

There was a roar of laughter.

How to react?

I felt myself grow hot.

I was back on the sofa in Crawley and the staff were hooting at Alf Garnett, the funniest man on earth.

It must have been a bloody hot day when he was born.

I could have turned around and walked out. I didn't.

I could have stood there, stony-faced. I didn't.

I could have allowed myself to be laughed at. A helpless victim.

Or I could laugh along, laugh with everyone. Like a man who was sharing a joke and wasn't the butt of it.

I laughed. With all the officers of Vine Street. With the comedian. As he giggled his way through every cliché about black people he could think of. Their primitive nature and intellectual limitations. Their love of bananas. Their sexual endowment. Their inevitable weakness for roasted missionary, which they must surely cook in large pots in some faraway jungle. There was nothing this man would not say or imply for a laugh.

How they all laughed. In my case it was a nervous, awkward, embarrassed laughter. Many of the staff were my juniors, some worked for my shift.

Come on, can't you take a joke?

My skin itching with the heat of the situation, I distanced myself, as usual, from the pain his words inflicted. Even while I laughed, I asked myself whether I should challenge him. What could be achieved by doing this, here, now, as 80 people laughed with him? Not at me. *With* me.

When I wasn't laughing, I forced a false smile. I forced it so long and so hard that my muscles tightened until they twitched. But I kept smiling. Eventually, and I may have imagined it, I sensed the laughter had become constrained. A bit awkward. Finally, he stopped.

I left immediately.

The next day, colleagues approached me.

"That was outrageous."

"Why did you put up with it?"

"How could you laugh along?"

I didn't want to discuss what had happened. I was still experiencing misery. And my main priority was not to show it. I didn't want to discuss with these well-meaning colleagues how I managed the routine racism which I had lived with so long in the Met.

I said: "It wasn't the time or place for me to object. Because no one else did. Unless the mood had changed or people had stopped laughing, I couldn't have stopped it. So I went along with it."

I couldn't explain to them that the jokes were about me being an outsider. If I hadn't laughed, if I had immediately walked out, if I had objected, then I would have been behaving like... an outsider. *Come on, if you're one of us, you can take a joke. We all take the piss out of each other.*

A fellow inspector shook his head.

"I was offended for you," he said. "I don't know why you laughed."

I said: "Never let them see you bleed."

"You know," he said, "you could take it further. I'll be a witness."

Did he voice his disgust to the organiser of the evening, and is that why the organiser found me to apologise?

"It's okay," I said. "I'm not going to complain. I would if it had been a police officer making the jokes. But complaining won't have any effect on that comedian."

"So you don't want to take action?"

"No. I just won't be going to any more socials like that again."

I hadn't handled it well and I wanted the whole thing buried and forgotten. But I did notice that, even if they had remained silent during the comedian's monologue, this was the first time people seemed to recognise that racism could cause offence, even pain.

TWENTY-FOUR

Soon after this, I was told that every black officer in the Met was to go to Bristol. For something called a wastage seminar.

I said: "What is it?"

Human Resources explained that the Met was haemorrhaging black officers and the seminars were designed to find out why.

"So... everyone there will be black?" I asked.

"Not everyone. But there will be a lot of black officers and staff."

I said: "I don't want to go."

Human Resources were astonished.

"Why ever not?"

"Because I've spent my career trying to be accepted by the people around me for who I am. Trying to persuade people not to judge me by the colour of my skin. And you're asking me to leave my desk and cross England for some seminar which is all about... the colour of my skin. No!"

"You are expected to attend."

I said: "Look, I've spent my whole working life trying not to be different. So please, just let me get on with my job."

Human Resources and the Equal Opportunities Unit were firm: I must go.

My colleagues at Vine Street got wind of it. I was highly embarrassed. Throughout my career, although no one had voiced this to my face, I knew that people suspected I received special treatment because I was black – that standards were lowered for me and inadequacies tolerated just to keep another token black officer in the Met. And now, what was the Equal Opportunities Unit doing? Giving me special treatment. It was all just embarrassing.

I was too busy, I was off that week, I had meetings to go to... I ducked and dived and tried to avoid it. But Human Resources would not budge.

Finally, I said: "Isn't it a bit racist to corral all the black officers together like this?"

Human Resources had thought of that.

"We've already told you some white officers will also be required to attend."

No escape, then. I was to be bussed – with all its ugly historic connotations – with other black people to Bristol. There was not a lot of chatting on the buses. We were nearly all black, just a handful were Asian or white, and probably not one of us wanted to be there.

When we were all gathered together in Bristol there were about 80 of us, both officers and civilian support workers, and we were in fact one of four separate meetings. The very senior officer from the Equal Opportunities Unit who opened the meeting explained why we were there. More black officers were leaving the Met than joining and, if the current trajectory continued, in a few years' time there would be almost no one of colour. At these seminars, they hoped to learn what our experiences had been. What we thought. How we felt. Why we left. What they could do to change things.

We stared at him in silence. I had now been in the Met ten years and I had never told anyone about how it felt to be a black officer, mostly because I was sure there was no possibility of being listened to. And I doubted they would listen today. I felt miserable as we were put into groups. I didn't want to talk about my colour and all the abuse I had been subjected to because of it. I had trained myself not to talk about it, and I was happier that way.

"We're asking each group to tell us what problems you face, what goes wrong for you and what works well... We want you to know this is a safe environment: you're talking to each other about this and comparing experiences. We're not taking notes to put on your file, we're not spying on you."

I doubt any of us believed that, but we started to talk. I was still reluctant. As an inspector, I was one of the most senior officers there: most black officers left long before they got to my rank. So, at first, I listened to others.

Listened to how the incessant use of racist language wore them down.

How they daily witnessed assumptions about black criminality which often proved misplaced.

How they felt they had to deny the existence of racism in order to gain acceptance from their colleagues.

How they had been passed over for promotion for reasons they suspected were to do with colour but could never prove.

How banter could humiliate them. How there was absolutely no point complaining to a manager or other senior officer about this banter because there was no hope of support.

By now I was joining in with a few experiences of my own.

How we had to laugh along with so-called banter or be condemned for oversensitivity.

How we kept our heads down and didn't complain because we feared victimisation if we did – or worse, being labelled a troublemaker.

How some senior officers used racist language as a means of bullying.

How officers who insisted they weren't racist said things like: "Black people have such a sense of rhythm!" and thought they were being nice.

How the black community sometimes expressed hatred for us and how it was their insults which hurt us the most.

How many white officers believed that for us standards were lowered to get a few black faces into the force.

How we were, in fact, often treated as the token black.

How we feared that crime against members of the black community was treated less seriously.

We had stories about all of this, every one of us. But there was more.

How isolated we often were by our colour because neither the black community nor white colleagues truly felt we belonged with them.

How there were sometimes National Front posters in the canteen and no one except the canteen staff seemed to find this offensive.

How it felt to be not really accepted by some white colleagues. Because they had a deeply buried and perhaps not even admitted assumption of superiority. Or because they actually expressed great disrespect for black faces or black culture and associated this with criminality. Even when their colleagues in the police force were black.

We talked, we laughed, we told. I'm not sure that any of us – and certainly not me – had realised that others were out there experiencing the same thing. It was truly cathartic.

By that night we were friends and felt we could say anything to each other. About 50 of us decided to go clubbing in Bristol. I was dancing but couldn't help noticing a black lad who was not dancing or having a good time. In fact, I realised he was not in our party at all. I watched him milling about. Something about him alerted me. And then it seemed that he was edging towards the handbags which the women had left where we'd been sitting. I carried on dancing, but I did not take my eyes off him. And, sure enough, I saw him slip his fingers inside a bag.

Before he could withdraw his hand, I was at his side.

The music was loud so I spoke right into his ear. But I did not shout.

"I shouldn't do that if I were you."

He looked at me and grinned.

I did not grin back. I said: "Do you know who all these people are? They're police officers."

His face was horrified. He looked around at 50 black people dancing madly and then back at me. He shook his head.

"You're having me on."

"I'm not. This is a conference for black police officers. So if I were you…"

"I wasn't doing anything!"

I raised my eyebrows.

"I know what you were doing. *You* know I know. Time for you to leave."

He got up, still shaking his head incredulously, and slunk away. When I told the owner of the handbag she laughed. He'd picked the wrong place to steal a purse. On the other hand, he might have thought that the chances of seeing 50 black police officers from London enjoying themselves in a Bristol nightclub were infinitesimal.

To say that people were a lot happier on the buses home than they had been on the way out is an understatement. It wasn't just that we'd had a chance to talk about the great unmentionable, our colour, and all the difficulties that gave us in the police force. Socially we'd had a good time, too. For me, the Bristol seminars were a watershed. We'd discussed shared experiences – shared cultural experiences and experiences of racism. This was the first time I'd had such a feeling of belonging since I joined the Met.

Soon afterwards, I got together with another black officer of similar rank for a drink. He felt that the seminars had been so good they should continue in some way.

"Let's see if Human Resources does anything," I said cautiously.

He said: "Why wait for Human Resources? We can do something ourselves!"

"Like what?"

"Form a network."

A network. Started by black officers, for black officers. I instinctively shied away from the idea. I had spent the last ten years not making a big fuss about being black. And a network could be seen as... well, as a bit...

"Radical?" he suggested.

"Threatening. Although I suppose a social network... I mean, we all enjoyed being together. It would be good to meet again."

And so, after some discussion, two officers from the Equal Opportunities Unit volunteered to organise the Bristol Reunions – social events where we could dance and eat and drink and, most of all, talk.

I really enjoyed these occasions. I made friends, got what I needed to off my chest and ended up mentoring younger black officers (as well as white female officers, who suffered from similar problems). I tried to ignore the background refrain at all of our social events that we should form an association. There were plenty of younger black people who wanted to establish the rights and needs of black officers and make these known to the Met. After all, hadn't we come up with a series of recommendations to help retain black officers at the end of the Bristol seminars?

I was asked to join a working group to suggest how the recruitment of black officers could be improved. The head of the group commissioned an advertising agency to produce a poster and they came up with the famous shot of a uniformed officer chasing a black man. I expect everyone who looked at it assumed the black man was a mugger. The text explained

MICHAEL FULLER

that the black man was actually a plain clothes police officer, rushing to the same incident as his uniformed colleague. It was a great way of challenging assumptions, and we were proud of it.

"That's about recruitment," someone at a Bristol Reunion reminded me. "No point recruiting if they can't retain black staff. We came up with lots of suggestions to make life better for black officers: how many have they implemented?"

The answer was: not many. If any.

"That's why we need an association!" people cried.

As an inspector, I was still one of the highest ranked black officers, so there was some pressure on me to be a mover and shaker in forming a new association. But the idea made me fear for my job. The police are like the Army: they don't have a trade union. They are represented by a staff association called the Police Federation. Many officers felt that the Police Federation had not done enough to deal with the concerns of its black members. But if an association for black officers was too political, if it was considered a pressure group of some kind, then I might be regarded as a troublemaker. In which case, I anticipated I would certainly be asked to leave the Met. So when there was discussion about the possibility of a Black Police Association at every social, for a long time I was lukewarm about it.

TWENTY-FIVE

It may seem incredible now that black police officers meeting together could be seen as a subversive act, but that was certainly a worry. If we took things on to any more serious a level than the Bristol Reunion socials, forming an association could jeopardise my job, even my career. And I was focused now on my career. I understood the only thing which might come between me and a senior job would be expectations. My own. And perhaps other people's – of me personally and of black people in general.

By this stage I'd spoken to enough people at the Bristol Reunions and entered enough exams and interviews myself to know that no one ever said you hadn't got the job or a place on the course because you were black. It was almost always because you didn't have exactly the right experience or qualifications. Some people, if they could see this was blatantly untrue, reacted by storming out of the police force for ever. Certainly, most got very angry and emotional if they suspected racism. I had learned to keep my emotions in check and I believed that dealing with racism in a calm, measured way kept fury under control. I always stopped and processed the insult before I decided the best way to deal with it and sometimes the best way was to ignore it. I was so good at this now that, even if an emotional reaction to an insult surfaced, it sometimes wouldn't surface until days later.

I knew, however, that my controlled response wouldn't work if, for instance, I was simply told I could progress no further for lack of qualifications. That was one it would be very hard to fight. And so, I decided to pre-empt it. I would simply ensure my qualifications were so impeccable that racism would have no place to hide. After all, I had taken enough exams already to know that I actually liked academic work.

As I moved on up the ladder, I started studying part-time for an MBA. A Master of Business Administration is internationally respected and a career-booster, whatever line you're in. An MBA would not only teach me management, leadership, marketing, accounting – everything high-flyers need – but would be very hard for promotion boards to ignore.

And what if, despite the MBA, I was still thwarted by racism? In that case, the Met would lose yet another entirely committed black officer. Not in a storm of anger. Not without trying to sort the situation out. But leave I would. Because staying put and quietly harbouring fury and resentment for years was not for me. And if the worst did happen, I would need somewhere else to go: an MBA would probably take me there.

I was studying in the evenings when, after some time behind the scenes, I went to my next front-line job. It was back to west London for me, this time as a chief inspector. Well, specifically, a detective chief inspector. That meant I was out of uniform and in charge of all the detectives at the police station.

Another first day. I drove to Shepherd's Bush Police Station and parked at the back, but it didn't matter which entrance you used, this place was shabby. The building, the area. Shepherd's Bush was a poor, largely white, working-class area in those days, but it had some black communities as well as expensive streets and the buzz and glamour of BBC Television Centre in its midst.

As for me, I entered with a slight sense of déjà vu. Here I was again, inside another old, run-down police station, sniffing that familiar smell: cleaning fluid and stale smoke. Everyone smoked in those days. They smoked in offices, in corridors, in the Gents, on the front desk, anywhere they wanted to. As a non-smoker, you didn't question it, you simply put up with it.

I took a tour (the cells, the control room, the front desk) and then was introduced to all the detectives. One of the detective inspectors, Simon, who was reporting directly to me, was an experienced older man who greeted me warmly and seemed ready to share his knowledge. Which was just as well, since I had spent much of my career in uniform and most of my detective background had been in Special Branch. I knew I had a lot to learn here and, specifically, a lot to learn from him.

And there was something important you had to know about if you worked at Shepherd's Bush. Something which had somehow seeped into the very mortar of the place. Three officers from this police station, two detectives and the constable who drove them, had been murdered by armed robbers, and murdered very cold-bloodedly. The murders had provoked public outrage, with a thousand people lining the route to Westminster Abbey for the funerals and the Prime Minister in attendance. The staff here were so shocked by this event and so conscious of it that it was hard to believe it had actually taken place 25 years earlier. The murders were one of the first pieces of essential information I was given that day.

My office was two flights up. As I moved up the Met hierarchy, my offices gained in altitude as well. The corridor from the stairs was dimly lit and off it, I found my own sparse space, next to Simon. Beneath him in the hierarchy were about six detective sergeants, situated downstairs in a big office, each with his own team of six or so detectives. The DI took charge of the day-to-day operations while it was my job to look at the bigger picture.

My aim: crime reduction. I became immersed in violence and robbery while all the time the Bristol Reunions were gradually turning into an association of black police officers. Black officers were now leaving the Met at a rate which was four times higher than white officers and, despite the Bristol seminars, the Met had not gripped the problem. For instance, there was an equal opportunities committee – but it was rumoured that no black officer had even been invited to join it. I had begun to admit that those who wanted an organisation to support black officers might be right.

This new, black police association felt very radical on the one hand. On the other, I knew that something must be done, and not in the angry, hot-headed way some people wanted. Of course, I, too, sometimes got very angry indeed, even though it could take me days, even as much as a month of consideration, before I decided that emotion was justified and I could allow myself to feel fury. It took a lot of the people who came to that first meeting about 30 seconds.

Because I was relatively senior and generally regarded as being calm, I was asked to chair the early meetings of an organisation which so far had no name and no defined aims. My misgivings were many. I was sure we would be regarded as dangerously radical and that I was ending my career. It was a surprise and a relief when I received word through a senior officer from the Met's Commissioner of that time, Sir Paul Condon, giving his full support to set up the new organisation, telling me to carry on because it was essential that the Met stopped leaking black officers.

And so, one cool evening, about 17 of us gathered in a drab and nondescript office block in Pimlico around a great oval table. The meetings were formally minuted by a black sergeant who worked in the Equal Opportunities Unit. The administrator was a white woman sergeant who was very good at her job. Everyone else was black.

This meeting and those which followed it were the most passionate and lively I had ever attended, let alone chaired. There were certain key questions to be decided. Not just the name of our organisation (if we called ourselves the Black Police Association, Asian officers might feel excluded. And did 'black' have a political meaning? Or was it purely about ethnicity?) but fundamentals like: who could join?

The most controversial part of this question was: should we allow white members of the Black Police Association? And, the most difficult part of that was: could we continue to receive help from the small group of white officers who had played such a significant role in the formation of our association? The highly respected white chief superintendent who had organised the Bristol seminars and whose invaluable support for setting up the association had been entirely sincere, helping us get started and trying to improve things for us; were we going to tell him we were excluding him? And what about the white sergeant who had also taken on the big burden of administration; was she going to get her marching orders because of her skin colour? Wasn't defining people by their skin colour the very thing we were objecting to?

For me this was really awkward. Although these meetings, like the Bristol seminars, gave me a real feeling of belonging, unlike most of the participants I'd been brought up by a white mother figure. Excluding white people made me feel extremely uncomfortable.

"Oh, come on!" said someone. "How's it going to look if we're a Black Police Association and the membership pictures are full of white people?"

"That would put a lot of black people off joining."

"I don't feel I can talk openly about the treatment I'm getting from white officers if they're sitting here taking notes about us, can I?"

"But you know, a lot of white officers will feel threatened by us if we keep them out."

"Let them feel threatened! There's a reason we need this association and it's them!"

"I'm tired of being treated like this, I want some support, the Met needs to hear a few home truths…"

"Remember, Michael, remember everyone, there won't be any black officers left in the Met if they keep leaving at this rate, that's a fact!"

The temperature was rising. The speaker had leapt to his feet and his voice was raised. I could see there was a danger that the organisation would split before it had even formed or that it would just fizzle out in its early stages.

I said: "Remember that we're here to pull together. I think that a good aim for our organisation would be to offer support to black colleagues and improve relations between the police and the black community because—"

But I was not given a chance to finish.

"Support! You mean we get treated like rubbish and then the organisation pats our hand and says: 'There, there.' We need to be about more than support, we need to be about changing things."

"We can't change things if we can't speak freely about how we're treated."

"Wrong! We can only change things if we have the support of white members."

"If they come here they'll just be spying on us…"

"I don't agree with that!"

"Neither do I; we need to get white officers on our side and we won't do it by excluding them."

"There's a gay and lesbian group; you think they let straight people in?"

"There's a women's group; you think they let men in?"

"We can't decide our aims until we've decided who our members are."

"We need to include something about the public in our aims, something about the black community…"

And so on. It took not one meeting and not two but many, many meetings to arrive at an agreement over membership – which did indeed, after a democratic vote, exclude white officers as full members. So our great supporters, the Chief Super and the Sergeant, could only become associate members. We would be called the Black and Asian Police Association and our aim would be to improve the working environment of black personnel in the Met and to improve relations between the Force and the black community.

Those were the aims. Now it was time to work out how we'd achieve them and formally start the organisation. I simply could not continue to chair it – pressure of work was too great. We had a name, a constitution and clear objectives as well as formal recognition from the Met and the Home Office. An interim executive was appointed and I handed over the chair once the association was formally launched a year later. I remained committed, although I had a tendency to show up at the BPA socials rather than the meetings. Holding things together for that year of set-up had been demanding and now something new was keeping me very busy in west London.

The rise in gun-related crime.

TWENTY-SIX

A drug had arrived in Britain which brought with it a wave of criminal behaviour. There was serious crime wherever it was traded in the UK, and a mass of petty crime in its wake because those who rapidly became addicted would do anything to buy it.

Cocaine had been around for a while and, at least at first, it had been so expensive that its use was restricted to the parties, clubs and homes of the rich and beautiful. But now crack was here and crack was for everyone. Crack is a form of cocaine which, when smoked, gives its users a high like no other. Coming down from that high creates hideous problems of its own – often heroin or prescription drugs like Valium are used to ease the legendary pain and paranoia of the come-down. And the user almost instantly requires, needs, insists on smoking more crack.

A characteristic of crack is that continued use can itself make individuals not just extremely violent but supernaturally strong. Safe restraint under these circumstances is a policing nightmare: I've seen seven big policemen struggle to restrain a small crack user. But worse, far worse, than the addicts was the specific crime which arrived in London with the crack itself. It brought a new word to the English language: the word was Yardie.

No one knows its exact origin. Yardies emanate from Jamaica, specifically downtown Kingston, where there is large-scale government housing built around huge courtyards, known as 'The Yard'. And all human life teems in these yards, including criminal life. In the early 1990s, the word Yardie was used freely by the British media to refer to any frightening black drug dealer.

I personally had not yet encountered Yardies. Who were these Jamaicans? I read books about them, asked relatives what they knew (not much), pricked up my ears when people talked about them in the barber's, but the best source of information was other cops. My own experienced DI for a start. And soon, of course, I learned on the job.

This education started with one of the most grisly murders I had seen so far. A drugs deal was taking place embarrassingly close to the police station, on Shepherd's Bush Green. The dealers argued (as so often) and one shot the other. While an air ambulance was called to the wounded man, we traced the footsteps of the perpetrator and, with the public's help, pinned him down to a row of nearby houses.

We surrounded the houses and a firearms team was despatched.

"Go in," I ordered.

"Too dangerous," they said. "It's a big area and he's armed and we don't have enough firearms officers. We need another two firearms teams."

My heart sank. I felt sure the gunman would escape if we waited for more firearms teams. But, of course, they were right: it was not safe to proceed.

While we waited for the firearms teams, I walked to Shepherd's Bush Green. The air ambulance was arriving, a doctor jumped out and within moments he had opened the wounded man's chest and, ventilator on hand, was carrying out heart massage, with blood spurting everywhere. This is a manual procedure which is truly shocking to watch. Everything had happened so quickly that there was not yet a cordon up around them and passers-by were startled then horrified.

The victim died. Back at the house, our teams finally went in and found... nothing. The perpetrator had used that tried-and-trusted London escape route, adjoining lofts. He must have slipped along the top of the houses, down through one of them and out of it before we were even in the road. By now I was beginning to understand how hard it was to catch these Yardies. But I was still determined to do so.

Experienced colleagues shook their heads.

"He's gone and that's the last we'll see of him."

I said: "He's committed murder. On Shepherd's Bush Green. People heard it, saw it, there are witnesses. Why wouldn't we investigate this like any other murder?"

They looked surprised.

"Well, because... these are Yardies..."

I looked at them, waiting.

"And," they added, "the victim was a drug dealer. Yardies are always sorting each other out."

I remembered my early days in Fulham when the really tough career criminals, the C11s, used to tell us to leave well alone and let them resolve their own disputes. It would have been easy, when a man who had been beaten up at the pub asked us to clear off, just to walk out of the pub and let rough justice take its course. But what I'd learnt was: walk away and the violence escalates. The next day you'd be sure to find someone sitting glassed on the pavement – or worse, run over in the street. And it seldom ended there.

I said: "Nope. We need to talk to witnesses, get statements, find him and arrest him. For murder."

No one objected, but they could not hide their surprise. I noted it with interest. What was it about these Yardies which meant experienced cops just shrugged when they died? Were they displaying an indifference to black deaths? I preferred to think not. If I wanted to understand, I'd have to learn about Yardies.

The more I learned, the more fascinated I became with these Jamaican criminals. They were men who often – usually

– entered the country illegally with the sole aim of getting involved in the drugs trade, generally to sell. Their method was to intimidate local dealers off their patch. They were extremely violent. For them, human life was low-value. They were fully armed and would kill people for no apparent reason and without apparent remorse: in fact, they were ruthless, pulling a gun and firing it at the least provocation. Some made their money by selling drugs, some by robbing other drug dealers, often shooting them in the process. They had chaotic lifestyles. Some were addicts, but many weren't.

Our overall strategy was to get the Yardies arrested and then they could either be deported or jailed. But first we had to catch them and one thing I learned from Simon, my DI, was that rather than simply closing in and pouncing on them, we could make more effective arrests by gathering intelligence first. Simon was a specialist in financial investigation and financial information often told us exactly what was going on at street level. Could that barber with £1 million in his bank account really have made so much money with his clippers, for instance?

But arrest was an extremely difficult process with this new sort of criminal. Intelligence told us a lot about most targets' habits: your old-fashioned British burglar could generally be relied upon, for instance, to be home, have finished his cocoa and be snug in bed at 3:00am. Yardies were unpredictable and at that time could be in a crack house, on the streets, in someone else's flat. They were often cuckoos, preying on the vulnerable by simply taking over their flats and moving in. They could do that anywhere, any time. And, if we did find them, they would almost certainly be armed and so violent that arresting them safely was a challenge. The last thing I wanted was more dead officers from Shepherd's Bush.

The Yardies were such tough young men that injury seldom deterred them. However, we managed to arrest one after he was injured in a fight with another dealer. In the past he'd been shot nine times. And he was only in his early twenties. He cheerfully showed me his old bullet wounds and when I remarked that it was amazing he was still alive, he shrugged. He didn't mind either way, he said in that careless but strangely charming Jamaican manner. I was a man with many responsibilities – I had been responsible all my life, including my childhood – and here was someone truly carefree. I had a strange sensation of looking at the world through a different lens, a world where you lived only for the moment and cared about nothing, and no one. Not even your own life. Total fecklessness did have its attraction. Fleetingly.

His ankle had been badly broken in the fight and two uniformed officers escorted him through A&E. Unlike CID officers, they'd had few dealings with Yardies and this one was 23 years old and seemed particularly small and inoffensive. They were told to take him up to his room at the hospital, where he was due for an operation as soon as a theatre became available.

"This man is very, very dangerous," I told them.

The younger constable nodded seriously. The older one clearly did not believe that the slight and injured Yardie lying on a trolley could be dangerous at all. I thought he had fallen asleep but now he opened his eyes. He had been listening. He flashed a winning smile at us. The older copper disconcerted me by smiling back.

Alarmed, I said: "You do not, repeat not, let him out of your sight."

The constables readily agreed but their reassurances sounded a bit routine. The Yardie continued to grin ominously. Apparently oblivious to the pain in his ankle, he was still grinning as they departed for his ward on the third floor. I had a nasty feeling about this one.

Once on the ward, he said he needed the toilet. Despite my dire warning, the two constables let him limp there by himself, dragging his leg behind him. No one will ever know how he managed to jump out of a small third-floor window but all the evidence showed that he did. He was a lone operator who was brave enough to do one of the most dangerous jobs in the world (he actually made a living by robbing drug dealers) and now he had fooled us by carrying out a near-impossible feat of athleticism despite his broken ankle.

After his spectacular escape, the Yardie was never seen again. You might think a small black man with nine old bullet holes and one broken ankle would be noticeable on the streets of London, but he apparently evaporated. That was Yardies for you. I doubt, however, that he lived much longer: many died young and few even reached his grand old age of 23.

Of course, their deaths seldom had natural causes. But I can't pretend that the British public – outside the black community – was upset or even interested that Yardies were killing each other across London. Most of this huge spate of stabbings and shootings went entirely unreported, unless white people were caught in the crossfire.

To me, black-on-black murder was as important as any other kind of murder. Time again I would stand over the bodies of young black men. In the streets. In houses. On the pavement. Each body had the shine and round perfection of youth in all respects but one – that small, bloody, fatal bullet wound in the chest. I would feel deeply saddened. For what the deceased might have been. For life's joys which he would never now experience. It did not matter to me that he had been a drug dealer or a man who robbed drug dealers or a drug user; none of it mattered. He was a murder victim and I wanted to see his killer convicted.

As I had learned on Shepherd's Bush Green that day, before I knew anything much about Yardies, my colleagues were bemused by my keenness to investigate Yardie homicide. I suspected this was because there was an unconscious belief that what went on in the black community could stay in the black community. The result was that these murders went largely unsolved – although I had proved they could be because, after weeks of work, we had finally arrested the Shepherd's Bush Green killer.

"Whenever we try to make inquiries, doors just get slammed in our faces," the detectives explained when I ordered an investigation into the death of another young, black male. "People live in fear of these men, governor. There's no way anyone's spilling the beans when we show up asking questions; they're all terrified, so we're just wasting our time."

It happened that some of these detectives were extremely talented. They had allowed themselves to be defeated by the lack of co-operation from communities, by that fear which silenced victims' friends and families and left witnesses voiceless. But they were also hampered by an assumption. The assumption was that black victims are nearly always themselves criminals.

I'm not sure I could fully admit to myself that this assumption existed then. What purpose would it serve to recognise officers I respected, officers who were my colleagues, as unknowingly racist? How would it have helped me to acknowledge that the good work they did was limited by their attitude to the black community? Years later, I had no choice but to acknowledge it. Because, at about that time, a teenager called Stephen Lawrence was killed in south London, a case I knew nothing about until the rest of the country knew about it, too. Later, everyone learned how half-hearted the investigation into his death had been. At least partly because the police assumed Stephen had died because he was involved in criminal activity. An assumption they made because he was black.

I did not know, when I told my detectives to investigate black deaths, how counter-cultural this was at the time.

I said to them: "Every death deserves a proper investigation. No matter what you think you know about the victim. No matter how hard it is to persuade witnesses to come forward. We have to try."

Perhaps it took a black officer to see what was necessary and do it. Ironically, because I had spent my career trying to persuade others to ignore the colour of my skin. Now it was the colour of my skin which meant I was unable to turn my back on what Yardies were doing to each other and to the innocent and vulnerable around them. It was the colour of my skin which meant I empathised with the affected black communities. I may have been brought up by a white woman in a white world, but my roots were in London's West Indian culture with my father and the relatives I still saw on Sundays and holidays and family occasions. I had absorbed this world by osmosis. I still absorbed it regularly at the black barber's shop, where Mac was semi-retired and his son Winston had taken over, but the customers still all hotly joined in the debate of the day. It was inconceivable to me that the lives of these people were less deserving of protection. Unthinkable that crimes with black victims were less worthy of investigation.

Introducing this new approach was like turning an oil tanker. But no one actually opposed it. From now on we would go into black communities, ask questions, find witnesses, pinpoint killers and carry out the armed raids necessary to arrest them.

It was very hard work. Yardies' chaotic lifestyles and false passports made things harder still and great determination was required. But I am glad to say, to their great credit, the officers soon shared my enthusiasm. In fact, most were pleased to leave petty burglary behind and concentrate on the challenge of such serious, drug-related crime. As for me, soon there were few nights of the week when I was not woken to give permission for yet another armed raid on a Yardie den.

TWENTY-SEVEN

My work had great breadth – Yardies weren't the only criminals in Shepherd's Bush, far from it – but it was inevitable that
some people saw me as a black man focusing on black crime
with black victims. And didn't like it. That's the only way I
can explain an unpleasant incident which occurred.

I was in my office one day examining the plans for yet
another operation to take some drug dealers by surprise, and
I was so immersed that I hardly noticed the sound of two lads
joking together as they walked down the dim corridor which
ran by my room. For no apparent reason, they stopped right
outside my open door.

One of them said: "Bananas!"

I looked up in time to catch sight of him going on his way,
laughing with his mate.

Did he really...? Did he actually walk past my office
and say...?

No, surely not. I simply could not believe the evidence of
my own ears. He can't have done.

I was a DCI. I recognised the pasty-faced cop as a mere
constable. In fact, he was a junior who had been seconded
to work in plain clothes with the crime squad, the way I had,
back in Fulham. I remembered how I had suggested putting
the Betamax video recorder seller on *Police 5* and the old
sweats had laughed at me. That must have been ten years ago

now. I had been young, keen, anxious to do well. Insulting a senior officer would have been inconceivable. Had these two lads somehow picked up the idea that it was all right to insult a senior officer if he was black?

Bananas was an insult I had encountered before. I didn't fully understand it but I couldn't think of one good interpretation. Whichever way you looked at it, shouting "Bananas!" at a black person was wholly racially offensive.

So, of course, I must have misheard. It was impossible that any police constable would behave that way. Well, anyway, not towards a DCI. Totally impossible.

Not so long afterwards, when I was once again at my desk, the same pair passed my room. Once again, for no good reason, they walked past my open door, momentarily stopped and one of them shouted: "Bananas!"

This time I was actually looking up from my work. I saw them deliberately pause at my door, I saw a face – eyes wide, comedian smile. And I heard the word clearly, delivered in what I feared was an attempt at an African accent.

Spinning on his heel, the constable continued up the corridor with his mate, laughing loudly. Suddenly I remembered that day in the juvenile court, when I had been about to give evidence against the lad who had nearly killed me while stealing a pair of jeans. Those two shouting, laughing kids had run in and run out again. Disrespectful. Indifferent to justice. Childish. And no one had been in time to stop them.

I leapt to my feet. I'd been suspicious enough last time this had happened to think hard about how I should react. Now I was ready.

At the door, I called to the two constables.

They turned and stared at me as if they couldn't imagine why I had stopped them. I thought I really must have misheard. I surely must be wrong.

But there was my own voice, booming up the corridor sternly: "Come here."

They walked to me, their faces curious, surprised.

I said: "I heard you."

"Heard what? Sir?"

Tall, blond, wide-eyed and innocent. *Too* innocent, innocent to the point of insouciance. I hadn't misheard, I knew I was right.

"You shouted 'Bananas!' as you passed my room. Just to whom is that comment addressed?"

"What, guv'nor?"

"We don't know what you're talking about, sir."

They could hardly wipe the grins off their faces.

It was my word against theirs and they knew it. I was powerless.

"If I hear that again, there'll be trouble," I said.

They exchanged looks of cartoonish bewilderment. Then they carried on their way and I went back to my work. Shootings and stabbings were important, those two idiots were not.

But it was hard to concentrate. The incident jangled around inside my head like a chain, clanging and banging. They had been telling me I was primitive, an ape, less than they were. No matter how much more senior I was, no matter how much older. I was determined to catch them out if they did it again.

They did it again.

"Bananas!"

Once more I leapt to my feet.

Once more, grinning, they protested their innocence.

"What are you talking about, guv'nor?"

"Guv'nor, what do you mean?"

"We didn't say anything."

I returned to my desk, humiliated once more by these small people as they laughed loudly in the corridor. Of course, I had the option of ignoring them. That might be easier. That might make them stop. But then I would simply be allowing them to treat me this way. You can choose whether or not to be insulted: the first person to say that to me had been Margaret, all those years ago, and I had made the choice thousands of times since. But I knew that this time there was no choice: I was being insulted by two of my junior officers and I must tackle them.

"*What?*" said Simon when I mentioned the 'Bananas!' problem. "They're saying *what?*"

"There's nothing I can do about it."

"But this is outrageous. Report them!"

"They'll just deny it. There are no witnesses, they make sure of that. So my complaint would go nowhere and people would say I'm imagining it."

The DI's face was like thunder. It happened that not long afterwards he was in a position to help me.

One morning, he was sitting in my room, just around the corner from the door and not in the immediate eyeline of anyone entering. There had been a pause in our conversation while I looked something up and so there were no voices to warn the two approaching constables that another person was present. I heard them talking and laughing their way down the corridor and raised my eyebrows to alert the DI.

I knew I had them as they paused outside the door. They were braver this time and looked into my office.

"Bananas!" they said. And then walked on. The DI jumped up, but I signalled him to wait.

As usual, I went to the door and called them.

"You two!" I said. "Come here, please, and explain what you shouted at me and why."

As usual, they shrugged and looked wide-eyed.

"No, guv'nor, not us, we didn't shout anything…"

As usual, they were smiling. I guessed this was something of a joke down in the office. I had guessed that some time ago. So I took great pleasure in seeing the smiles suddenly drip down their faces like custard pies in the slapstick I used to watch on TV. Every muscle in their cheeks literally turned from up to down. Their eyes popped once more, not now in imitation of a monkey, but in horror. Because the DI had appeared in the doorway behind me.

I said: "What did you say?"

"Nothing, guv'nor."

The confidence was drained from their voices. Simon was a tough man, the veteran of many murder investigations, who was known for his cool. And he was on my side and keen to be an honest witness. Today, if anything, he was angrier than I was. But he remained silent.

I repeated: "You said bananas. Why?"

We waited. There was a long silence.

"We all know what you said. I've got a witness to prove it."

No reply.

Now I had to decide what to do with them. I was in no doubt that I wanted them gone. They were junior constables who had been seconded to work with my team in plain clothes for a while and this was something of an honour. I knew that being sent back to their own stations, back into uniform, would be a humiliating experience.

I said: "You're moving, both of you. Back where you came from."

Their faces fell. I dismissed them but later called them up to my office, one at a time. Simon insisted on being there.

"I don't want to move, I haven't done anything wrong!" they each said, hot-faced.

The DI and I exchanged weary glances.

"I didn't! I didn't say anything about bananas! You must have imagined it."

Simon said: "So, we both imagined it, did we?"

I had already decided that being sent back to their stations was enough of a humiliation to be a punishment. If I insisted on a full investigation, they would be disciplined and their records blotted for ever. Probably that would make them even more entrenched racists. This way, there was a chance they would change.

Each one of them stuck to their line: "I didn't say anything, I don't know what you're talking about!"

I said: "Either move or face a formal disciplinary investigation. Is that what you want?"

Of course, it wasn't. They agreed under protest to go, faces sulky, lips pursed. I never saw them again. And the most important part of this incident to me? The support given by Simon, my detective inspector, along with a few others. Racism is a painful, humiliating thing to experience but the key to that pain is isolation. When others protest, offer support, turn that isolation back on the racists, the pain is greatly eased. Feeling alone with the hurt is far, far worse. I already knew that, but I was shortly to learn the lesson all over again.

TWENTY-EIGHT

Over the next few years I moved all over west London, tackling crime in general and robbery in particular. Each area was different, each had different crime profiles, different class and ethnic communities, and each required a different solution.

Burglary was universal although its style varied. Most of it was quite petty. Not, of course, to its victims. My job was to take an overview of an area and think strategically. The burglary figures in particular were rising at a rate which told me that the Met was starting to lose the war, and that was certainly the public perception.

I knew it must be time for a new approach: investigation hadn't changed much since I used to watch *Softly, Softly*. A crime was committed and then there were clues, suspects, theories, questioning and eventually it was either solved. Or not.

So, after a lot of thought and discussion with colleagues, the Burglary Control Programme was born. The idea was that we took a wider and more scientific approach, looking at the problem as a whole. Now each burglary was logged with information about when, where and what sort of burglary it was. We planned to feed this into one of those rather newfangled machines called a computer.

The only problem was that we didn't have one. In the early 1990s they were so new that applications for them were being found all the time but, as far as the Met was concerned, they only had one use: administration. Crime prevention? No way, computers were for payrolls! There was a lot of head shaking at our request and no computer was made available to us.

Happily, one large local employer was the BBC. Television headquarters in White City fell in our patch and they knew all about burglary there. It wasn't just theft from offices or of kit at the end of productions, it was employees' homes in the vicinity and mugging around the local Tube stations.

The BBC was on our Crime Prevention Panel and was happy to organise the loan of a computer for our new burglary programme. When it arrived, it was a huge machine and looked very modern. We walked around it admiringly. Staff from all over the building came in to glimpse it, as though a spacecraft had just landed in the office.

We loaded huge amounts of data into it about local crime. Then we employed a skilled crime pattern analyst to use the computer to work out what it all meant. Our underlying theory was that a small number of people in any policing area were actually carrying out most of the crime. Intelligence from tip-offs, undercover surveillance but, above all, the computer's crime pattern analysis, proved this to be correct. With a little help, we could rapidly identify the culprit.

The first time we tried it was around midnight. A family in Abdale Road had been burgled one night. A small upstairs window had been left open and a burglar had daringly scaled a wall to climb in, helping himself to jewellery and cash and then exiting casually by the back door.

We inputted all this information into the computer and then waited breathlessly for our analyst's report.

In an astonishingly short time, he produced the names of all the night-time burglars (actually night-time burglars are quite rare) who lived within a square mile of Abdale Road (burglars tend to operate within one square mile of home) and who had a history of climbing, especially through high, open or openable windows.

Three names came up. We checked to see if any of them were in jail. Two were. We went straight to the house of the third, a known burglar who was quite simply astonished to see us. He was so confident of our incompetence that he had not even bothered to hide his haul yet and so surprised at our arrival that he made no attempt to create some elaborate story to prove his innocence.

The computer was our new secret weapon. It could do all sorts of tricks. Not only did it help us solve crime, but it enabled us to actually predict where, when and by whom crime might be committed. As a result, cops would visit vulnerable areas and encourage householders to increase security because they were at imminent risk of a break-in. All of this caused an impressive drop in the crime statistics at a time when domestic burglary had been increasing year on year and the public suspected that the police had simply given up trying to solve it. The Burglary Control Programme reversed that: in our patch alone there was a fall of more than 14 per cent within the first year. In a change of approach we also targeted the criminal rather than the crime by collating intelligence and running surveillance operations on the small number of our known burglars, who would sometimes commit at least 20–30 burglaries in one day. By successfully prosecuting them we had a huge impact on reducing the area's burglary problem. The programme was later developed into a London-wide anti-burglary campaign which ran – and still runs – right across London called Operation Bumblebee.

If only our computer could have helped us catch Yardies. But at that early stage, their erratic behaviour proved more than a match for a rational machine. However, it could help with street robbery.

This was a big problem around Paddington. Our own eyes told us that quite young kids were snatching handbags and then running on to their rabbit warren estates and crime pattern analysis gave us an accurate picture of where and when. The victims were usually old or vulnerable in some way and the robberies all happened so quickly and the kids hid so well that there was no chance of anyone catching them.

We decided to use undercover techniques. In other words, dressing up as old ladies. There was much hilarity at Paddington Police Station as cops, both male and female, put on their petticoats and tried to carry their walking sticks daintily. I must say they looked very plausible. The officers who were in disguise were told not to resist the kids. When their bag had been grabbed, a team of up to ten hidden officers would then apprehend the thief.

It worked. The main object of the exercise was to turn the tables on these juveniles. Their elderly victims had been living in fear. Now, the fear was passed straight back to the perpetrators. And, indeed, most of them were terrified when they were caught. Although the penalties were not very serious because they were juveniles, there were a lot of parents who were furious to hear that their son or daughter had been caught stealing in the street and were more than willing to take their children in hand. Some children stopped with crime at that point. Others stopped snatching bags and started stealing from vehicles instead.

We persuaded BMW to loan us a honeypot vehicle which the kids could not resist breaking into, for the radio or whatever else they might find. Once again, a team of officers caught them in the act. They were taken to court and dealt with by the criminal justice system – and perhaps more harshly by their parents.

I moved from station to station tackling crime statistics but I was unhappily aware that I was not being promoted. And I knew there was no possibility of such a thing. At that time a government review of the police hierarchy had recommended the abolition of one rank – mine. This was immensely frustrating because it meant I could actually go down a grade as a result of the 1993 Sheehy Inquiry, examining the ranks, pay and conditions of service of the Police. And, as if this wasn't demoralising enough, an incident occurred which almost persuaded me to leave the Met.

Police canteens, everyone had agreed at the Bristol seminars for black staff, could be a hotbed of racism. You might walk in and see people huddled in groups, dropping their voices while they glanced over their shoulders at anyone black. Sometimes you'd catch snatches of conversation which you'd tell yourself you really couldn't have heard, even though you knew you had.

One day in the canteen at Paddington, I was standing in the queue a little way behind a group of junior officers. Racism is not acceptable, whether a black person is in the room or not. But perhaps if they had known I was there, they might have modified their language. In fact, I suspect they did know I was there and simply didn't care. They were talking in the loud voices of those who are comfortable they will not be challenged.

I heard them use the word 'nigger'.

I went through the old routine. Surely not, I must have misheard. This was the mid-1990s and I am glad to say that the use of this word by police officers in public was now considered unacceptable. Because, for many people, including me, it was offensive to hear. Offensive, unnecessary, unacceptable. So, even given the nature of police canteen culture, they wouldn't be saying that word in such loud voices, would they?

Yes. They used it again. And then again. And then again. Over and over again.

I looked at the colleague who was standing next to me.

I said: "Can you hear them?"

His face was very red. He turned away.

I said: "Can you?"

His face burned. Suddenly the choice between shepherd's pie or chilli con carne absorbed him entirely.

I looked around the room. Wasn't anyone going to stop them? Everyone could hear.

There were a few red faces, mostly turned away like my colleague's. So I stood in the queue listening to loud voices talking about niggers and there was something immensely tiring about the tedium of its constant repetition, as if nigger was not a word but a large, heavy weapon which they were bludgeoning me with again and again and again.

I had to do something.

I did stop to think about what I was about to do and about the possible consequences. But I was sure: I knew that challenging them was the right thing.

Staying very calm, keeping my voice low, I walked over to them.

I said: "Excuse me, I can hear what you're saying clearly. That language is just not acceptable."

The canteen was immediately silent. Not a fork scraped, not a coin clinked, not a plate clattered and not a word, anywhere, was spoken. For a hideous moment I was reminded of that bar in St. Louis. The white bar where no black man was welcome, where I had been frozen out not by any figure of authority but by the customers.

The three officers now sat upright and stared at me. Two large blond men and a woman who looked at me with an insouciance I had seen on the faces of the 'Bananas!' cops. Rudely. Their look said: how dare I interrupt them!

"What are you talking about?" demanded one of the men. And in a tone that no junior officer should employ to one who is much more senior.

"You are using the n-word and, even if no one else in here does, I find it very offensive."

And apparently, no one else did. They were all too busy

gawping silently. A few faces burned like my colleague's. But no one supported me: they chose not to.

The three officers' eyes bulged. The two men puffed their chests out like the pigeons who strut around the park. The woman shifted her weight evenly on to both legs as if she was about to argue with a traffic offender.

"Just what do you mean?" the second man said. His voice was sneering.

"We didn't use the n-word," said the woman.

"I heard you say—"

But the man who had been talking about niggers burst in now.

He said: "No! You didn't hear us properly! We were talking about Nicky! Someone called Nicky!"

The others seized on this.

"Yeah, Nicky!"

"That's right! We've got a friend called Nicky. We were talking about Nicky, not any n-word."

They all nodded to each other. Nicky. Yes, Nicky. Our friend Nicky. They were smiling. I did not look around – I did not want to see if anyone else nodded.

I said: "Very well, this will be investigated."

I went back to my place in the queue. The canteen slowly turned from stone to a living mass of individuals. Surely someone would support me? Many must have heard that language. I waited for someone to tap me on the shoulder and tell me so.

No one did.

"How," I asked my colleague quietly, "could you not hear them?"

He was calmer now, the pink patches on his face turning to white.

"I think you're attuned to that sort of thing," he said wisely. "I think you're sensitive and you hear insults cutting through all the noise, whereas to the rest of us it's just... well, noise."

Ah, so that was why everyone else in the canteen was apparently deaf: my ears were attuned to insults. Because I was so sensitive.

"Are you saying I imagined it?" I demanded.

We were sitting down now, our meals on trays before us. I had not touched my food. I studied his face, waiting for a reply.

He finished his mouthful and considered.

At last he spoke: "I'm saying I don't know because I didn't hear them."

I could not like that man any more, I could not like anyone in the canteen, I could not like the world at all at that moment. Because every person in that room had closed ranks on me. Isolated me. I was a man who had just been left alone on a small, bare island, watching people he had thought were his colleagues sail off into the distance. The canteen was a noisy, gossipy, clattery sort of a place but I was surrounded by a silence which went on for miles.

When I told my boss what had happened he gave me his full support and urged me to call for the investigation I had threatened. That felt good. It helped me to gather the strength to fight, as I knew I must. Sadly. I'd joined the Met to fight crime, not to fight other officers. But I was confident of my success and so was the boss. The three junior officers would be investigated then disciplined.

So there was an investigation.

And they weren't disciplined.

Because no one else in the canteen had heard them mention niggers. No, they had been talking about Nicky.

The investigators had decided that I must have misheard the whole conversation.

This news had the effect of a physical blow. And the blow was very deep and very painful. I knew I had done exactly the right thing: I had drawn the unacceptable nature of their behaviour to the offenders' attention and, when they had dismissed my complaint, I had appealed for justice through exactly the right channels in the right way.

But first there had been no witnesses. And then there had been no justice.

I am a stranger to bitterness. But not on this occasion. This time the system – the one I had been taught as a boy to believe in and use clearheadedly to combat racism – the system had entirely failed me.

The whole police station knew that the tribunal had not found in my favour and it was difficult to go to work for a while. When I arrived, rooms of people stopped talking. Voices dropped. There was some unkind laughter. The hardest thing was to face the young men and woman who had a friend called Nicky. To witness the expressions on their faces if they saw me. Their smug grins. Their disrespect for my seniority.

I walked into the building every day with deliberate steps, holding my head up high, and I'm not going to pretend it was easy. From now on, in the canteen, I always ensured someone I could trust was with me. I even asked people to get their coffee with me so that I'd always have a witness.

"But," said my boss, who was horrified by the whole incident, "you did the right thing confronting them; they'll never talk that way in public again. So you may have lost the battle, but you won the war."

He had been wholly supportive and he was upset this incident had happened on his patch.

Gradually, people seemed to forget and things returned to normal. But I could not forget. My bitterness did not go away. No wonder so many of my colleagues in the Black Police Association were leaving the Met, usually leaving with the same anger and frustration I now felt. Some of them, at much lower rank than me, admitted they were simply worn out by daily banter about their colour, by being told they were oversensitive or had a chip on their shoulder if they forgot to laugh one day. Others had nervous breakdowns, finding themselves the victim of racial bullying which was often perpetrated, doggedly and without respite, by just one person. And this wasn't confined to black officers. Women had similar problems: they would sometimes ask me to mentor them through the bullying. It began to feel like an intractable problem and, to many female or black officers, it was so intractable that they left.

I went to the barber's, a place for members of the black community. If a white man had entered, apart from having a very long wait for a haircut, I had often wondered if it wouldn't be a bit like that white bar in St. Louis I'd walked into. None did so. Right now, I wanted to immerse myself in the black community, the warmth of Mac's shop with hair on the floor, his son Winston flourishing a broom, reggae playing, men arguing loudly about politics or music.

There was a loud voice in my ear.

"My son went to get his mother some shopping last night and how many times do you think he was stopped on the way home?" demanded the man in the chair next to mine.

I did not reply. I did not need to – everyone else was.

"Two times!" guessed a customer in the queue.

"Three?"

"To the shop, no, it's just downstairs, it can't be more than two…!"

"Three times!" said the man in the chair. "It was crazy last night. They were stopping everyone!"

"I got stopped five times last week," piped up a young man. "And the most they found on me was a carton of orange juice."

"What you think about that?" demanded the customer in the chair, turning to me.

Mac paused with his clippers. He knew, I knew, that the whole conversation had been aimed at me. I had been outed as a policeman years ago. Mac looked ready to intervene as usual, to tell people to leave me alone. But the place was noisy now. Everyone was joining in with a stop-and-search story which they believed exposed police prejudice or rudeness.

My eyes met Mac's for a moment in the mirror but he said nothing and carried on clipping. I looked down and tried not to listen to the angry customers. I was thinking how I'd been deluding myself that, as a police officer, I could ever be accepted as a full member of this community. And for even longer I'd deluded myself that I belonged in the Met. It was clear to me now: I belonged absolutely nowhere.

TWENTY-NINE

I thought it was time to think seriously about leaving the police.

I had just completed my MBA and I was sure it would help me if I started searching for a new job. I was even headhunted. But did I really want to walk into a maelstrom of corporate politics and racial issues somewhere else? I began to think of running my own business. The idea was exciting. I smelled a challenge, a change of lifestyle, a world outside the strict hierarchy of the Met, where I would be entirely dependent on my own skills and hard work to succeed.

The MBA had shown me how to set up a business enterprise. And I'd had an idea.

A chain of cafes which focused on coffee. Cappuccino, latte, you name it, all made from a variety of interesting blends from around the world. And the cafes might play jazz music, clients could lounge about on sofas or at tables, there would perhaps be books to read and if people wanted to sit there nursing one coffee all day while they read or worked, they could. It would be a warm and welcoming environment.

I developed my business plan, constantly boring family and friends with its details.

"What do you think?" I asked a group of mates who'd come over one night. And I probably wasn't talking about my coffee shops for the first time.

They looked embarrassed when faced with this bald question.

"I mean, do you think it could work?" I said.

There was a long silence.

"What's wrong with a good old-fashioned English tea shop?" asked one. "Where the teapots don't pour, the staff are grumpy and the scones are stale? That's what the British expect when we go out."

"Or there's the pub," said another. "That's where people go to relax. We don't need coffee shops too, they're just not what we do."

I was sure the British could be persuaded to fall in love with coffee. Wasn't 18th-century London a seething mass of coffee houses where thinkers and businessmen met up to talk over the ideas of the day? There was a coffee tradition, it had just died out. Maybe I could resurrect it.

I persuaded someone to introduce me to a pair of venture capitalists. They were money men; they must surely understand my vision, and if they understood it then they must certainly share it.

We met in their very glossy Mayfair offices. A secretary brought us shining cups and a pot of tea and then poured it for us, elegantly using a strainer. Thin biscuits were served on a bone china plate. Langues de chat.

I delivered my presentation. I could hear myself. My enthusiastic voice, falling onto the china, the upholstery, the silk curtains. And the deaf ears of the venture capitalists.

Their faces impassive, they interrupted me before I had even finished.

"London," they said, "is a city of pubs and tea shops. No one's going out in London just to drink coffee."

I said: "Other nations love coffee, and London's full of tourists. But I think the British could love coffee too. I'm suggesting that we try the idea out in just one coffee shop. In a good central location. If it takes off, we could unroll my franchise plan... I've got it here if you'd like to look at it..."

One of them said: "Who will use this coffee shop?"

"Everyone who wants to go and sit somewhere and watch the world go by. Or to work in peace. Or listen to music. Even people like you. Between meetings, a bit too far from the office, you might drop in for a coffee."

They looked at each other and shook their heads.

"We'd go to the pub," they said.

"Not everyone wants to sit in a smoky pub and drink. Certainly not in the morning!"

They shrugged.

"Thanks, but it's not for us."

"Don't you want to see the figures in the business plan?" I asked, disappointed.

They shook their heads.

"No point," they said. "Daft idea. Coffee will never take off in London."

I wonder if they ever go into Starbucks, Costa or Caffè Nero these days and think of me.

When I left their office I told myself that there were other venture capitalists around, people with more vision than these two, but gradually, and to my friends' relief, I let coffee shops go. I had learned a lot from the experience. I'd learned that you can have a good idea, you can have a strategy, but if you don't have a clear plan and good staff to deliver it, you're sunk. It will never get anywhere. For some ideas, timing is everything. It was the wrong time for coffee shops.

The result of this was that I became even more despondent at work. As if I hadn't been despondent enough after the Nicky episode, when the system had so let me down. When racism had been condoned. When injustice had triumphed. Coffee shops had been my escape route and now the door was firmly shut.

Perhaps I could promote myself out of the doldrums? Promotion would take me to superintendent and at that level there could be no junior officers telling me they had friends called Nicky. I made my application.

I did not pass the assessment. When I asked for feedback, the head of the assessment centre was uninterested. He shrugged his shoulders and told me that I had simply failed to use certain key words in my assessment exercises. He might have said: "Try again!" He might have been supportive. Even just sympathetic. But he said: "Well, if you don't like it, go and look for a job elsewhere."

I think I would have done just that if it hadn't been for a reassuring senior colleague.

He said: "Look, Michael, don't take this to heart. You're more than capable. Do a strategic role in an acting superintendent capacity somewhere, then come back and undergo the assessment again and next time just remember to use the right words at the assessment centre."

I said: "That's ridiculous."

He gave a small, helpless gesture to remind me that a lot of things are ridiculous.

So, in the knowledge that wallowing in self-pity and regret was going to get me nowhere, I did as he suggested. For a while I moved into the Home Office, where I advised HM Chief Inspector of Police on crime and terrorism. This was a suit job. Back to the polite middle classes of the Civil Service. They weren't half as jokey as the people who work in police stations but they were friendly and treated me respectfully and, if they had friends called Nicky, they didn't talk about them in the canteen.

When I retook the Superintendent's assessment, I'd learned the key words.

I passed and was given a choice of posting. I knew which one I wanted.

"Guess where?" I asked my wife. By now we had children and she was in perpetual motion but she paused for a moment to think.

"A nice leafy backwater, I hope," she said at last. We had a friend who was the same rank as me and had contrived to spend his entire career in places where nothing much happened. "Somewhere like Richmond, maybe? Or Twickenham?"

"Streatham!" I announced happily.

Her face fell.

"You always choose the hardest option," she said. "Why do you enjoy making life hard for yourself?"

"Hard? You mean interesting!"

I grinned back at her, because my idea of a good place to go was somewhere with lots of crime I could get my teeth into. Like Streatham.

THIRTY

How could I have forgotten how many black people in south London hated the police? Or maybe I just assumed things had changed since the Brixton riots. I was wrong. Streatham is very near Brixton and in fact the place still reminded me of the Brixton of the early 1980s. Its former grandness was a sort of ghost presence. Now the quaint architectural features on fine buildings were barely discernible. Most of the big houses had been converted to small flats, added to, boarded over, neglected. There was a high street where traffic was incessant and most of the shops small. There was widespread poverty. There were sprawling concrete estates, most of them built in the last 25 years. And there was rising crime.

So, how to deal with the crime here? I'd willingly accepted the challenge but now I could see how tough it was going to be. None of the tactics I'd tried in west London would work. For a start, the whole history of the place was different. There had been various deaths in police custody which had inflamed community-police relations. Stop-and-search powers had been extensively, perhaps *too* extensively, used. And the community's memory of the nearby Brixton riots, while these were almost 20 years ago, was still raw.

Although I was in uniform again, as a superintendent I was far from the front line. I was determined to cross the great divide between the office and the streets and so I went out on the beat as often as I could. Remembering the riots and my days on the beat at Fulham, I braced myself for strings of insults from the black community. But... they didn't happen. I was not now singled out for abuse by black people because I was a black police officer. I didn't know if this was because the world had moved on or because my rank gave me a sort of invisibility; the silver braid and flat hat both said seniority.

The junior cops did take a lot of flak, though. There was anger and disgust everywhere. It was yelled from across the road, hissed as they walked by, shouted from cars – or it was directly confrontational. Watching groups of black lads swearing and shouting at young officers did take me back to my days as a callow probationer. Back to Fulham. On one hand these constables were subjected to a different kind of attack, because they weren't being yelled at by their own community and there was nothing personal about it. But on the other hand, it was a similar attack. Because it was all about their uniform, their job.

Worst of all, the locals sometimes succeeded in preventing arrests. Crowds would surround officers as they struggled with handcuffs. Men, women and kids shouted, yelled, grabbed the suspect, pushing and pulling to help him run away. It was ugly, it made life miserable for cops. I knew from my own experience how you could hate coming to work if you knew you were going to face abuse. But the same experience had taught me that withstanding it is possible.

Senior officers may have been immune from abuse on the street but there was a forum where we had to take it on the chin. The Lambeth Consultative Group met regularly at Lambeth Town Hall. The group was a struggling attempt to improve communication between the top brass from the four police areas here – Streatham, Brixton, Kennington and Vauxhall – and a panel from the community. In fact, it had been set up as a result of recommendations by the Scarman inquiry into the Brixton riots. Onlookers were allowed in, and were highly participatory. Meetings were always full of noisy, angry activists.

Officers from each area stood up to give an account of what they had been doing and, if the public didn't like it, the response was rapid.

Getting slowly to my feet, I might begin: "The number of stop and searches we carried out during this period increased from..."

The word 'increased' in the same breath as the words 'stop and search' was enough to flick the anger switch. There were immediate howls, hisses and boos, so loud that there was no way anyone could hear the actual figures at the end of my sentence, not even me.

"Why? Why the increase?" people shouted.

"What are you doing to us?"

"Why do you want to treat us this way?"

"Do you really think you'll control us by stopping us every time we set foot outside our doors?"

The Lambeth Consultative Group had a clear policy on stop and search. They thought it shouldn't happen and had imposed an unofficial ban. Because they believed only black people were stopped. For them, stop and search was a police control mechanism, not a legitimate means of tackling crime.

It happened that stop and search was proving very useful to me. I hated its indiscriminate use. The idea that only members of the black community might be stopped was repellent. But, properly employed, it was a good tool. We had a big street crime problem in Streatham, geographically concentrated around the Railway station, because the muggers targeted people coming home from work. Returning to Streatham was becoming seriously hazardous, whether you were an office worker rushing home at six or a drunken businessman stag-gering back at eleven: the street robbers were always waiting to pounce. Some of them were as young as 12 and looked harmless enough to commuters – until they found themselves surrounded, knocked off their feet and relieved of their valuables. Late at night the assailants were older and more likely to carry knives.

So we stopped and searched suspected street robbers, even quite young ones, if we saw them hanging around the Tube station. We used intelligence to help us pinpoint known offenders, look out for them hanging around the train station, take their knives away, and arrest them for carrying an offensive weapon before they could mug someone with it. I was convinced that we were preventing a lot of crime with stop and search. It was, however, an unfortunate fact that most of the muggers were black and their victims white, so it was easy to accuse us of discrimination – and the Lambeth Consultative Group of course did so.

Many angry black people came to the meetings to make political points and if you tried to explain police strategy, they simply thought you were defending the indefensible. It wasn't easy to take their anger and ceaseless criticism but at least they didn't single me out for attack because of my colour. I took this, at least, for progress. Surely it must mean that, even if there were invisible battle lines between the activists at the meetings and the police, the assumption that the community was black and the police were white must be crumbling a little? I felt relief at this. No one was calling me a traitor any more.

Perhaps I was changing a bit too, because I couldn't help secretly admiring some of the activists. They were fighting for their beliefs and their community and, although I might not always agree, I thought it was good that they were monitoring police activities on behalf of black people and making their voices heard. I just wished they would occasionally listen, too. That was the most you could hope for. You couldn't expect them to trust a police officer: they never would.

Some of them made good points and asked really challenging questions which were hard to answer; I'm sure I wasn't the only officer who went home and thought about their questions afterwards. One of these was a young activist called Lee Jasper. He was an arch critic of the police, that much was obvious, but it seemed to me that he was particularly articulate and certainly worth listening to. He would always hold us to account. I made sure I remembered his name. Given his feelings about the police, I don't know why I thought we might work together again, but I did.

I sat in those stormy meetings wondering how things could ever change, because the history of poor policing in black neighbourhoods went so deep with these people. After the meetings I'd get on with the day to day – burglaries, domestic violence, drug-related gun crime – but my work was never without the wearying, undermining inevitability of ugly police-community relations. I may have persuaded large numbers of prostitutes to move out of the area with a resulting drop in crime figures which astonished even me. I may have targeted the street muggers with great success. But no one at the Consultative Group was thanking me for any of that. A drop in crime figures meant one thing to them: we were protecting the white community and convicting the black community and never the other way around.

Their greatest anger was reserved for violence and, worse, deaths, which occurred in custody. I'm relieved to say there were no such deaths in my time at Streatham but there were accusations that black people had been subjected to police brutality during detention or questioning in the custody suite. The accusations were repeated at meetings with hot fury.

I was discussing this with the Chief Inspector at Streatham when he had an idea. He suggested that we put CCTV into the custody suite. This is universal now but at the time it was really innovative. I liked the idea a lot. It would stop any false

accusations and would keep any bad behaviour by police officers in check. I discussed it with the Chief Superintendent and
he agreed that we could trial CCTV at Streatham.

At last I had done something to earn, if not the praise, then
the acquiescence of Consultative Group members. But now
police officers were objecting: they hated the intrusion. The
Police Federation was soon involved. Videoing members doing
their jobs, spying on them, even filming their jokes and private
moments: it was a complete invasion of privacy. We argued
that officers should see CCTV as a form of protection and,
after endless discussions, cameras were finally installed in the
custody suite and cells. We waited to see what would happen.

The Consultative Group whooped and cheered when we
announced that there had been a huge drop in the number of
complaints. As far as they were concerned the cameras were
keeping police brutality in check. They may have been right,
but we didn't know how right; in fact, we'll never know what
proportion of the accusations prior to the installation had
been based on fact. We did still have a few complaints, and
then we would sit with the complainant's solicitor and watch
the video footage – and invariably, the complaint would be
dropped for lack of evidence.

Gradually, the other areas in Lambeth, then the whole of
London, introduced CCTV to their custody suites and cells
and it became common practice. None of this won us any
points with the Consultative Group, however. They were still
as angry and mistrustful as ever and the problem of relationships between the black community and the police remained
an open sore.

And then, one day, I was given the chance to do something
which might help bring about change. Quite suddenly, I was
moved to Scotland Yard. A huge missile was heading for the
Met and I was being asked to help the Force dodge it.

THIRTY-ONE

I have already mentioned the name of Stephen Lawrence. Everyone knows it, and for reasons which he certainly never would have wanted. Stephen would now be in his 40s, and the indications are that he would have been an urban professional – if he had lived. But his death went largely unnoticed by the general public when he died as a teenager in 1993. Famously, he was stabbed while standing at a bus stop in Eltham.

Around that time there were many young black men dying of stab wounds for reasons said to be related to drug or gang warfare. The police did not prioritise their investigation. Since, during the same period, I was trying to persuade my detectives to take Yardie-related murder more seriously, I was uncomfortably aware of the widespread assumption of criminality on the part of the victim when young black males were stabbed or shot.

But this was not a safe assumption. Stephen was not killed because he was involved in a drugs war. He was a serious student who planned to become an architect. It rapidly emerged that he had died because of his colour and for no other reason. His killers were unknown to him and, standing at the bus stop, he had done nothing to provoke their racist attack.

Stephen's parents were not prepared to accept the police's failure to make any arrests. They did not believe the investigation had been conducted thoroughly or compassionately. They wanted to see his murder properly investigated and his killers arrested. They started a long and dignified quest for justice.

Suspects were in fact arrested but charges were soon dropped due to lack of evidence. An attempt at private prosecution by Stephen's family failed, also for lack of evidence, but the fact that it was widely publicised and led by the high-profile barrister, Michael Mansfield QC, indicated that anger at Stephen's murder and the police's failure to investigate it thoroughly had already spread outside the black community of south London.

Pressure grew and, four years after Stephen's death, an inquest was held. His alleged killers, who had so far evaded prosecution, were now in court – but a coroner's court. A coroner is powerless to attribute blame and he could only look at them very hard when he gave the verdict of 'unlawful killing in an unprovoked attack by five youths'.

The *Daily Mail* decided to go one step further: it named the suspects and printed their pictures. But it was now impossible to prosecute the five: they had already been put on trial in the Lawrence family's private prosecution and the trial had collapsed. No one at that time could be tried for the same crime twice.

The spotlight moved from Stephen's killers to the police's failure to investigate and arrest them. Media disgust prompted the Home Secretary to order a public inquiry into this failure. It was chaired by Sir William Macpherson.

Stephen's family's determined journey to bring their son's killers to justice was, at this time, far from over and they had no way of knowing then that after a change in the double jeopardy law, it would ultimately lead to two convictions. The Macpherson inquiry, however, was an important milestone in this journey and now, in 1998, five years after Stephen Lawrence's death, everyone knew that Sir William Macpherson's report would soon be published.

Criticism of the Met would be inevitable. Almost certainly the report would recognise that police racism underpinned the desultory nature of the investigation into Stephen's murder. I didn't need the Consultative Group to tell me about the Met's attitude to black victims of crime. They insisted that the police believed black victims were simply less important. Because they were assumed to be criminals.

I didn't need the Consultative Group because I heard words to this effect hurled about the streets of Streatham daily. But now this viewpoint was not to be confined to south London. It was almost certainly going to be stated publicly by an independent judge after an independent inquiry.

Naturally, when the Macpherson report was published, the Met wanted to be able to say that the failures of the Lawrence investigation had been addressed and there were already new measures in place.

But what should those new measures be? They were asking me for ideas.

I knew this was a chance to do something really important. A chance to suggest how, ultimately, the Met could change its relations with the black community. And, most exciting of all, my suggestions would not, could not, be ignored: the Macpherson report, appearing shortly, would see to that. Whatever happened to me next, wherever I went, I knew that in some ways this opportunity could be my greatest contribution.

I worked for Deputy Assistant Commissioner John Grieve, a man of fair and open mind, who told me to think outside the box and come up with some really new and radical suggestions. And I had two months to do it.

Research was vital. I spoke to academics, Victim Support, community representatives, religious bodies, police officers, any organisation which I thought could help. I even went to the American Embassy and spoke to the FBI in order to learn how the Americans were dealing with their terrible and well-publicised racially motivated murders. But perhaps the most important piece of research came from our computer.

Crime pattern analysis had progressed since those early days in Shepherd's Bush when the computer had been regarded with awe and staff members had dropped by just to look at it. Now we proposed to use it to analyse a crime which many police officers didn't really recognise as a crime at all. The crime could take any form – murder, violence, theft – but it was specifically motivated by one thing: racial hatred. Stephen Lawrence's death was caused by the racial hatred of his assailants. Was his murder an extraordinary, one-off event? Or had there been more Stephens? And if so, how many more young, black men had been killed by racists, the victims wrongly assumed to have been criminals?

We soon had an answer. There were at least eight similar cases. Eight more Stephen Lawrences whose families had felt too helpless in the face of police assumptions of criminality to insist on a proper investigation.

What about other racially motivated crime? It might not end in homicide but it could all the same be serious crime. We were amazed by the results of the analysis. There was racially motivated crime – now called hate crime, but then the term was unknown – in very large quantities and right across London. But until now it had been invisible. Many cops never really saw it as crime at all. Unless it was very serious, they might not even log it.

We offered the analysis at Scotland Yard. John Grieve listened thoughtfully and so did the Commissioner, Sir Paul Condon. But there were many others who preferred not to hear.

I tried to explain to them something I had learned long ago. And if I'd ever come close to forgetting it, the Lambeth Consultative Group had certainly reminded me.

"Racially motivated crime is bad for the victim, but it's disastrous for the victim's community," I said. I was presenting my findings and proposals to a group of very senior police officers.

They looked at me stony-faced.

"Racial tension escalates if we don't deal with race crime properly. These communities need to see that we'll take their concerns seriously and act immediately to protect them," I said. "Or we can't expect them to trust us or co-operate with us."

I could hear my own voice. "We" were the police force where I'd spent my entire working life. And "them"? My family's community and, to some extent, mine. But for the purposes of this conversation with these people, it was essential for me to be us and not them. I looked down at my hands, folded on the table. They were so very black. And on the other side of the table the folded hands were so very white.

I told them about my visit to the FBI.

"The Americans have quite scientific ways of measuring community tension. Riots there are seldom a total surprise to the police. But handling crime well in black communities, particularly race crime, means we can try to reduce or de-escalate that tension."

One man spoke. He said: "I can't see what you're saying. If there's a violent crime then of course we investigate it. Why do we care or do things differently if the perpetrator was a member of the National Front or just very drunk?"

"We have to care," I said. "Because the community cares."

"What are we? The Thought Police?" asked one.

But another said: "So what, exactly, do you want us to do differently?"

I told them: "Any crime motivated by racial hatred should be treated as a 'critical incident'. Just like in the USA. It should be recognised and investigated and prosecuted as vigorously as any other crime. If we try to ignore it, communities will retaliate."

I looked from face to face. Every one of them was scep-
tical. But they were willing to talk and we did, for a long time.
I'm not sure I succeeded in convincing them that hate crime
really existed, let alone that we should address it. When I got
up to go, I shook their hands. They were friendly enough.

"Not sure how I feel about all this, but it's very interesting," said one.

"Fascinating," agreed another.

"I've enjoyed talking to you, even if I don't agree with
you," said a third. "I think this is the first time I've really sat
down and talked about race crime."

He spoke politely and truthfully. He meant no harm. I
smiled at him. It would have been unkind to tell him that he
was part of the problem.

I proposed that we set up a Racial and Violent Crime
Taskforce specifically to tackle hate crime in the black communities and show them that we were serious about dealing with
it, rapidly and effectively. John Grieve was wildly enthusiastic
about this proposal and so was the Commissioner. And they
took on board another suggestion: I thought that selected
community members from those communities that suffered
from hate crime should act as independent advisers to the
police. Not an angry monitoring group shouting abuse at
the platform from the floor as in Lambeth. I meant a group
of advisers from inside the black communities who were
respected by and actually worked with the Met.

This was an American idea. In the UK, while we had
developed and devised community policing, the police had
almost no history of working closely with outside advisors
on an equal level. The possibility, at that time, of the public
having a say, making suggestions, getting involved, giving
advice – well, it was simply not acceptable to most senior
police officers. The Met employed more than 30,000 people
and was a huge and impenetrable monolith, with its own

complex, mysterious system of ranks and its own way of looking at things.

John Grieve might have been on board straight away but the reaction of the grizzled senior officers was predictable when I told them about the idea. They looked as though I'd just lobbed a petrol bomb in their direction.

With the Commissioner's approval, John Grieve ignored the naysayers and set to work. He formed a task force to target racist crime in the areas our mapping indicated suffered most. And he went about finding suitable independent advisers.

THIRTY-TWO

There were many more lessons to be learned from the faults of the Lawrence investigation. The treatment of the Lawrence family throughout had been appalling and I suggested that a trained and sympathetic family liaison officer always be appointed for each murder inquiry to improve communication between families and murder investigators. Just one police service, Avon and Somerset, had introduced this idea and, after consulting them, we were convinced it should be a part of national policy.

It happened that during this period I visited my GP about a minor ailment and he asked me what I was up to. We got talking, and he told me how doctors continually review each other's cases. Not to sanction or discipline other professionals but to help put things right – or at least to help everyone learn from whatever has gone wrong. That GP visit led to my next suggestion: that any unsolved murder case should be regularly reviewed and the forensic evidence re-examined. That's what I'd want if one of my family members had been killed and no one arrested.

John Grieve fully approved of this. Elsewhere, I was met with a row of shaking heads.

"Look, suppose the Senior Investigating Officer missed something, some crucial line of inquiry…"

"Exactly," I said. "Because everyone's human, everyone makes mistakes."

"If you reopen an investigation and discover something like that, then the officer's career could be at an end."

"Imagine it. The increased number of complaints and disciplinary procedures."

They waited for me to reply. I didn't know how to tell them politely I thought bringing a murderer to justice and some closure to a victim's family is more important than trying to find mistakes made by the Investigating Officer.

At last I said: "Well, it's a question of attitude. When doctors review cases, they're not trying to catch each other out. They're looking to review the case together to ensure things aren't missed. I suppose we're talking about teamwork."

"And you're suggesting that once an investigation is closed the case is reviewed... how often? Every five years? Have you any idea how much that would cost?"

"It's very expensive and time-consuming to keep sifting and resifting through the same evidence."

I said: "But everything might have been different in the Stephen Lawrence case if the evidence had been reviewed more often."

"Unless there's new evidence, what's the point?"

I had to think about that. I said: "Well, the evidence might not change, but time changes other factors. There are developments in forensic science, for instance."

They didn't like it. They didn't like my proposal for a police liaison officer for every homicide either. There were other recommendations which they didn't like but, despite all that head shaking at Scotland Yard, both John Grieve and Sir Paul Condon were looking for groundbreaking solutions. So they set about implementing them. Most are still in place today.

I could not fault the determination at the top to put things right. My brief was to look at how we could improve our procedures so that no one else suffered as the Lawrence family had suffered. I think I fulfilled that brief.

But... were we all ignoring something?

It was something everyone preferred to ignore, including me. I'd spent my police career training myself to do so. Why would I start talking about racism within the Met now? The only time I'd ever really discussed it was back at the Bristol seminars for black officers and staff, and sometimes too at those early Black Police Association meetings I'd chaired. Now I went to BPA socials not to talk about racism but to dance the night away. I had mentored a few young black officers but recently, the people who came to tell me about bullying were mostly women and discussions about racism had morphed into discussions about sexism or bullying in general.

I had come this far in the Met by not talking about my colour. By not discussing racism. By not shining a light on it but letting it stay quietly in the shadows. If it ever became too public and too brazen, then I took action – not always successfully, as the Nicky incident had proved. Otherwise, I left it alone. Police racism was an ugly beast in the corner which I didn't want to poke.

Soon after my recommendations had been made and implemented, the Macpherson report was released.

And in headlines everywhere were these words.

Institutional racism.

The Black Police Association, now a thriving and focused body, had made its own damning submission to the Macpherson inquiry, which spelt out some of the problems black officers and staff had experienced. And in the submission of Dr Robin Oakley of the University of London, 'institutional racism' had been referred to and defined.

He described it as: *"Usually covert rather than overt, unintended so far as motivation is concerned, acted out unconsciously by individuals, and an expression of collective rather than purely individual sentiment. Particularly on account of the latter characteristic, this may be appropriately referred to as a form of 'institutional racism'."*

I experienced a deep-down, gut-felt recognition of what was being described: I think every black officer must have felt the same sense of recognition. But rationally, I could hardly understand it. After years of suppressing such thoughts, I had to read and reread the definition of institutional racism in order to process it.

Many white cops could not process it either. They had a different gut feeling: they were deeply offended.

One white officer said: "My wife's black! How dare anyone call me a racist!"

Another said: "Well, I know I'm not racist and neither are my mates. How could we be racist and not know it?"

"Unconscious bias? I'm conscious that I don't have a bias, that's the end of it."

Nobody could see themselves as part of the problem.

And almost nobody asked me for my opinion, or wanted to know if I had personally experienced racism within the Force. Perhaps they did not want to hear the answer. Perhaps I did not want to hear the question either.

But at last a couple of colleagues said: "Michael, what do you think about this institutional racism thing?"

By now I'd had time to consider the Macpherson report, but it was very hard for me to reply honestly. To express something I'd spent years not saying.

I said: "I agree with Sir William Macpherson – he's got it right."

The colleagues had clearly been hoping I'd disagree. They looked angry. I could see they were going to jump to the Met's defence.

"The racism is mostly unwitting," I added quickly. "Very few people actually think they're racist."

That just seemed to make things worse.

One said: "Listen, we police more in the poorer areas of this city. We know that's where most of the policing problems are. And more black people live in those areas and are both victims as well as perpetrators of crime. It follows that of course it's going to look as if we're racially biased."

The other said: "Okay, so you've heard the junior cops talk about black people a certain way. That's how society talks about black people. It proves we're no different from anyone else, but it doesn't prove that we show prejudice out on the streets."

It would have been so much easier to back out of this conversation.

I said: "The Lawrence case has proved that there is institutional bias and racism, whether conscious or unconscious."

They stared at me with hostility, their faces reddening.

I said: "It proves there's a link between prejudice in the criminal justice system and what happens to black people. They're more likely to be stopped and searched, more likely to be arrested, more likely to be convicted and their sentences tend to be harsher. Black police officers have to wait longer to be promoted, are more likely to be disciplined and their punishments are likely to be stiffer. And, of course, they're much more likely to leave the force. As for crimes with black victims, they're less likely to be solved. The statistics are all there if you want to look at them."

The Black Police Association would have been proud of me. Even I could hardly believe I was saying this out loud. I'm not sure my relationship with those colleagues ever really recovered. Although I had never realised it or thought about it, this relationship, like so many, was built on my silence.

The Met in my view eventually accepted the findings of the Macpherson report and despite an initial backlash from some officers, the senior officers debated how they would address the problem of racism within the police force itself. They introduced one very important measure: senior officers were to be held responsible for racist language or behaviour among their juniors. This sent out a message that racism was to be taken seriously. I remembered, almost 20 years earlier, how, as I had waited for the bus to disgorge us into the Brixton riots, I'd sat listening to officers hurling racial abuse around. How the Inspector had sat doing his crossword and pretending not to hear them. Now an inspector would have to put a stop to that kind of language or he, too, would face disciplinary action.

The other solution offered to combat racism within the Met? Training, of course. Diversity training. I regarded this with some cynicism because in my experience such training is never widespread enough nor sustained long enough – not once the media spotlight moves on. However, I must admit that there was some good training: black kids participated, talking to officers about their lives, their communities and their experiences with the police, and there is no doubt its reach, although limited, was powerful.

I'd seen so many reports relating to the police and race, but the Macpherson report filled me with hope. It had already forced the Met to look hard at itself. Change – for black officers and black communities – could surely not be far off? And I was proud of my own contribution. It had taken just eight weeks and, when I left, John Grieve presented me with a biography of General Patton and inside he had written: "Thanks for a very important two months of your life."

I think he was right.

THIRTY-THREE

One day I was walking through a housing estate in south London when I heard music. That's not unusual; sometimes it blasts from every window in every flat. But this was live music. A steel band. The rhythm, the tune, the sheer exuberance of it made me want to dance.

Of course, I didn't. I was a chief superintendent by now and chief supers definitely don't dance on duty. All I could do was walk in time with the beat and add a spring to each step and hope no one would notice. A group of men lingering in some sinister shadows did notice. As soon as they saw a lone police officer, a couple of them moved to stand in my way, and a few more shouted insults. I walked on, ignoring every attempt at intimidation. To my relief, they melted away.

The music played on and everything about it was at odds with its environment. Steel bands suggest freedom and sun, but as I drew closer to the sound, I was threading through a dark, concrete labyrinth. This was the Winstanley Estate, one of London's most notorious housing warrens, a maze of walkways and high-rise flats, squat towers and long, uniform slabs of lower buildings, forsaken public squares and occasional shops which looked as though they were operating from behind barricades. There wasn't much sky on offer. Just more concrete wherever you looked and occasionally some mud.

I was breaking my own rules by crossing the estate alone – I had told my cops to stay in pairs. But broken bricks on the ground and a smashed sink reminded me of another rule: don't walk under walkways where anything can be tipped on your head.

In the 1960s, the Victorian streets here in Battersea were swept away in what was then called slum clearance. And the Winstanley was built to replace them, a beacon of hope reaching to the sky. The buildings may have changed but the people didn't and it remained an area of unemployment, extreme poverty, social deprivation and, of course, crime.

That's why I was here.

On the Winstanley Estate it was probably easier to buy drugs than it was bread or carrots, so widespread was the dealing. Along with it went theft, mugging and prostitution. A number of flats had been taken over by cuckoo drug dealers, who simply moved in and took over, leaving the rightful tenant either cowering in a corner or just deciding to disappear. And, of course, the drugs turnover and all that vying for turf meant there were frequent shootings and stabbings here.

The sound of the band was quite loud now. I passed a couple of junior officers on the beat. They, too, were walking in time to the music. They stopped when they saw me. Officers knew that I liked to get out on the front line but still they were taken aback by the sight of a chief super at Winstanley, the office being the usual habitat of the senior ranks.

"Where's the music coming from?" I asked.

"Community centre, guv. Local steel band."

The band stopped now. We talked for a few minutes. In broad daylight, not 30 feet behind us, I could see, over the shoulders of the cops, two men buying drugs from a dealer. The transaction was casual and their behaviour barely furtive. This was typical of the Winstanley Estate. The dealers terrified the neighbourhood but they themselves had no fear of anyone, not even the police. I looked around the forlorn square and saw more dealers milling around, eyeing each other, looking for their customers. They were completely unconcerned by our presence; in fact, they prided themselves on the idea that, if the police showed up here at all, they were too intimidated to take any action. I was determined to change all that. Our Estates Policing Initiative was in its infancy. I was determined it would succeed.

The music started again.

"I should search those men," I told the young cops, resuming my journey towards the steel band.

Battersea is in south London but it had none of the anti-policing history of Lambeth and the public did not regard us as their enemies. It was easily possible to stop and search a drug dealer here without being surrounded by angry people who tried to intimidate the officer while pulling the suspect to safety. So when I had announced a massive increase in police presence on the estate, most residents had been pleased. They wanted to be relieved of the relentless crime, drugs and violence which surrounded their children. The Winstanley had been labelled a sink estate – no one wants to live there.

Finally, I arrived at the community hall. The band was a large one, and its members were bashing away in a fashion that looked so haphazard it was incredible they produced music which was both rhythmic and melodic. You couldn't hear them without smiling. And a lot of people were smiling. Kids of all colours had been attracted in by the sound, just as I had, and some were dancing, while others were joining in with makeshift instruments. The steel orchestra, as they were known, were called the Melodians.

Nervous glances were thrown my way: that assumption that if the police are here there must be trouble somewhere. But I clapped enthusiastically at the end of a piece and smiled broadly. Kids rushed to the front. During the pause, a member of the band came over to me.

He said, a bit anxiously: "Is there a problem, officer?"

I said: "Not at all. I like your music. Do you live around here?"

He lived on the estate. We chatted as we watched kids swamping the band. The players let them try the instruments and showed them what to do. A couple started making something that was almost music. Others simply banged the drums enthusiastically. A few kids danced. How much more they could gain from this than sitting in bored groups watching drug dealers and even running for them.

I said: "I have access to a community fund."

The other face of Battersea, the people who lived in grand houses, held a police ball in the park each year. It was a fundraiser and some of those funds were earmarked for community groups. I had already given money to a man on this estate who taught karate each week to kids. He thought it gave them some self-respect, discipline and useful skills. Their parents agreed, but many couldn't afford the 50p for the class.

The steel band man was still looking at me anxiously, as if a community fund was something which might get his band closed down.

I said: "Maybe with a bit more funding you could expand your activities here?"

His face broke into a broad smile.

I saw that smile, that band, and its ever-expanding activities as a symbol of hope for one of the UK's most notoriously crime-ridden estates. And it certainly needed one.

My new strategy was to move in a huge policing team, consisting of probably 20 officers. We worked with the local authority to analyse where the greatest crime areas were on the estate and get CCTV there. We asked for better lighting to make it harder for dealers to lurk in dark corners. And the local authority also appointed a housing officer who would

Children playing in the garden at Fairmile Hatch Children's Nursery. *(Donated)*

Pet Donkeys 'Neddy' and
'Peppy' at Fairmile Hatch
Children's Nursery. *(Donated)*

'Shake' our cross-bred
terrier proudly displaying his
obedience certificates and
prizes (1970).

Left: Fairmile Hatch Children's Nursery – aged two years old washing up with George. *(© Newspaper Photo)*

Below: With 'Auntie' Margaret Hurst in photo booth. *(Donated)*

Left: At Alderbrook Primary School, London, SW12 which I attended from February 1964 until June 1965. *(Donated)*

Above: Cross Country running for Met Police Cadets 1976.

Left: Riding 'Meg', a friend's pony, outside the children's home. An unusual sight in Crawley New Town in the 1970s.

Sussex Police Volunteer Cadet Corps, Crawley Unit, winners of the county orienteering competition 1975. *(Donated)*

Class of 1978 – Hendon Police Training School Graduation Photograph.

(© John Everitt Photography 01424-812984)

Above: With PC Mark Jordan – Winners of Police Cadet Scholarship to attend Sussex University October 1978.

(© Commissioner of the Metropolitan Publicity Branch)

Left: Newly promoted Detective Chief Inspector at Hammersmith and Shepherds Bush – July 1991.

With Detective Sergeant Jane Fields at Battersea where I was chief superintendent, hosting a visit from Helen Mirren to the Domestic Violence Unit – March 1999. *(© Met Police)*

Publicising the logo at the Operation Trident Launch, July 2000.

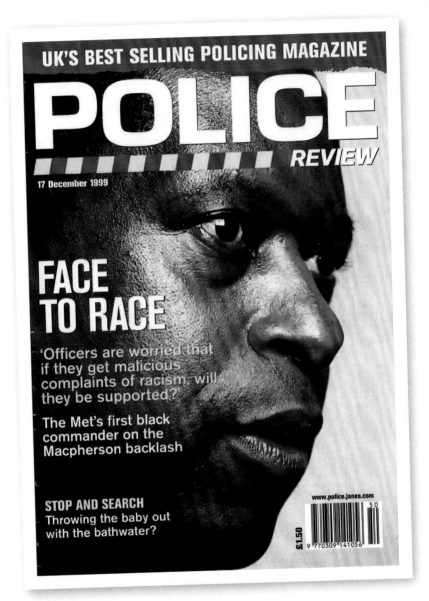

Front cover of *Police Review*, 17th December 1999 – I was Interviewed by
the Editor, Gary Mason, regarding the backlash from Met officers following the
Macpherson Inquiry report which labelled the Force as 'institutionally racist'.

At Kent Police's 150th Anniversary celebrations, with the Archbishop of Canterbury, Dr Rowan Williams (14 January 2007).

A portrait photograph taken by John Ferguson on 12th December 2006, as part of the *Daily Mirror's* Black Britannia Exhibition in March 2008.

share intelligence. So, whenever a criminal took over a flat, we quickly knew about it.

I'd learned when I'd been tackling Yardies that information was an important part of the battle. But here, it wasn't hard to gather, because the local community was on our side. After Streatham, Battersea felt like a warm embrace. Everyone wanted to get rid of the drugs and violence which had overtaken their area.

Gradually, we did improve the quality of life for the people of Battersea, and not just at Winstanley. I became a patron of the band. Its rising star – the steel band is now a steel orchestra which has performed all over the world – coincided and perhaps contributed something to the area's change.

As for me, I was a rising star too.

With some mixed feelings.

The higher you climb, the more isolated you become.

Long ago, back at Vine Street in Mayfair when I was an inspector and in charge of a shift for the first time, although I liked and got on well with all the cops who worked for me, I first encountered the invisible barrier which meant I was the boss. I think everyone feels more comfortable when the barrier's in place. But sometimes being alone on one side of it can lead to feelings of isolation. The more you achieve and the more staff under you, the more substantial the barrier – and the greater the isolation. I remembered a man who had stood alone one night on Piccadilly Tower. Down in the street, across an air barrier of hundreds of feet, was a crowd, urging him to jump. Sometimes I understood why he had turned to us when we arrived and said: "What took you so long?" At the time I'd assumed he was an attention-seeker. These days, I saw him as a man suffering from acute isolation.

Now I was a chief superintendent there were probably a lot of people who wanted me to jump. For instance, when I tackled the street robbery problem in Streatham it had made me a hated man at the police station. I had simply adjusted shift patterns so that more officers were working in the evening when the muggers were busiest. It was the obvious thing to do but no one wanted to see less of their families or work anti-social hours and the Police Federation had soon become involved. I argued that the safety of local people was important enough to justify a change in working patterns. I got my way, but the price was my popularity.

That was when I realised I was prepared to forfeit popularity to do a good job. I'd seen others compromise over the implementation of measures which were needed but made them unpopular. I was not prepared to compromise. Result: isolation.

It affected me and reminded me of an incident back in Vine Street when I'd walked alone across the park with a suspect package in my hand, the police and public cordoned off far away. I understood why the careers of others sometimes halted at this level for no apparent reason: they'd had enough of the long walk.

I knew I could deal with it. The only black kid in the class, the only black bobby on the shift, the only black inspector in Vine Street, the only black senior officer for miles around... I'd been isolated by my colour all my life. And perhaps, although I still avoided talking about it, by the knowledge that I was almost certainly the only officer at my level who had been brought up in care. Yes, I knew about isolation. And I knew I was strong enough to go on.

So I applied for admission to the Met's stratosphere. Commander was the next rank up from chief superintendent and for a place on the Strategic Command Course there were more interviews and lengthy assessments.

Once I was accepted, there was more studying. The Strategic Command Course at Bramshill Police College meant I would acquire another qualification: a post-graduate diploma in criminology from the University of Cambridge.

Soon I was walking down narrow streets which were very different from the concrete walkways of the Winstanley Estate.

Bicycles whizzed past, not actually touching me but close enough to displace the air I breathed. The pavements were so narrow that my coat sometimes grazed against ancient stone walls. Through the small, forbidding doors built into great archways, I glimpsed quads. Squares of cobblestones, squares of immaculately mown grass, oases of still timelessness in this thriving, thronging town.

My college was more modern but it retained the old college structure and was built around courtyards. I crossed one of these to my staircase. Up to my sparse room. The window looked out across the green quad. Crossing it now were small groups of students, talking in low voices. At night the groups were larger and louder, usually drunken. But on this dim winter day, the world was busy studying. There was the deep hush of academia. Of all those people thinking.

At mealtimes I was sitting at long, bare polished tables, my head bowed, watched from on high by the portraits of the great as I listened to grace in Latin.

I said: "Amen."

And I thought: this is ridiculous.

The lecturers were clever, interesting people but certain lecturers hadn't changed their notes for years. Some of the pages were yellow. Were they having a secret competition to see who could read most monotonously? Clearly, these lecturers had no interest in teaching.

More fascinating than their yellowing lecture notes was the research they were immersed in. Sometimes they joined us at mealtimes and we'd sit for hours afterwards, our elbows polishing the tables as elbows had done here for years, and they'd talk with animation about their fascinating research, speculating, answering questions, mulling over theories. Could these be the same people who droned on in lectures?

I knew, the way I knew I could never be a Freemason, that I did not belong at Cambridge. I could never be part of this world of privilege. My grandfather was the tailor who hid his money in the roof until the rats destroyed it. My mother had left her baby alone to do some menial job so that she could feed us both. My father had arrived in the UK to take lowly work in factories and dry-cleaners which the British evidently thought was beneath them. None of that should exclude me from anything. But Cambridge, with its history and traditions, invited self-exclusion. Of course, black people are admitted. There were a few wealthy, privately educated black people from overseas and I suppose there must have been some black British students there, too. I just didn't meet any of them. Perhaps, like me, they found it hard to relate to Cambridge values.

On finishing the Strategic Command Course, I was told by my course director that I had done reasonably well but her prediction was that I would never reach the rank of chief constable for reasons that were not made clear or obvious. I was disappointed. However, I thoroughly enjoyed the course and learned a lot. But I was glad to return to London. I sat in Mac's barber's shop, Mac now wielding the broom, his son Winston clipping my hair, at least four men so involved in some noisy political debate that they were on their feet, and I felt as though I'd come back to reality.

THIRTY-FOUR

Early evening on a cold winter's day.

Westminster.

Embankment.

A hold-up, so we diverted up towards the Royal Courts of Justice, and then continued east.

As a commander I had my own driver now. Nice bloke, it turned out he lived on the Winstanley Estate.

"No, really, guv, it hasn't gone back to how it was before you came. I mean, there's crime, of course there's crime, but nothing like it was," he said, as we stop-started our way across London.

Finally, we reached the Hackney Empire, an extraordinary confection of a building, designed to entertain, inside and out.

"My old man used to come here," said the driver. "Told me he saw Charlie Chaplin but I never believed him. He always used to say: 'Every famous comedian had to do a turn at the Hackney Empire.'"

There was no evidence of comedians tonight. People were streaming inside but they were not smiling. They were all under 30, mostly male and exclusively black. Some spoke the language of the London streets: a stylised half-patois which had evolved from West Indian patois. They eyed the car with a keen and threatening interest.

"Doesn't look too promising..." I said, as a few insults were hurled our way.

The driver began to look concerned.

"You going to be all right in there by yourself, guv?" he asked.

I got out. More anti-police insults were thrown at the car, at me.

"I'll be fine," I said, trying to sound confident. "Just make sure you're out here in case I have to make an emergency exit."

I walked in with the crowds and they gave me a wide berth. Those who were near me fell ominously silent. A few started muttering in low, threatening voices.

I was glad to meet up with the organisers.

"Thanks for coming," they said. "Are you okay to make a speech?"

By now we were in the main auditorium, a wedding cake of a place, with balconies and friezes and ornate plasterwork. I looked up: the theatre was full, everyone was talking at once. The noise was like the sea, rising and falling but always there.

"You didn't tell me I'd have to make a speech..." I said. I wished I'd done more research on this event. There were at least 300, perhaps 400, people here and the hostility towards me made me wonder if I should be here alone. It seemed that every face was turned towards me. Not one of those faces was white. For so many years I'd been the only black man in the room. Now, the way they were looking at me, at my uniform, made me feel like the only white man in the room.

I heard a young man say in a loud voice I was supposed to hear: "What's he doing in our ends?"

His friends immediately joined.

"Did anyone ask him to come?"

"We don't want him here."

The organiser was looking at me with concern. "Don't you want to speak?" he asked.

No. But I knew I could not pass up the chance to address all these black kids. They were the people whose help we needed most to make Operation Trident a success.

"I'd love to," I said, faintly. "Thanks for giving me the chance."

The organiser called for the attention of the audience and gradually, they quietened down. He explained that we were going to watch a short play about the impact of gun crime on families and communities. The audience was being asked to put themselves in the position of the characters. One of these had a terrible dilemma. In the end, he'd have to decide whether to help the police stop gun crime, even though it would mean leaving his friendship group behind. It wouldn't be an easy decision, warned the organiser. After the play, the audience would be asked what he should do. There would be a vote.

A vote? No one had told me about that, either.

The young people were noisy. They responded to the man's words with shouts and catcalls, but they listened.

"Right," said the organiser. "Now I'm going to introduce you to Commander Fuller from the Met."

I expected some catcalls but instead there was a deathly silence which was even more ominous. My hand was shaking as I stood up. I tried to steady my voice. I felt small and very vulnerable.

I said: "I run a police initiative called Operation Trident. We set it up with community members because there's so much gun crime in London now and we're trying to tackle it. Too many young black people are dying. I know what a terrible thing gun crime is because it's my job to work with the victims' families. It's misery for families, it's terrible for communities. We want to stop it but we can only do that with your help. We want you to tell us what you know. Who has the guns? Who is using them? Where are they? If you tell us that, we can do our job and protect everyone. I'm asking you to help me because we, all of us, want to stop this loss of black lives. There are leaflets, badges, posters which explain how you can tell us what you know. We'll take care of you and make sure no one hurts you because you've talked to us. So, help us. Help your community. And save black lives."

I sat down. The eerie silence persisted. It felt as though it might be the sort of silence which comes before a big animal pounces. But the organisers were quickly on their feet.

"Thank you, Commander Fuller. Right, now it's time for the play, so sit back and enjoy it, everyone."

My heart was beating fast. What did that silence mean?

But the audience was ignoring me now because the play had begun.

It was a community effort, with young actors and lots of in-jokes. This was not the kind of audience to watch in silence. They whooped, they shouted advice, they yelled abuse, they screamed with laughter at the community jokes.

On the stage, a young man saw his friend killed and then had the choice of helping the police or not. There were lots of factors to make the decision difficult, and the main one was that the police were so rude, stupid, aggressive, insensitive, so everything police officers should not be. There was a lot of whooping every time one came on stage and soon it was clear that the police were the enemy of the community.

I sat still in the erupting theatre, worrying.

With this representation of the police, there was no way any member of the audience would vote to support us. The antagonism towards the Met was obvious. And something about the energy, the exuberant hostility of the crowd, told me that this situation could turn nasty if the vote went against the police. I had stupidly, thoughtlessly, put myself in danger.

Operation Trident began because black-on-black gun crime in London was now reaching epidemic proportions. For a long time, this crime went unreported or under-reported. For instance, after a drive-by shooting in south-east London, every car in one street had bullet holes in it. The police crime report simply referred to 'criminal damage'. There was no mention of the sub-machine guns which had inflicted the damage.

But now gun crime was so widespread that it could no longer be ignored. There were large numbers of murders and they were virtually all going unsolved. Newspapers were starting to say that the situation was out of control. There were gang wars. There were turf wars over drugs pitches. There were petty disputes over parking spaces which resulted in a shoot-out. Guns were fired at young people queueing to get into nightclubs. Police officers dealing with disturbances found themselves unexpectedly dodging bullets.

It was, of course, mainly about drugs. Any drug really, but crack in particular. No one talked about Yardies any more, but the violence they had introduced to certain areas had now spread right across the capital. And the gunmen didn't come exclusively from Jamaica – we had developed lots of our own homegrown seriously violent criminals as well. That careless-ness about life, about death, even their own, bred an utter ruthlessness. Yardies had brought this attitude to our shores, but now it had seeped into local gang culture. One thing Yardies could not do was organise themselves into gangs. But drug gangs had certainly started to behave more like Yardies.

What about the people who used the drugs? They were certainly not all street addicts. In fact, there was evidence that a lot of drugs ended up in the hands of the white, wealthy middle classes, and particularly those who worked in the City of London. No doubt they all thought we should do a lot more to make the streets safe, without ever asking themselves how they contributed to the problem and how many deaths had been caused further down the food chain to bring them their drugs. Perhaps they would ask themselves now that this crime was beginning to affect everyone, black or white: if a whole road was being sprayed with bullets by angry gang members, the bullets were proving colour-blind.

As a new commander, I had to find a solution and it was Operation Trident. The other commanders regarded this job as a poisoned chalice. I certainly knew it would be hard. I saw community involvement as the key. If only communities afflicted by gun-toting drug dealers would trust us and help us, I believed we could defeat this problem together. And that ugly chasm between the police and the black communities which, despite all the changes we'd made around the time of the Macpherson report, still persisted: well, if Trident was successful, that chasm might close a little.

The bedrocks of Operation Trident were intelligence, good community relations and carrying out operations to arrest the gunmen. We could not have one without the other. We needed the community to tell us when a girlfriend was keeping guns for a dealer, or where people had noticed weapons buried in the park, or what the neighbours had seen or passers-by heard. We needed people to trust us enough to report crime. Whole communities had more information about some of these dangerous men than the police did. We needed that information so that we could arrest perpetrators and develop preventative initiatives. We had skilled, competent and tenacious investigators, led by two excellent officers, DCS (Detective Chief Superintendent) Dave Cox and DCI (Detective Chief Inspector) Steve Kupis: but without the community playing their role, our investigators were handicapped.

I was far from the front line of crime now but my new front line was the community. I had already spent 18 months in meetings, large and small, trying to persuade black communities all over London that we were sincere in our intention to rid their neighbourhoods of weapons and the men who used them. Everywhere I went, I met hostility: the hostility which arises from both anger and fear. Anger because they believed they had been let down in the past. Fear because these were intimidated communities. They were well aware that many of the murders were carried out by contract killers who were happy to shoot as many people as they needed to.

Of course, I wanted an independent advisory group for Operation Trident and, of course, it should consist of members of the affected communities. I was the man who had advocated an advisory group to help combat hate crime after Macpherson, so I was certainly going to use one for Trident. I knew where to look for a chairman – Lee Jasper, the activist who was a critic of the police and had made his points so intelligently and incisively when the Consultative Group hauled us over the coals, back in Lambeth. If I could persuade him, along with other respected community figures, to challenge and advise us, people might be more likely to believe our sincerity about reducing the number of young people killed in the gun violence.

"There's no point talking to you if you don't listen," Lee Jasper said.

"We'll listen," I assured him.

"You never have."

"We will this time."

The independent advisory group was founded and the marketing of our operation to the black communities of London began: we were soon marketing Trident as hard as Kellogg's once marketed cornflakes. The aim was to tell everyone how important it was to give us information – as well as to transfer the fear of gun crime from potential victims to criminals.

I told the advisory group that I wanted a logo for Trident.

"Well, if you want to get through to people, don't make it look like a police badge," said the advisory group. "Or no one will be interested."

"How should we do it, then?"

They considered for a while and then agreed: "Urban. You could make it look like street graffiti."

Not everyone in Scotland Yard liked the sound of this.

"Graffiti! Like something sprayed on a Tube train? Are we going to start approving of that?"

"You're going the wrong way about things."

"We're the police, not some bloody youth club."

I had a choice. Did I listen to my colleagues, or the advisory group from the black community we were trying to reach?

That was a no-brainer. Our new logo was popular immediately and even gained a certain kudos with London's kids, who were often seen wearing our badges.

The logo appeared on leaflets and posters everywhere – in nightclubs, pubs, community halls, on the street – and we had Trident business cards which we'd leave anywhere someone might pick them up and decide they wanted to talk to us. Including houses we raided or any place where we made arrests.

Soon, there were 160 officers working in different murder investigation squads, building up expertise all the time. Computers were getting much more sophisticated now and were able to carry out quite detailed crime mapping and analysis, helping us produce a list of the top ten criminals.

When government minister Mo Mowlam visited us and we showed her the crime map, she looked at a street in Hackney and asked why there were so many dots on it.

"We call that Murder Mile," I explained. "Eight murders already this year. There's a big gang warfare thing going on there."

Her face fell.

"I've just bought a house in that road," she said.

And now, here I was, a stone's throw from Murder Mile, watching a play about gun crime with some of the young perpetrators perhaps sitting not far away from me. Yelling, stamping and catcalling as the police on stage bungled their way through an investigation. As the play drew to a conclusion, I could feel my heart beating hard. If the final vote went against the police – and there was every sign it would – then a rapid exit would almost certainly be required. This was beginning to feel like a humiliating situation at best and at worst a dangerous one.

My anxiety heightened as the play ended to wild applause and stamping.

The organisers appeared on the stage.

"Right everyone, you've heard Commander Fuller and you've seen the play. Let's have a show of hands. Put your hand up now if you believe that we should support the police to defeat gun crime. Come on, if you believe the police should be supported, hands up!"

I could hardly bear to look. I busied myself recceing the exits.

From the corner of my eye, I could see one or two hands go up in the front row. That meant nothing. There were always hands in the front row. Behind me, all around the room, was the noise of people muttering to each other. It sounded as if they were talking and ignoring the vote.

"Hands up if supporting the police is right!" repeated the organiser.

There was a long pause.

I had to look.

I turned around and saw that at least two-thirds of the audience had their hands in the air. I could not believe it. I felt a huge smile start inside me and then spread right across my face. It was not returned by any members of the audience.

"Yes!" said the organiser. "It's clear. You're saying: 'Yes! We don't want gun crime and we're going to support the police in stopping it!'"

There was a lot of noise now and the show was effectively over. Despite the vote, I felt no warmth in the room towards me. Many eyes still glared.

Still smiling, thanking the organisers, I exited at speed now. I hoped to find the car right outside where the driver had said it would be. I didn't want to hang around in this hostile environment so near Murder Mile one moment longer than I needed to.

There was no car. It had disappeared.

I walked down the street. The cold winter air nipped at my face and my ears. I looked up the side roads. Behind me I could hear the voices of hundreds of young people streaming out of the Hackney Empire.

No car.

I knew there was no Tube for miles and that no train at the station would take me anywhere I wanted to go. Instinctively, I started walking west. A few streets away, I called the driver. It was a moment before he responded.

"Where are you, sir? Paragon Road? I'm just around the corner, I'll be there in two ticks..."

Soon I was inside the car and we were merging with the late evening traffic. Lights were on, meat hung outside the halal shops, greengrocers stood by mountains of fruit, young men stood talking and smoking in groups.

"Why didn't you wait outside?" I demanded. "I told you I might need to make an emergency exit!"

"Sir, it was too dangerous hanging around."

"What happened?"

"Lads."

This was an unmarked police car, but of course Hackney youth would know at once what it was.

"What did they do?"

"Thought I was spying or something. Surrounded the vehicle and... well, it all got a bit hairy."

I said: "Things could easily have got a bit hairy for me inside. The mood of that crowd could have turned very ugly and I'd have had no means of escape."

The car was picking up speed now. It felt warm and safe.

"All's well that ends well," said the driver.

THIRTY-FIVE

The black community did support Operation Trident. Over 3,000 pieces of information flooded in. Some intelligence we received was very general ("A big drugs lord has just arrived from Jamaica!") and some of it required an immediate response ("Ludo's on his way round to Rollo JJ's and he's going to kill him!").

The only way to respond was with armed operations. There was some public disquiet that so many police were armed now but really it was not possible to deal with ruthless men who bristled with weapons by simply waving truncheons around. We generally discussed our tactics with the advisory group after an operation. They didn't spare our feelings.

If we successfully arrested a suspect without anyone getting shot, the next problem was evidence. We needed witnesses who would agree to make statements. You might think that no one would give evidence against a contract killer, particularly if that killer was a member of their own community, or even their own family. But people sometimes did, even if they were terrified. No one really thanked them for this dangerous and selfless action: no thanks could be adequate. But we did offer them places on the witness protection programme. Of course, that meant leaving their home, their families and all who loved them. It was a big ask. One witness refused all offers of protection and was in fact shot and injured on two separate occasions. This brave woman did still give evidence at the Old Bailey and her former partner was jailed on the basis of it.

Our raids picked up many hundreds of weapons, a lot of them military or trophy guns which had been brought back by soldiers from various wars and sold on. We had them all destroyed, but more kept coming. I had my photo taken with some of the weapons we seized and there are at least ten UZI sub-machine guns in the picture. We found there were illegal armourers who hired out guns for specific jobs: a contract killing could cost as little as £100.

Drug dealers' lives were cheap.

Our operations were complex and demanding and some-times I ached to join the others out there on the street. But it was not appropriate. My role was strategic now and even involved me tracing my way back to the roots of so much of this crime: Jamaica. And if we thought things were bad here, in Jamaica there was a crisis.

Cocaine arrived there from Colombia, by air or more usually by sea, and then was carried on to the UK and other countries. The gun crime which always travelled with drugs was now so extreme that Jamaica had declared a state of emer-gency and a number of countries had agreed to help, including the UK, not least because British nationals had already been caught up in the crossfire there.

For Jamaica the crime was a downwards vortex: shoot-ings deterred tourists. The fall in tourism caused the locals economic hardship. Which increased the crime rate. Which deterred tourists. And so on.

I thought a joined-up approach to the crime in both coun-tries would be productive and, for the second time in my life, I contacted Ossie and Marigold to tell them I would soon be on a plane bound for Kingston.

On landing, I stepped into a wall of heat. I had forgotten the loud, brash way the people talked, their slow walks and that relaxed, carefree attitude to life.

Land of my fathers.

Ossie and Marigold were older of course, but as vigorous as ever. They welcomed me warmly the way only family can welcome you. When I was with them, they gave me a sense of belonging to something. They urged me to stay with them, but I declined. I was working with the Jamaican police and based myself at a central hotel.

In London, we spent a lot of time ensuring our officers remained safe. Now, talking to the Jamaican officers, I understood how gun crime had reached such a level that here cops risked their lives out on the beat every minute of every day. But whatever help we wanted to give was undermined by one ugly fact which we kept hitting like a brick wall: corruption. Corruption in the police force was endemic. It was a good idea to spend government money on Jamaican crime to stop it haemorrhaging into the UK. But not if that money just went into people's pockets.

We would have to support anti-corruption projects or smaller projects where we could control the cash flow. I was keen to focus on the transportation of drugs to the UK. One project targeted the mules who carried the drugs. They were nearly always women, and invariably very poor women, who had generally been duped into carrying the drugs in every known orifice and any other place about their person they could find.

Whatever they had been promised on their arrival at the airport in the UK, what was waiting for them was generally rather different. Sometimes it was just the barrel of a gun. One woman had simply been picked up at the airport, killed and her stomach cut open to remove the bags of drugs she was carrying. Most of the women were doing this to earn money to improve life for their children and had no idea that if caught, they would spend many years in jail far away from those children.

I wondered how we could intercept these mules. I had all sorts of ideas. But something unsettling happened and my ideas were put on hold for a few days.

The phone rang in my hotel room.

It was the receptionist.

"Mr Fuller, there are some men down here looking for you. About five of them."

"Men? What men?"

"They asked for your room number. I told them that you aren't here at the moment. I suggest you leave before they return."

I did. Jamaican police informed me they had just learned there was a price on my head and from now on I would need protection. I was horrified (although of course I secretly hoped it was a high price). And, as I changed hotels, I did feel that if criminals thought my visit to Jamaica was a chance to put an end to Operation Trident in London, then maybe it was having an impact.

Under constant protection now, I made a point of visiting many parts of Kingston, including the poorest parts. Which were shockingly poor and not in a nice, pleasant rural sort of tin shack way that my mother was poor. Not that I intended to visit her this time – I was too busy.

I spoke to as many people as I could and one day I was chatting to a woman police officer who was surrounded by children. She was running an ad hoc education programme for them in an area of serious crime: there had been about 1,500 murders in the last year in that one square mile.

Was it all the children around her that reminded me of Auntie Margaret? I had spent much of my career telling myself not to think about the woman who brought me up. Her influence on me was inestimable but she was dead and there was no point looking back. That was my reasoning. And now this Jamaican policewoman suddenly brought Margaret into my mind. I didn't know why. She looked nothing like Margaret and sounded nothing like her.

"What would you do about all this crime?" I heard myself asking her. As if she really was Auntie Margaret and we were sitting in the kitchen in Crawley, chatting.

I waited for her to say what most Jamaican mothers might be expected to say: more policing, more arrests, more money to sort the problem out.

Instead, she said: "Education! That's the only thing which will help and it won't help tomorrow or next year. It won't help for years and years. But it's the answer."

I stared at her and realised that's what Margaret would probably have said.

"Of course," she went on, "the politicians aren't interested. They want a quick fix which will work before the next election. But if they would just invest in education for the long term, they would give hope."

At that moment I saw my life as a long, long walk through crime. Blue lights. Long nights of shoot-outs. The bodies of young people, peppered with gunshot wounds, still clutching their own weapons. Endless operations to arrest an endless stream of criminals. I had seen generations by now: as one died or matured or went to jail for life, his son arrived on the scene with a gun. A parade of criminality which stretched far into the past, far into the future.

And the answer is not more police operations. The answer is education.

I knew that this Jamaican policewoman had given me one of the more profound moments of my career.

I tried to immediately apply her words to the drugs mule problem. Not in the way that she intended, not on the scale that was needed, but I did want to educate these women about the consequences of their actions. Since they were illiterate, a reading programme would have been good. But for now, a respected local artist designed posters showing what happens to women who carry drugs to the UK.

The posters were colourful, charming, engaging and shocking. They had such a dramatic effect on the drugs mule women that passenger numbers from Kingston to London dropped sharply.

I had one other revelatory moment with Operation Trident.

Back in grey London, where, after those strolling Jamaicans, everyone who walked down the street seemed to be turbo-charged, I went to a meeting about youth crime. I gave the speech which I had given so many times but still passionately believed in, reaching out to the community, inviting them to trust the police and work with us.

At the end, just as I was leaving, someone tapped me on the shoulder.

I swung around and, without knowing that I recognised the big, broad, black man who faced me, I felt nauseous. I even started to shake as though in shock. It was a moment before my brain followed my instincts.

A dark night. High over the shop fronts in west London. The flash of a blade, a precipitous drop below us, a fight for my life.

"You know who I am!" said the jeans burglar, grinning from ear to ear. "Don't worry!"

I stared at him. He had very nearly killed me, and that had certainly been his intention. And, not so long afterwards, he had threatened to kill a teacher.

"I'm here as a youth worker," he said. And he told me his story. How he'd been jailed a few times and woken up one day and realised that he didn't want to do this any more and he didn't want to be that person any more. When he came out of prison he did not revert to his old ways. He stayed away from crime and others who committed it. He changed his life.

"I've got a job working with young offenders," he said. "I try to support them and help them turn their lives around so they don't go back inside."

I was still suspicious. I could hardly believe that this cheerful, open-faced man was once the angry, violent offender I had known. The lad who I had been sure was heading for a life of crime and prison.

"What made you change?" I asked, hoping that he had some secret formula.

"I changed myself," he said. "Prison changed me."

"Were you on some kind of rehabilitation programme?"

He laughed. "If only! There aren't any really."

If only. If only our prisons tried harder to rehabilitate. If only there were more stories like the jeans burglar's. If only I hadn't spent my career meeting the same criminals over and over again.

The jeans burglar, who I had thought was a hopeless case, proved to me that people can change and sometimes they do.

"How's your mum?" I asked, remembering her tears: in the police cells, in court.

He smiled again, warmly.

"Happy," he said.

THIRTY-SIX

Operation Trident worked in lots of ways. Most obviously, we succeeded in transferring some of the fear in the community back on to the gunmen who were causing it. Within five years we had arrested the ten most wanted criminals, along with many others. We had seized and pulverised tonnes of guns and knives. Who knows how many lives might have been saved as a result.

Just as important, I believe Trident was one of the first examples of the community and police working together. Beyond the front-line operations and arrests there was a lot of prevention activity: programmes like the one the jeans burglar worked on to help steer offenders towards safety and employment when they left prison, programmes to prevent kids being swayed by gangsta rap culture, programmes to offer positive choices.

As the Jamaican policewoman had said, it was all about education. Of course, the effects of such programmes are slow and it is hard to find funding for any initiative which takes so long to show results. And after five years, crime had dropped to a point where the Commissioner of the day said that Operation Trident "no longer justified this level of policing and resources". A compliment of sorts, although I reminded him that this is the sort of crime which always returns.

By now I was a Deputy Assistant Commissioner of the Met. I'd started making history when I'd become the first black commander. Not surprisingly, I hadn't heard the words wog, coon, bananas or Nicky for quite a while. But I did have the problem many black people encounter when they surpass others' expectations. The banter stops and the chatter starts. Chatter which says you only got the job because you're black.

This had been a problem from the beginning of my career, but as I climbed higher I became more aware of it. No matter how good my exam grades, the chatter was that the pass mark had been dropped for a black man. If I was promoted, I couldn't help noticing that double-checks were always carried out on my qualifications. By now I had an MBA, a diploma in marketing and a postgraduate diploma in criminology. So no one could say, ever, that I was underqualified and couldn't have the job. Not when the real reason was my colour.

Once I was based in Scotland Yard as a commander and my life became a bit more regular, I had thought I could find time for some more studying and had decided to take a part-time course which would lead to a post-grad diploma in law. This would help any further moves up the ladder I might make – although I was getting near the top now. And, along with my MBA, it would make me highly employable when the day came to leave the Met. I'd already studied a lot of criminal law. Basically, the course was not just about under-standing but about memorising. Laws, precedents, cases. I had to find any cracks and crevices in my brain and just cram law into them.

While still in charge of Trident, I passed my postgraduate diploma in law. As Deputy Assistant Commissioner, I really was not sure there were too many places for me to go now in the police and, when a vacancy for Chief Constable of Kent came up, I applied with no real hope of getting the job. It involved days of interviews with many different people. All my experience had been in London and Kent was a county with a diverse range of policing problems from tackling illegal immigration, policing the Channel Tunnel and the threat from terrorism, to its many rural areas. I really thought I stood no chance at all. No one was more amazed than me when I was appointed.

The most interesting reaction came from the press. There was an assumption by some that all black men must have a criminal past, or at least that I must be lying about having so many qualifications. Newspapers checked my degrees and diplomas with each institution, flew to Jamaica to take pictures of my mother's shack, dug up long-forgotten school friends, harassed my elderly father and finally revealed to all the world that I had been brought up in care – something I had rarely mentioned to any colleague. I doubt they have ever gone to so much trouble for a white chief constable.

Chief constable is about as far as you can go. So now I was in charge of an organisation of more than 6,000 employees and a £300 million budget. That meant I could introduce policies which were truly inclusive. No one in Kent would have to endure the prejudice I had – I wanted everyone to feel they had been treated fairly. Responsibility at this level means you have the opportunity to make many such changes for the better – but still, responsibility is a heavy weight to carry. I loved the job. The Kent public were very welcoming. But it could certainly sometimes feel lonely at the top, despite having good people around me and a supportive police authority.

For me, the great aloneness had never been as hard to bear as it might have been for others. Like every black copper, I had developed a resilience. The resilience which comes from not quite belonging. I certainly belonged entirely to policing – but perhaps not to the police. Only BPA get-togethers ever made me feel that here were people who understood and had shared my experiences. And one of those experiences was isolation. From other officers. And from our own black communities because we were police officers.

For the future, my dearest policing wish is not just the thorough integration of black officers, but for them to be respected and welcomed by black and white communities alike. That, of course, would require a revolution in police-community and black-white relations. But, when I was still chief constable, there was a promising portent of the future.

It was 2007 and the Black Police Association had gone from strength to strength, although retention of black officers was still poor. So many of my BPA contemporaries, especially if they reached a senior level, left around that time feeling hurt, angry or aggrieved and such departures generated a number of lawsuits for the Met, most of which were quietly settled out of court. The number of black police officers did not (and still does not) reflect proportionally the size of the black community.

But in October 2007, something happened which amazed me. During their annual conference, the National Black Police Association organised a march of solidarity through St Paul's in Bristol. It culminated in a ceremony at the Trinity Centre to remember the officers from ethnic minorities who had died on duty.

I had policed so many marches. Now I was marching myself, through the streets of Bristol. And I will never forget the sight of black communities lining the streets as we moved through their city. They were not shouting at us to go home. They were not insulting us. There were no cries of "Coconuts!", that angry word I had heard so many times.

No, they were waving and cheering the black officers, proud of the work we do and the status we have achieved. It was astonishing. It was thrilling. Black people were championing black officers. Warwick Road, Stapleton Road, the Trinity Centre: not one insult, only smiles for the 300 or so of us, the black officers of Britain's police forces and the USA.

I had spent years trying to involve black communities in our work and persuading officers that criminality cannot be assumed from skin colour. I had challenged prejudice and aspired to build genuine trust and community confidence wherever I had worked. As I watched the crowds enthusiastically cheering us, I now felt that our contribution was finally being recognised. For the first time in my career I felt kinship and a sense of belonging. It gave me great hope for the future.

EPILOGUE

When I sat down to write this book I thought about my childhood in detail for the first time. After Margaret Hurst's death I made a determined effort not to think about it all. I've seldom talked about it either, certainly not about being brought up in care: I didn't want other people's sympathy and I didn't want their assumptions and the stigma that comes with it.

But writing this book awoke my own curiosity. I began that audit of my childhood which is an inevitable part of ageing. For me, however, it was more difficult than most.

People brought up by their own relatives are told the stories, the mythology, of the family and they carry this around inside them all their lives, defining who they are and where they came from. Kids brought up in care don't have that – although I was lucky enough to have a little Jamaican mythology.

However, I did have something else, something firmer which could not be revised or whitewashed as mythology can. I had notes. Those social workers, whom I had regarded as such a threat and a nuisance all through my childhood, had written notes on me at the end of each visit. Those notes, I reasoned, must still exist somewhere.

And it wasn't just that I wanted to find a dusty file which told me more about myself. I figured that Auntie Margaret must have written notes, too. There would be words by her and about her in the files. And, as much as I was starting to wonder who I was, there was something I wanted to know even more: who was Margaret Hurst?

When I look back, as an adult, on what she did, I am astounded. She lived with us and, although she had some time off and some help, she devoted all her waking hours to us. Like a mother. Her love, devotion and dedication to caring for us, plus the continuity of my care with her, are probably the reason that I am one of the few to look back on a childhood in care as idyllic. But, who was she? I know what music she liked, but if she had a backstory, I don't remember it. If she had relatives, I don't remember them. I do know that wherever we went she made friends and good friends too, intelligent, supportive people who obviously valued her highly. *But that's all I know.*

I put in a request to see my files at the archive where I discovered they must be held. I told them what I wanted to see, and learned they had 40 days in which to contact me.

In the meantime, my research took me to an old London County Council pamphlet about the care services provided in the early 1960s. All the women in the pictures wear aprons and have perms. All the children are white.

The LCC took 5,000 children into care each year all over London. I know from talking to other people, from looking at pictures of iron beds in prison-like rows, that most of those places were not as lovely as Fairmile Hatch and that many of the staff shared none of Margaret's qualities.

We were a show home, a sort of exhibit for the council's changing policy: "*It is in the new small house, on housing estates and elsewhere, that the Council can more nearly realise its aim of providing substitute family life for the children in its care. Here, the children's lives follow almost exactly the same lines as those of children from normal homes. A comfortable house, a small garden, a garage – no one would know that it was technically a Home and not a home. In many of the homes, a married couple are in charge and 'Mum' sees 'Dad' off to work and the children to school each morning. The children and the houseparents play a full part in the life of the community and are generally accepted as one of the families 'belonging' to the town… in the summer, the whole family go off for a fortnight's holiday. It is a holiday of the housemother's own choosing, not one selected for her by a well-meaning official."*

I went back to Surrey. First, I saw the primary school. It seemed to have shrunk almost beyond recognition, although I knew its windows, it was so small. When I was six, I won a beautiful book as a handwriting prize: *A Day at the Farm*. I loved its pictures and looked at it a lot, but most important of all was the way it stood for an achievement. I still have it.

Next, I went looking for Fairmile Hatch itself. I knew that the house was no longer there: it had closed completely as a children's nursery five years after we were moved to Crawley. There were rumours that it had burned down, been pulled down, but no one had ever said the Lodge was gone. And there would be the lane, the woods, perhaps the grounds…

It was strange to drive on a road I had pedalled along so many times. As a boy I knew where I had to swerve the bike to avoid ruts, where the edge of the tarmac fell away. I knew it like a map. It had been inside my head all these years. And now the map was still inside my head, but the landscape had no relationship with that map. The road broadened and veered to the right and then it was unrecognisable. There were turnings and buildings and signposts which hadn't been here before. I stopped the car. I didn't know where I was, I couldn't see a single landmark. Not a rock or a tree or a rise or a fall or a building or… anything at all from my past. As if it had all just been swept away.

I must be in the wrong place. I would recognise the woods, that's for certain.

I drove on and found some woodland. But it was the wrong woods. Not our woods.

I drove back, looking, looking all the time for something which felt familiar. But now I was completely lost. Lost in a world of luxury mansion houses with manicured gardens. The undulations of my childhood had been entirely recontoured. There was nothing, not even a small sign, to say that a great house which was home to many children over the years once stood here.

Back at home, I decided to try another avenue of enquiry. I did remember some of the young nursery nurses at the home, either in the nursery itself or with Margaret. They had been training and a few had worked with Margaret for quite a while. One or two of them had kept in touch through Gill and Tony, the houseparents who had taken over in Crawley after Margaret's death. 'In touch' is too strong a phrase, but there was a link, and I had even received letters when my appointment as chief constable had been so widely publicised.

So it wasn't too hard to find Judy's phone number.

I remembered her as a tall, affectionate helper, neatly dressed in her staff apron. Retired now, she was living in the south west. She was a bit taken aback when I rang her after 50 years using the internet to establish her phone number. But she rapidly recovered.

"How wonderful to hear from you! I probably seemed very grown-up to you in those days but we were just girls, I was only 17. We used to climb out of the windows of the main house at night and go and meet the boys from the rugby club! You didn't know that, did you?"

We chatted and laughed as our two perspectives of the same place, a place from long ago, sometimes collided.

"And Auntie Margaret..." I said. "Can you tell me anything about her? Her background? Where did she come from? Did she have family of her own?"

"Family? Hmmmm. Well, you know, she was quite a forbidding sort of person. Correct. I'm not sure I ever would have dared to ask her a personal question like that."

"What can you remember about her?"

"She was a very nice woman. But I mean, far above us, with all her education and experience. A bit on the plump side, I used to think then, but today nobody would even notice. A lovely smile…"

Yes. She did have a lovely smile.

"Michael, Fairmile Hatch was simply one of the best homes to work in. I went to plenty more after that, and nothing came close. And your Auntie Margaret, she ran the house like clockwork and she was a very strict, no-nonsense type, of course, but one of the kindest. Terrible things went on in other places I worked."

Very strict. That was true. I always thought it was good to be strict. The kids who came and went, some of them didn't seem to know which way was up. But they knew where they were with Auntie Margaret.

"What else?"

"That's all really. I never knew much about her."

It sounded as though Margaret was as much an enigma to Judy as she was to me.

Then I asked a question which had been bugging me for a while, ever since I started all this research. I had to ask it carefully because it referred to a memory so strange that I sometimes worried that I must have dreamt it.

I said: "I remember this man coming to the home. He wore a white coat and he had thick, black-rimmed glasses and he wasn't very nice really. I think he… this sounds crazy… I think he conducted experiments on us. He put electrodes on my head. With some sort of paste—"

"Oh, I remember that paste! I scrubbed and scrubbed but could I get it out of your hair? No, I could not!"

So, it had happened. I felt relieved.

"The paste was like bubblegum in my hair. But it was to keep the electrodes in place. And the man was in a room and we went in, one by one. He had a big box and he kept playing with the switches. I don't think I had to do anything much but all the same he seemed to think I was doing something wrong. He kept playing with the switches and getting more and more annoyed. Finally, he said he hadn't got the results he wanted and I left feeling like a real failure. It was horrible. What was all that about, do you know?"

"I certainly remember the paste in your hair…"

"Did all the children have the electrodes?"

"I'm not sure, Michael…"

My friend Kevin, the superintendent's son, didn't. I remember that much. And I have since wondered if this might have been some sort of racial experiment. Because I kept telling whomever was in charge that I didn't want to do the experiment and I was told there was absolutely no choice.

"Who was he, that man in the glasses?"

"I don't know who he was, but I seem to think it was something to do with alpha waves. I feel… I feel a bit guilty that I… I didn't say something at the time. It was sort of… wrong. But, you know, I was only 17."

She said she'd try to remember more. And she was still in touch with some of the other nursery nurses and would ask them, too.

"By the way, you don't remember what happened to Mrs Ward, I suppose? The supervisor of the nursery? Her son Kevin was my best friend but we completely lost touch."

"I think she might have gone to Croydon. But I'm not sure really, I'll ask the others."

I arranged to phone her back in a week's time.

I wished she had told me more about Margaret. Perhaps the next step was to find the grave. That at least might give me some information. I thought Margaret was in her late thirties when she died but I wasn't sure. A gravestone would tell me. Margaret was a Quaker at the end of her life and many of her friends had been Quakers. Perhaps someone at the Friends Meeting House could help.

"Well," said the Friend at the end of the phone. "That's Hurst, is it? H-u-r-s-t?" She wrote it down painfully slowly. "Well, I'll see what I can find out. It might be some while before I get back to you."

I thanked the voice. I hoped she wouldn't forget.

I did speak to the other nursery nurses. It was very pleasant, talking to them, but they could not help me find the Ward family and said they had no knowledge of the experiments. If Judy hadn't confirmed it, I would by now have assumed I'd dreamt the whole thing.

By now I had done enough internet research of my own to know that children in care were used as guinea pigs in psychological and other experiments in the 1950s and 1960s. But most of these had been documented and had not taken place at Fairmile Hatch. Nothing I read seemed relevant to the strange experiment I remembered. The reluctance of the nursery nurses to talk about it, however, meant that I remained suspicious.

To my delight, the Society of Friends did phone me back. They had located Margaret's headstone. It was very overgrown and the woman who rang assured me that they would now be tidying it up. I now learned that Margaret Hurst had died on 20th December 1974. She was 32.

The next call was from an archivist. The 40 days' waiting period for my files was nearly up.

"I understand that you've asked to see your file from your childhood in care..."

"Yes! Have you found it?"

"It's not a question of finding it, really. It's a question of what you can see."

"What do you mean? It's my file, isn't it?"

The archivist was kind.

"Well, the trouble is that your information is all on the same file as the children you were in care with. And because of that we can't give you access to it for many years."

"How many years?"

"Seventy-five."

"Seventy-five!" I felt a strange, physical feeling, as though something, an organ the size of the heart, really was dropping down through my body.

"I'm very sorry," said the archivist.

"Why can't you redact the information which isn't about me?"

"That is a massive job."

"But I want to know what my file says!"

I felt like a swimmer gasping for air now.

"You made an application under the Data Protection Act, but I understand that you're asking for years of notes. So this is what I propose to do. I'll read it to you, leaving out anything which doesn't directly relate to you."

"Read it to me?"

"I shouldn't really be doing that, but it's better than nothing."

I had to agree that it was better than nothing. And I realised that if we followed the correct procedures then redacting my file would be so time-consuming that probably nothing is what I would get.

I met him at the town hall. I waited in a modern office and he bustled in behind a huge pile of files.

"You might want to write this down," he said kindly. "Because sometimes people can get a bit overwhelmed and then they need to check the facts afterwards."

I swallowed. Getting overwhelmed was not something I enjoyed.

I reached for my notepad and prepared to listen to him as he opened the first of the big, brown files which contained the story of my life.

"Now, when you rang you mentioned some rather interesting experiments. I've searched high and low for something on that. There's nothing, nothing at all."

By now, this came as no surprise. If the experiments were dubious, if they even were racial in nature, probably the authorities would not want to admit to them. I made a quiet resolution to continue researching, although I wasn't sure exactly how.

And so the archivist, scanning the pale pages of my file and seldom looking at me, told me my own story. It is strange to hear about a baby and know that baby is you. You cannot receive information with the total detachment due to someone else, even if you feel you have nothing in common with that long-ago baby.

My mother flew in from Jamaica to be with my father and they had a baby but the relationship foundered and somehow she was left alone with me and very little money. She had to work, she could not cope with the baby as well. Someone contacted social services and at her request, I was taken into care, into a nursery in south London. I don't know why, but I was soon returned to her. And then, when I was about two years old, the landlord complained about a baby crying, a baby who had been left alone while the mother was at work.

So one day the social workers came, accompanied by the police because they anticipated a fight. They got one. My mother fought to keep me, fiercely and loyally. I heard that with some emotion. I could not remember her demonstrating any love for me, ever. Even more shocking, I fought to remain with her. I screamed, I shouted, I yelled for my mother. The fact that I had any attachment at any stage to her was even more astonishing than her attachment to me. The archivist had to read it twice. It was like feeling tectonic plates move. The whole world was rearranging itself. My mother had loved me. And I had loved her. I was forcibly removed from her care.

Although the room we shared, me sleeping in a collapsible cot, was clean and tidy, social services felt I was neglected and they were concerned about my diet. I was taken for a month's stay in hospital. I had a consistently high temperature due to some sort of infection. And anaemia. But despite treatment, the high temperature remained. The doctors concluded that I was traumatised by the separation from my mother.

When I was taken back to the care nursery, I did not thrive. I was unhappy and longed for my mother. They tried putting me in different wards with different carers. Finally, the social workers decided to send me to the country. To a nursery called Fairmile Hatch.

Here, things improved a lot. The most remarkable finding in the notes now was the frequent attempts by both parents to take me back. My mother tried constantly. And, amazingly, so did my father. He worked shifts and was told this was impossible, given his work pattern. And then, he met a young nurse.

She also worked shifts but she told the court she could organise these around Dad's and that between them they would care for me. I was taken out of Fairmile Hatch, and brought to the house in south London to live with my father.

The archivist's voice was careful and precise.

"It seems you lived there for a year."

"What!"

"During that time a baby brother was born to this woman, the nurse."

"What! How old was I?"

"Er... five. They intended to marry. But... oh dear, the reasons aren't at all clear from this but their relationship broke down. And the woman left. Er... are you still there?"

"Yes," I said hoarsely. I leaned back in my seat. This was too much to write down. Outside, there was a police siren. I heard it without listening to it. "I lived with Dad for a year? A whole year?"

"You went to school in Balham."

A year had been condensed in my memory into a series of weekends. Time's telescope. I tried to remember. Perhaps there had been a classroom, a bully in it, a fight over something small. Perhaps there had been a woman at home who was kind to me but not my mother. Had there really been a new baby? I looked hard, very hard, for the baby. But these were shadow memories, shadow people who had disappeared into the past's darkness.

"Then your father could not cope alone and so... well, you were returned to Fairmile Hatch. You weren't very happy about it."

He read me a passage describing the outrage of an angry six-year-old who thinks he is being taken for a trip to visit his friends' house and finds that he is actually being left there. As he spoke, my heart froze. My father told me we were going away for the day but in fact it was for the rest of my childhood. The heartbreak. The betrayal. I felt tears stinging now as the archivist spoke. Even though my rational adult mind was sure that my father thought this was the kindest way to return me to the council's care, even though I am sure he was as upset as me, even though he desperately wanted to keep me. Despite all that, I was a child again and my heart was breaking with fury and hurt.

"And then..." said the archivist, "well, it's remarkable, really. The next entry is from the supervisor of the home..."

"Mrs Ward?"

"Mrs Elizabeth Ward. She says there has been an extraordinary change in you. You are now living in a group of six children in the Lodge at Fairmile Hatch with a woman called Margaret?"

"Yes. Yes."

"She wrote this just a few months later. Somehow you have entirely changed into a happy, outgoing child."

Margaret's magic. I smiled.

"There is a copy of a letter here from Margaret Hurst to your father. It very politely encourages him to visit you. Apparently you won a prize at school and you would like to show it to him and Margaret wants your father to know that he would be more than welcome to visit. A very nice letter. I will try to send you a copy."

I could imagine how, after that terrible scene at our parting, Dad did not want to risk upsetting me again. And Margaret was telling him it was all right to visit.

And so my childhood whizzed by in the soft, persistent voice of the archivist. Much of the detail was dull. Whole years were missing. There were endless complaints by my mother that she could not afford the train and taxi fare to visit me. There were long discussions about the cost of these visits and whether I should be moved closer to my mother. There were my mother's attempts to take me to Jamaica. My father's objections. My mother's applications to take me back to live with her, endless, persistent.

"Why did the court say no?"

"Well, it says here that they thought she was too chaotic, moving from rented room to rented room: the court believed she couldn't cope."

I sat in that modern office, the sun going down outside, the evening traffic thickening. And my mind was not in the room at all, but in the past.

The archivist had said I would be overwhelmed.

I was.

By my parents' constant and determined attempts to take care of me. By this great and astonishing evidence of their love. By the court's protection of me. By Margaret's wise comments. And, by the social workers. Those hated social workers. I saw now how hard they worked in my best interests, to do the right thing by me, how well they protected me from the many mistakes my parents might have made.

Some of their comments were irritating.

"Too intelligent for his own good." That was the one which had infuriated Margaret. "Tries to appear more intelligent than he is." That one infuriated me. But their aim had been to keep me safe and this they had done by leaving me with Margaret.

It was all there in the notes, my unfolding life. The arrival of Shake. The closure of Fairmile Hatch (now revealed as not so much a financial but a philosophical change from large institutions to smaller family units like ours). The move to Crawley. My desire to join the police. My lack of interest in Malcolm X. Constant discussion by social workers about whether I should be moved. Margaret's illness. Margaret's death. My story. Told through the scribbled notes of other people. People who were just doing their job.

"Well," said the archivist as we reached the end, "I'm sorry there were so many gaps there, but it's inevitable when someone's file goes back so far. And I realise that hearing your own story can be a very emotional event."

I pride myself on being an unemotional person, but even I could not pretend that I had heard all this with entirely dry eyes and a disengaged heart. I knew I would have to allow the tectonic plates to shift further by recognising not just Margaret's great love for me, but, finally, my parents' too. I was brought up in care, but my parents loved me. How powerful that statement feels.

And now I had to understand how my mother was a young, lonely, poverty-stricken woman in a foreign land far from family, friends and support and how hard that must have been for her with a young child. And how terrible it must have been when that child, who was all she had, was taken away. I had to recognise that my father tried hard and really wanted his son to be with him. I had to acknowledge that everyone did their best.

"Let's see," said the archivist, quietly closing the file and meeting my eye for perhaps the first time. "Some people might regard all this as a rather unpromising start. So, would you mind satisfying my curiosity? May I ask what you've done with your life?"

He knew more about me than anyone else on earth. And he knew nothing about me.

I said: "At 16, I became a police cadet. At 45, I was Chief Constable of Kent. I've got a degree, two Masters, three further postgraduate qualifications and three honorary doctorates. By the time I left the police I was qualified as a barrister and I then became Her Majesty's Chief Inspector of the Crown Prosecution Service."

It was the archivist's turn to be silent.

"Well," he said at last. "Well... Who'd have thought that?"

ACKNOWLEDGEMENTS

My grateful thanks to:

My wife, Helen, whose help and support has been invaluable throughout my career and in the writing of this book.

Gill and Tony Walker for their friendship and understanding.

The former nursery nurses at Fairmile Hatch for sharing their stories and photographs.

My agent, Mark Lucas, who has encouraged me so enthusiastically to tell my story to the world.

CEO Perminder Mann and my publishers, Blink, who have shown such interest in my story, including editorial assistant Madiya Altaf, and, of course, my kind and patient editor, Joel Simons.

TIMELINE FOR
SIGNIFICANT EVENTS

1958	Father and mother arrive from Jamaica, West Indies
1959	Born East Dulwich, London
Nov 1961	Admitted to Fairmile Hatch Children's nursery
May 1965	Moved to The Lodge
April 1968	Moved to children's home in Crawley, Sussex and attended Ifield Junior School
September 1970	Attended Ifield Comprehensive School
December 1974	Death of Margaret Hurst
September 1975	Joined Hendon Police Cadets
January 1978	Passed out of Hendon Police Training School
January 1978	Police Constable, Fulham Police Station
Oct 1978 – July 1981	Sussex University
April 1981	Brixton disorders – 10-12th April
July 1981- Dec 1982	Police Constable, Fulham Police Station
November 1981	Scarman Report published
June 1984 – Mar 1985	Sergeant, Kingston Police Station
Jan 1987 – Oct 1987	Detective Sergeant, New Scotland Yard
Feb 1988 – Jan 1990	Inspector, Vine Street
1990	Met. Police hold Bristol Wastage Seminars — all black and Asian officers required to attend
April 1993	Stephen Lawrence murdered in racially motivated attack
April 1993	Founding Chairman of the inaugural meeting of the Black & Asian Police Association
July 1991 – June 1996	Detective Chief Inspector Shepherds Bush, Hammersmith & Paddington
June 1996 – Dec 1997	Detective Superintendent – Home Office – Advisor and Specialist Staff Officer (Crime & Terrorism)
Dec 1997 – July 1998	Superintendent Operations – Streatham Police Station, Lambeth Borough
July 1998 – Oct 1998	Superintendent Racial & Violent Crime Task Force – New Scotland Yard
Oct 1998 – Nov 1999	Chief Superintendent Battersea Police Station
Nov 1999 – Oct 2002	Commander Serious Crime Group – New Scotland Yard
Oct 2002 – Jan 2004	Deputy Assistant Commissioner – New Scotland Yard
Jan 2004 – April 2010	Chief Constable of Kent
April 2010 – April 2015	Appointed and served as Her Majesty's Chief Inspector of the Crown Prosecution Service and Serious Fraud Office

INDEX